SUNDAY *in Canada*

SUNDAY *in Canada*

The rise and fall of the Lord's Day

Paul Laverdure

GRAVELBOOKS

Editor: Paul Nathanson.
Production, Cover, and Book Design: Duncan Campbell.
Cover Art: Kathleen Moir Morris (1893-1986), *After High Mass, Berthier-en-Haut,* Oil on canvass, 1927, Gift of William James Morrice to The Montreal Museum of Fine Arts. Photography by Brian Merrett, The Montreal Museum of Fine Arts.
Printer: Marc Veilleux Imprimeur Inc.

National Library of Canada Cataloguing in Publication

Laverdure, Paul
Sunday in Canada : the rise and fall of the Lord's day / by Paul Laverdure.
Includes bibliographical references and index.
ISBN 0-9688813-5-1
1. Sunday—Canada—History. 2. Sunday legislation—Canada—History.
3. Canada—Religious life and customs. I. Title.
FC95.L38 2004 263'.3'0971 C2004-902442-6

The author acknowledges and thanks the assistance provided for the publication of this volume by the Carmelite Sisters of St. Agatha (Ontario), the Grey Sisters of the Immaculate Conception (Pembroke, Ontario), the Poor Clares of Alexandria, Ontario, the Sisters, Faithful Companions of Jesus (Toronto), the Sisters of Saint Martha (Bethany, Antigonish, Nova Scotia), Les Soeurs de l'Assomption de la Sainte Vierge (Edmonton, Alberta), Les Soeurs de la Charité d'Ottawa, and the Ursulines of St. Angela's Convent (Saskatoon, Saskatchewan).

Printed and bound in Canada.

GRAVELBOOKS
194 Second Avenue North
Yorkton, Saskatchewan, S3N 1G7
1-306-783-1832
drpaul@sasktel.net

To the memory of
Lise Mongeon Desrosiers

Remember the sabbath day, to keep it holy. Six days you shall labor, and do all your work; but the seventh day is a sabbath to the LORD *your God; in it you shall not do any work, you, or your son, or your daughter, your manservant, or your maidservant, or your cattle, or the sojourner who is within your gates; for in six days the* LORD *made heaven and earth, the seas, and all that is in them, and rested the seventh day; therefore the* LORD *blessed the sabbath day and hallowed it.*—EXODUS 20:8–11

CONTENTS

LIST OF ILLUSTRATIONS

I was in the Spirit on the Lord's Day, and I heard behind me a loud voice like a trumpet saying, 'Write what you see in a book . . .'—REVELATION 1:10–11

INTRODUCTION

WHY DO SOME CANADIANS HAVE A SUNDAY HOLIDAY? If it is to go to church, could those people not do it before or after working hours? Why is there a whole day set aside for rest? And why Sunday? Could not Canadians get their worship or their rest in some other way or on some other day? Probably. But Canadians, and Americans, and almost every western country influenced by the Christian religion, have Sunday.

Before beginning any history of something as insubstantial as time, specifically Sunday, we need to define what exactly we mean by some important words and, more importantly, what did Canadians mean when they used these words. No definition of religion or of Sunday can be offered without inviting criticism. So-called neo-orthodox theologians emphasize that religion is transcendent: a reality or an idea of the totally otherworldly. Sunday, for these people, must be taken out of the ordinary, made sacred, and dedicated solely to God. People who believe in this kind of Sunday also believe that the loss of a sacred Sunday is part of the lamentable decline in religious belief. On the other side of the debate, liberal theologians say religion is immanent: a phenomenon or an idea of the sacred permeating and sustaining the individual, society, and the world itself. For these people, any kind of a day, whether Sunday or any other day—or even the briefest moment—dedicated to rest is a religious event, since it helps sustain life. Religion is implicit in the ordinary. A person does not need to put aside a day for God. God is everywhere.

Although it is undeniable that proportionately fewer people experience Sunday as it was understood a hundred years ago and understood today by neo-conservatives, liberal theologians would argue that religion and Sunday have not declined, that only a literal, biblical, or even fundamentalist form of the Christian Sunday has declined, and that Sunday is still a rest day, showing the continuing influence of Christianity in Canada. The decline of Sunday observance does not necessarily mean secularism, only the decline of a form of Christianity that, in the grand sweep of religious or even of Christian history, is a recent arrival. The Canadian federal law, the Lord's Day Act, creating Canada's Sunday, was created and died in the twentieth century. The various laws, whether British or Roman, that inspired the Lord's Day Act, were usually just as ineffective or haphazardly applied in their own times and places. Yet Sunday continues.

This debate about the connection between the sacred and the secular is reflected in the very word of religion. From its Latin roots—*religio* (obligation, bond, reverence)—to the present, religion has always referred to people being bound to God and to each other as the result of a divine command. Religion has come to mean the personal or institutional system of attitudes and practices that unite the service and worship of God with the service of humanity in God's name. The student of religion must therefore recognize the constant tension between this world and the other world. The student of religious history must also recognize that people hold a range of beliefs about the exact role of religion and of Sunday in their lives.

Since religion cannot be defined without implying the secular, religion itself must be studied in relation to the secular world. From its own Latin origin to the present, the word "secular," like "religion," has gone through several meanings. Its earliest meaning referred to time. The Latin *saeculum* referred to an age, a duration of time, unlike eternity, which was timeless. A *saeculum* meant the age or time it took for one generation to arrive in the "secular" world and to return to the eternal. Religion, through liturgy and prayer, bound time to the eternal, helped the eternal to break into and influence the temporal and, religious practitioners hoped, helped the temporal to influence the eternal. At the very least, religious ritual eased the passage of the generations in birth, marriage, and death. Death itself, however, removed the most experienced practitioners of religion, leaving a new generation to continue or to begin again its relation with the eternal.[1] At its most fundamental level, then, the limits of the secular realm are defined by secularization, or the passing away of a generation.

A second meaning of "secular" which developed in European Christendom, refers to this physical (or temporal, time-bound) world. Secular clergy worked in the world as pastors, teachers, or diocesan priests; religious clergy worked in the monastery and dedicated themselves to worshipping God. Secular and religious property and activities referred to their uses for the temporal world or the eternal. Becoming secular, or secularization, really meant laicization, a passing of power to the laity. For example, the secularization of property was accomplished most often through the intervention and increase of political power. More than once have kings and governments unilaterally declared monastery lands to be property of the state and available for lay ownership and use.

Today, in our Western world, the secular is popularly understood to oppose religion. It is often thought that this world and the other do not, cannot, will not, and should not meet. Hence the triumph in the West of the separation of church and state. Furthermore, "secularists" wrest power, symbolism, and language from religious authorities to influence the world's morals, activities, and practices. How often do we hear about some business equipping itself with a "mission statement?" "Secularism" has only recently come to mean an absolute decline of religion over time, as if the secular and the sacred were opposite to each other, when the sacred is actually opposite to the profane, not the secular.[2]

The fact that "secular" as a realm, "secularization" as a process, and "secularism" as a creed became interchangeable words in contemporary use has fuelled an extraordinarily lively debate. David Martin protests the modern confusion about secularization as an attempt "to simplify that complexity in the interest of ideology or of an over-neat intellectual economy." This simplification strengthens secularist attempts to separate church and state or weaken the hold of religion.[3] Yet, as Owen Chadwick states, secularization cannot be understood without studying its partner, religion, no matter what the modern secular metaphysicians declare.[4] Behind the modern debate over the word "secularism" as in the debate over the word "religion" is the control of reality. The note of desperation on the part of some religious authorities comes from the fear of losing power and, ultimately, meaning in the lives of millions. As for the secularists, confidence in the inevitable complete secularization of the world has given way to an equally uneasy doubt. In reality, secularists and religious authorities are doomed to live together, perhaps for all eternity.

All three definitions of the secular recognize one element: that there is a tradition, or handing on, of religion.[5] In the first definition of the secular, religious power is passed on from one generation to another in an attempt to maintain contact with eternity. In the second definition, power or property changes hands from religious to worldly, or political, spheres of authority. In the third definition, religious authority is offered to a new generation but the new generation does not or refuses to receive it in its entirety. In this third definition, religion supposedly declines and, perhaps, disappears.

All three forms of the secular take place in time. The earliest meaning of the secular, or the *saeculum,* had time at its root. The cycle of the birth and death of generations took place in the secular, linear historical time of this world. Sacred time is cyclical (in Eastern religions) and circular (in western ones) and, therefore, eternal; there is no beginning and no end (in the East), while humanity's destiny is to return to our origin (paradise, in the West). To recreate history, control change and chaos, and share in God's eternity, people broke into and participated in sacred time through repetitive, cyclical rituals. Even the change from one generation to another in worldly birth and death recreated the sacred circle and the similarities between secular and sacred time supposedly established a relationship with God.[6]

In the Judeo-Christian tradition, secular time is also sacred time, since God creates time and participates actively in his creation through the prophets and direct intervention or providence. Shimon Eider argues that the Sabbath, the seventh day of the week consecrated by God for rest, is the centre of Judaism. By resting from all work from sundown to sundown on the Sabbath, Jews participate in God's creation of the world in six days and rest with God in paradise on the seventh. The instruction to observe the Sabbath day, to keep it holy, is enshrined in the Ten Commandments, both in Exodus and in Deuteronomy. Since then, strict observance of secular rest on the Sabbath has given rise to the word "sabbatarianism." Secular time is an integral part of later Christian faith, because time is part of both the secular and the sacred dimensions of Christianity.

Christianity, shaped by Hebrew scriptures, developed its own form of sabbatarianism. Christians fashioned a sacred Sunday from three sources: from the Greco-Roman Day of the Sun, from the Jewish Sabbath, and from the resurrection of Jesus which reportedly took place sometime on a Sunday night. Hebrew scriptures defined a day from sundown to sundown, so early Christians could calculate the three days from Friday evening to Sunday evening as the three days before the Resurrection. Roman law calculated days from midnight to midnight.[7] As Christians adopted the imperial culture of Rome, their sense of daily time shifted to accept the twenty-four hour day from midnight to midnight. After their expulsion from the synagogue, when Christians could no longer worship on the Sabbath with other sabbatarians, Christians began to treat Sunday, the first day of the Jewish week, as the Sabbath. This was natural, since Christians commemorated Jesus' resurrection day on Sunday, calling it the Lord's Day. The biblical texts of Genesis 2:2–3, describing the seventh day of Creation and Exodus 20:8, where Moses receives the command to observe the Sabbath, were linked with the apocalyptic Christian belief that the end of time described in Revelation 1:10 was to be revealed on the Lord's Day. Since Jesus' resurrection day was also called the Lord's Day, Christianity united the beginning and the end of Creation, the first and the last day of the week, in an eternal circle where the secular week became God's time. Similarly, Jesus became known as the Alpha and the Omega, the beginning and the end, and the union of the human and the divine, so that the sacred and the secular were found in the centre of Christianity.

The importance of sabbatarianism in Christianity can be seen not only in hundreds of direct references to the Sabbath in the Hebrew scriptures but also in hundreds of references to Sunday, the Sabbath, to the mystic eighth day of Creation, and to the Lord's Day in Jewish, Babylonian, Greco-Roman, and Christian scriptures, apocrypha, and pseudepigrapha. When one adds Christian patristic authors and church laws, it becomes clear that secular and sacred time, and their offshoot, the Sunday-Sabbath, form an important part of the Christian worldview. With the adoption of Christianity's Sunday-Sabbath as the imperial day of rest for worship by the Theodosian law code of AD 386, Sunday left its Middle Eastern roots to enter the imperial history of the West.

Against a growing number of literal seventh-day, Saturday sabbatarians or even strict first-day Sunday sabbatarians, theologians Thomas Aquinas, Martin Luther, John Calvin, and Richard Hooker thought it important to remind their respective contemporaries that Sunday is not exactly the Jewish Sabbath; their writings inform modern Christianity in the West. Nevertheless, with the rise of mass literacy, industrialization, and a middle class, a literal, biblically based sabbatarianism revived and re-entered modern Christianity. Many Protestant denominations, which emphasized the Bible and the conscience of the believer, adopted a more severe Christian sabbatarianism. Since the Second Vatican Council and the introduction of biblical studies into Roman Catholic consciousness, we see more and more Catholics adopting a strict Sunday rest day too, at least in theory. Since Christianity has been and is still the religion of most Canadians, controversies about the Christian Sunday have been, are still, and will continue to be an important part of Canadian life from generation to generation.

This book describes the rise and fall of Sunday as a holy day in Canada and the people who created it between 1900 and 1950, when our present Sunday holiday emerged. A history of Canada's Sunday, French and English, Roman Catholic, Protestant, and other, from east to west, tells us much about the rocky relation between church and state, religion and society, and the sacred and the secular, because they all meet and greet each other regularly on Sunday in Canada.

As Canada became an industrial and urban nation in the late nineteenth century, Protestant Social Gospel and Catholic Action movements fought to establish Christianity's moral authority on the ethical, political, economic, and social questions of the day. From today's perspective, the seeming failure of Christianity to influence modern Canadian history has led many historians—notably Richard Allen, Ramsay Cook, and David Marshall—to believe that Canada became secular. Yet, statistics about the phenomenal growth of other, recently arrived Christian Protestant churches and of other religions demonstrate powerfully that neither Christianity nor religion itself has been renounced by the majority of Canadians. "Secularism" could be another word for "tolerance."

Many writers point to declining attendance at Sunday religious services as one of the clearest examples of the dechristianization of Canada. These writers argue that the decline in the observance of Sunday as a special day set aside for rest and the worship of God is part of the secularization of Canadian society. True, but have Canadians, as a whole, become less Christian? Many people have stopped going to church, they have sometimes even dropped the name of Christian, yet they continue to live unconsciously Christian lives. They continue to rest on Sunday. Many of them claim to be spiritual or religious. This could be implicit Christianity.

Using previously unknown sources, criminal files, and private papers unavailable until now, I describe, sometimes humorously I hope, the Sunday enthusiasts, especially the Lord's Day Alliance in English Canada and the Ligue du Dimanche in French Canada. I also describe their original success in imposing their Sunday vision on all of Canada, then their long, losing struggle to shape a distinct Canadian Christian Sunday. I show that the decline of Sunday is actually the decline of a very narrowly defined Christianity and of traditional Christian and mainly Protestant religious authority. Religious and political fragmentation have taken Sunday away from the Presbyterian and Methodist clergy formerly in control of Sunday. The so-called secular Sunday Canadians now enjoy could in fact be a more Christian way of handling Sunday, since, as Jesus stated, "The Sabbath was made for man, not man for the Sabbath." Ironically, until the secular Sunday holiday we have now triumphed in 1950, most other Christians—French Catholic, English Protestant, white, black, or aboriginal—were persecuted for their differing interpretations of the sacred day. Naturally, Jews, Chinese, Japanese, and Seventh-Day Adventists were prosecuted in court.

Stated in another way: only 30% of the Canadian population now goes to weekly Christian services, but 80% still declares itself Christian. Many scholars look at Sunday attendance records and declare that Canada is a post-Christian or secular nation. I say with some sociologists and theologians that their definition of religion is too narrow, too bound by outdated definitions of what constitutes religion, and that we should redefine Christianity in order to take into account peoples' self-definitions. No matter how often some scholars declare the death of God, of Christianity, or of religion, God, Christianity, and religion in general stage resurrections. So it is with Sunday, since Sunday is also still with us as a special day set aside from the week. While it is certainly not the day of rest that it was at the turn of the century, it is still distinctive for most people today. As our definitions of religion must grow, our definitions of secularization in Canada must also grow. The two must be seen together.

So God blessed the seventh day and hallowed it,
because on it God rested from all his work
which he had done in creation.—GENESIS 2:3

ACKNOWLEDGEMENTS

PAUL RUTHERFORD ORIGINALLY THREW OUT THE SUGGESTION that, given my previous interests and academic training, I might be interested in the Lord's Day debate. Was I ever! I have since learned that Professor Rutherford makes a habit of freely tossing out ideas that change students' thinking. Thanks must also be made to John Moir who accepted to guide my studies in the doctoral programme at the department of history at the University of Toronto. The staff at the Thomas Fisher Rare Book Library at the University of Toronto must be thanked for their helpfulness and encouragement in my tackling the papers of the Lord's Day Alliance of Canada. They arranged for permission for the illustrations that adorn the present volume.

Elmer Ziegler, of the Favorite Music Company, graciously granted permission for the republication of the words to the song, "Sunday in Toronto."

Lorraine Mychajlunow, accession clerk of the Provincial Archives of Alberta, guided the application that convinced a hesitant William Joyce, Alberta's manager of records, that the Attorneys General's Sunday criminal files (sitting next to sedition and sex) and Lord's Day Act files (nestled next to the explosive Lubicon Indian files) could be opened for this study, with the proviso that names of people writing within the last fifty years would be suppressed in any published work. At the Provincial Archives of British Columbia, with the help of Frances Gundy, the archivist, Deputy Attorney General Ted Hughes granted authorization to examine the restricted criminal correspondence files at the Provincial Archives dealing with the Lord's Day Act for the years 1937 to 1957. This permission was granted on the understanding that the names appearing in the files would not be used and that any published writings making use of the restricted materials would be submitted to the Attorney General for examination. In Quebec City, Jean Simard, document manager in the Ministry of Justice, and Hubert Langevin, the director general, opened the restricted criminal files for 1900 to 1938 stored in the National Archives of Quebec. The Provincial Archives of Ontario criminal files up to 1938 were open for research until 1989; they were suddenly closed to the public, however, when the misnamed Freedom of Information Act was implemented. Upon application to the Management Board of the Freedom of Information and Privacy Act, correspondence files of the Attorneys General dealing with the period after 1938 were reopened with the agreement that personal information would be suppressed and notes would be destroyed one year after being made. Hazel Blythe, who guided my applications, authorized my continued access to pre-1938 materials to verify references to the formerly public materials.

I am grateful also to the late archivist of the French-Canadian Province of the Society of Jesus, Joseph Cossette, SJ, who granted access to the private papers of Father Joseph-Papin Archambault. The former archivist of the Archives of the Roman Catholic Archdiocese of Toronto, Sister Frieda Watson, CSJ, granted permission to use Cardinal McGuigan's political papers, although they had been closed to the public for cataloguing. The fact that I volunteered to catalogue them (and was then paid to do so) helped a great deal in gaining the necessary permission, and in keeping body and soul together, a research technique I have used in other projects and one that I wryly recommend to other historians.

Finally, I wish to thank Louise Bray, who helped me to compile and analyse Alliance accounting records, listened to drafts of each chapter, and married me.

Truly, I say to you, this generation will not pass away before all these things take place.—MARK 13:30

An ounce of legal restriction is worth a ton of moral suasion.
—JOHN SHEARER, PRESBYTERIAN MINISTER, HAMILTON, 1904

CHAPTER ONE

OUT OF HAMILTON

the Sabbatarians, 1900-1905

THE NINETEENTH CENTURY IN CANADA WAS FILLED WITH frustrated efforts to have uniform Sunday laws enacted and enforced. Railways operated on Sunday; stores stayed open; businesses boomed; parades celebrated small and large triumphs such as the suppression of the 1885 North-West Rebellion. Yet by 1900, there were provincial Sunday laws in place almost everywhere in Canada. Ontario since 1845, New Brunswick by 1899, the Northwest Territories from 1883, Prince Edward Island by 1861, and Newfoundland by 1893 had enacted and systematized the old English laws forbidding work, sales, political meetings, drinking, drunkenness, fighting, swearing, games, races, gambling, hunting, shooting, fishing, and public bathing on Sunday. Nova Scotia had laws forbidding offenses against religion, especially noise disturbing worship. Newfoundland prevented the killing of seals on Sunday, while Prince Edward Island regulated the

J.G. Shearer, General Secretary, Lord's Day Alliance, 1900-1907, and a Presbyterian minister.

schedule of its fish industry. The fines for infractions now seem small, between one and forty dollars. Although they were substantial in the nineteenth century, they had become more of a nuisance by the beginning of the twentieth century and less of a hindrance to Sunday activities.

Exceptions to these laws were by no means rare. Each colony before Confederation and each province after it defined necessity and mercy in widely different ways. Sunday streetcars were deemed a necessity in Toronto and in St. John's, Newfoundland. Fishing was considered necessary in Prince Edward Island, but only before 1868. There were no Sunday laws in Quebec's civil code, and so it was left to the few English-majority municipalities to pass various regulations about Sunday observance in their Montreal and southern Quebec enclaves. The Roman Catholic Church discouraged manual work but little else. Exceptions and differences were creating interesting legal tangles. A growing awareness of inequality from one province to another grew. The Canadian body politic was growing, but it was disjointed.

A desire to bring all parts of the Dominion of Canada into a more uniform shape took hold and was called Canadian nationalism. Political and religious fragmentation seemed to hinder nation building. The uneasy and half-hearted truces about the separation of church and state forged at Confederation—between Anglicans and Presbyterians, between Roman Catholics and Protestants, and between English-speaking and French-speaking Canadians—quickly gave way to a mad rush to remake Canada into a sectarian Eden. English Protestants tried to make Canada into a Christian nation—speaking English and renouncing Rome—while French Catholics talked about the need for emigration to the West to counterbalance the English in Ontario and the Maritimes. Industrialization and urbanization were transforming the East. The West, in the boom years of the late nineteenth and early twentieth centuries, was opening up to settlement by the railways, so both English and French Canadians looked west for the future of Canada. By 1900, however, so many French Canadians had emigrated to the United States that Quebec's intellectual elite lost the battle to have western Canada become a French and Catholic ally.

The question now was which form of Protestant Christianity would determine the future of the Canadian nation. The real threats to an English and Protestant hegemony were immigrants. Some were not Christian, others were Roman Catholic, many spoke neither English nor French, and most were more interested in work and wages than in Sunday rest.

In the late nineteenth century, religion in Canada adapted and grew rapidly in denominational unions, especially of Presbyterians, Methodists, and Congregationalists, to encompass the Canadian nation.

The challenge of a secular and industrial world did not succeed in shouldering religion aside; religious institutions and their members wrestled with Canadian businesses and railways for mastery over Sunday. Sharon Patricia Meen claims that the sabbatarian campaign was a conservative reaction to lost membership and to lost income from collection plates on Sunday. After 1888, she says, the churches were frightened by streetcars which threatened "to attract from church attendance the very class that provided the financial backbone of the churches' social and economic position."[1] Some other churches, notably the Roman Catholic, welcomed the streetcar as a means to bring people to church. Historians of religion have described sabbatarians as having been in continual struggle with the secular world from the founding of Christendom, however, so nineteenth-century efforts were not new conservative reactions. Historians have also pointed out that clergymen, reformers, missionaries, and revivalists all made new efforts to evangelize immigrants in the late nineteenth century; they could not bear to think that the people of North America would ignore

God. New immigrants and younger, energetic, usually newly ordained immigrant clergy—not lost members or income—allowed growing churches in an expanding country the luxury of a new religious crusade.

So, in the nineteenth century, sabbatarians made their presence known in Canada. John Charlton, a crusty Presbyterian elder and member of Parliament, continually pressed Prime Minister John A. Macdonald for uniform federal legislation, but the wily prime minister claimed that Sunday legislation was a provincial matter, since only provinces could make laws dealing with religious customs. Letters went out from the 1886 Hamilton Assembly of the Presbyterian Church, calling on the whole Christian church to "rouse public interest on an issue so momentous, secure legislation . . . and provide funds for the purpose of having the law enforced." In 1888, the churches sent representatives to Ottawa and the Lord's Day Alliance was formed under the Reverend W.D. Armstrong, convener of the Presbyterian Sabbath Observance Committee; its former convener, the Reverend William Thomas McMullen, had become moderator of the Church and strongly endorsed Armstrong's letter. One hundred representatives went to Ottawa. Forty-three were Presbyterian, thirty-three Anglican, ten Methodist, seven Baptist, five Congregationalist, and two Reformed Episcopal.[2] These churches were in the forefront of the Sunday struggles during the nineteenth century and began to co-operate more closely on a national level just before the twentieth century.

Religious differences had kept the churches apart in the past, but the formation of a nationwide (called the Dominion) Lord's Day Alliance was meant to overcome these differences. Regional and religious differences brought people to observe Sunday differently. Ontario, with its Protestant majority, was the heart of Canadian sabbatarianism. There, many Presbyterians, Methodists, Baptists, and Anglicans observed Sunday as a day of rest for the worship of God. Sunday was filled with religious services and the clergy of these Protestant denominations vigorously urged each member to observe Sunday, the Lord's Day. Looking closely at these Protestant denominations, however, one can see slight differences in how they viewed Sunday.

Ontario, as well as being the heart of Canadian sabbatarianism, was home to the Presbyterians, who were historically the soul of Canadian sabbatarianism. In 1901, there were over 840,000 Presbyterians in Canada, just over 15% of the population. Half of them were in Ontario. Presbyterians strongly identified Sunday with the Jewish Sabbath. Their standard of belief, the Westminster Confession, did the same. Both the Shorter and Larger Catechisms, memorized and studied in Sunday schools, repeated Exodus 20:8-11 to "Remember the sabbath day, to keep it holy . . . in it you shall not do any work." The Larger Catechism of 1648 settled that Sunday was the Christian's seventh day; everyone was to rest from employment and recreation on that day. The Shorter Catechism allowed works of necessity and mercy. In 1875, at the union of small groups of Presbyterians scattered in Canada, these confessions and catechisms became the subordinate standards of the Presbyterian Church of Canada. In the same year, it formed a Committee on Sabbath Observance. The highly respected and ascetic-looking principal, William Caven of the Presbyterian Church's Knox College, headed the Ontario branch of the Lord's Day Alliance. The Reverend Armstrong presided over the umbrella organization, the Dominion Alliance, founded in Ottawa. And John Charlton, an elder of the Church, continued his dogged efforts in the House of Commons.

Methodists found themselves only slightly less certain than Presbyterians about the eternal obligation on Christians of the biblical Sabbath. Part of Methodist hesitancy came from theological divisions among the Methodists themselves. In England, there were Calvinist, almost Presbyterian followers of George Whitefield and of Jonathan Edwards, who published his popular sermon "On the Perpetuity and Change of the Sabbath" in 1804.[3] There were also followers of Wesley, whose Anglican background emphasized freedom of the will to do with Sunday as it would. They moderated any Puritan strains in later Methodism. In North America, the distance from England and Anglican roots combined with rough frontier challenges to strip many theological subtleties from Methodism. Evangelical fervour for a Kingdom of God on earth remained, and a strict biblically based sabbatarianism gradually took hold of these pietists.[4] In 1886, in response to the Presbyterian Sabbath Committee, which sent out letters to all Protestant bodies of Canada, the Methodist General Conference formed its own Sabbath Observance Committee to denounce social visiting and worldly pleasure.[5] For years, the Presbyterian and the Methodist committees repeated each other's concerns, although the Methodists did not refer to the Westminster Confession and more often denounced the sale of alcohol on Sunday than anything else. If the number of pages in official conference reports is any indication, temperance in alcohol topped sabbatarianism and other moral and social reforms for Methodists. Although there were several thousand more Methodists than Presbyterians in Ontario and over a hundred thousand more in Canada as a whole, Presbyterians held the leadership in the Sunday question.

The number of Anglicans, heavily represented at the 1888 formation of the Lord's Day Alliance in relation to their percentage (over 13%) of Canada's population, seems to indicate a great interest in Sunday. The Ottawa numbers, however, do not represent average Canadian Anglican thinking. The Lambeth Conference of 1888, the Church of England's international synod, had just issued an encyclical urging all Anglicans to safeguard the Lord's Day. As Edward Pulker suggests, in deference to the events in England, Canadian Anglicans merely showed a brief interest and then subsided into their more usual indifference. Rightly so, because in the past, Anglicans and non-established churches in England had exhausted themselves over Sunday observance, or rather, non-observance. In the eighteenth century, Quakers had condemned Sunday sports and amusements, while Anglicans had condoned games, music, dancing and plays.[6] As Christopher Armstrong and H.V. Nelles have written, Anglican lay people were prominently in favour of the Sunday streetcar, and their ministers did not oppose them. The loose institutional organization of the Anglican Church fostered divisions, sometimes vague and sometimes sharp. High and Low Church Anglicans competed for influence in the hazy and broad middle ground. Generally, a line can be traced between Low Church Anglicans, who adopted evangelical attitudes, and High Church Anglicans, who adopted laissez-faire attitudes. Low Church Anglicans relied on the authority of the Bible, as did more radical Protestants in dissenting churches. High Church Anglicans emphasized rather the authority of the community and its leaders in interpreting the Bible and its Sabbath texts for contemporary problems.

Even the Lambeth Conference of 1888, which prodded Canadian Anglicans into a flicker of Sabbath interest, illustrated this division. While a motion to protect Sunday observance passed the conference, to the probable satisfaction of Low Church Anglicans, the motion mentioned only that God commanded rest one day in seven, leaving the church free to adopt Sunday. For Anglicans, as for Catholics, there was nothing intrinsically sacred about Sunday, although Sundays and holidays or feast days were important to the liturgical year. English Anglicans feared rather the growing tendency among the wealthy to spend their Sundays in amusements, golf, and travel, thereby hindering their attendance at Sunday services. The debate in England can be better understood when one learns that Sabbath observance received less attention than polygamy. Canadian Anglicans showed some interest in the Lord's Day, but their numbers at the founding of the Alliance in Ottawa in 1888 were inflated by the recent Lambeth encyclical and, probably, by the presence of Low Church Anglicans. More significantly, the Reformed Episcopal Church, a North American and very low church offshoot of the Anglican Church, sent a number of delegates to the Alliance meeting in Ottawa that was out of all proportion to its insignificant numbers in Canada.

Congregationalists, too, were few in Canada—just over 28,000 in 1891—but their theology was very similar to that of Presbyterians. They gave allegiance to the same Westminster Confession and thus to the Lord's Day Alliance. Congregationalists had rejected the state church of early Scottish Presbyterianism. In the New World, they found their position to be almost identical to the Free Church Presbyterians, who comprised the majority in the united Presbyterian Church in Canada of 1875. It is not surprising that they, too, attended the Ottawa meeting of 1888.

Baptists formed about 6% of the Canadian population and were known to be "determined supporters of the voluntary principle and the complete separation of Church and State." To many Presbyterians, however, the separation of the church and state meant only the freedom of the church from state control. It did not mean that the state could not be controlled by the church, since the church articulated the collective consciences of its members. How did Baptists reconcile the separation of church and state with their attendance at the Alliance? They believed that the separation of church and state did not mean isolationism. Baptists also believed they should inform the state of its duty to pass and to enforce Sunday legislation. For a relatively small community, a large number of Baptist representatives went to the Ottawa meeting. In the new century, however, problems of heresy and fundamentalism raised by biblical criticism and T.T. Shields swallowed Baptist energies, so that Baptists left to the early twentieth century the impression of isolationism. This impression is false.

Since Catholics formed over 41% of the Canadian population in 1901, no study of religion—or of secularism—can ignore Canadian Catholics and claim to shed more than a dim halflight on Canadian religious history. What was Catholic opinion of the Sunday question? In the late 1890s, Armstrong and Nelles state, English Catholics in Toronto supported Sunday streetcars. French Catholics believed, not without justification, that the Sunday question was a peculiarly English illness rampant in Toronto. French Catholic bishops, as the real or even as the nominal representatives of the vast majority of Canadian Catholics, were asked for support by Lord's Day Alliance secretaries in the 1890s but to no avail. While there are numerous pastoral letters denouncing Sunday dancing, games, or other activities, the problem was dancing, games, or the activity itself. As long as there was time for worship, there was certainly nothing wrong with Sunday work.[7] Sunday was just another day of the week, which the Roman Catholic Church had chosen for its weekly celebration of Jesus' resurrection. Like High Church Anglicans, Catholics did not believe that there was anything especially sacred or sabbatical about Sunday. Moreover, the anti-Catholicism of well-known sabbatarians—Presbyterians and Methodists—convinced many Catholics and their clergy to have very little to do with the Sunday question. *Saturday Night* denounced the Alliance because, the magazine incorrectly claimed, no Anglicans or Roman Catholics were members. It was not far off. In 1900, there were a few Anglicans on the executive committee but only one Catholic representative. D.J. O'Donoghue (1844–1907) was an Irish Catholic labour leader and an organizer of the Knights of Labour. He represented labour, in fact, and the fight for more humane working hours. He did not represent the Roman Catholic Church.

The Lord's Day Alliance of Canada mirrored its diverse origins. Its 1888 foundation statement included strict sabbatarianism and a Social Gospel conclusion. Presbyterians were comfortable with its strict sabbatarianism, while other denominations and labour representatives were able to accept its conclusion. The Ottawa founding convention wrote that the

> basis of this Alliance is the Divine authority and the universal and perpetual obligation of the Sabbath, as ordained by God at the creation of the world, enjoined in the Fourth Commandment of the Moral Law, and continued and maintained by the Church of God to the present day, and as essential to the best physical, intellectual, moral and social welfare of mankind.

Clearly, by 1900, Canadian Christians who worshipped on Sunday demonstrated a rainbow of varying opinions about the sacredness of Sunday itself. At one theological extreme were Presbyterians. On the other were Catholics, who did not attend the Ottawa conference (or any other ecumenical conferences). Close to Presbyterians were Methodists and Congregationalists. Baptists were close to the sabbatarian wing but preoccupied with maintaining a clean division between church and state as well as a division between heresy and Baptist orthodoxy. Anglicans seemed to straddle both positions with their High and Low wings, but it can be assumed that they were finally enticed into the Lord's Day Alliance only when the 1888 meeting voted to hire the Anglican evangelical layman and lawyer, A.E. O'Meara, as the first secretary. Born in Georgetown, in southwestern Ontario, brother of the principal of the Anglicans' evangelical Wycliffe College, O'Meara presented himself for ordination only in 1906. Naturally, Seventh-Day Adventists, Seventh-Day Baptists, and Jews believed that a Saturday-Sabbath was binding on all consciences and wanted nothing to do with the Alliance. Roman Catholics acknowledged that the biblical Sabbath was indeed from Friday night to Saturday night but believed equally that the Church had abandoned the biblical Sabbath.

Canadian Christians were so divided about Sunday observance that the young Hamilton Presbyterian minister and Ontario Alliance secretary, John G. Shearer, wrote, "little can be expected from any but the three churches, Methodist, Presbyterian, Congregational."[8]

There is little evidence that business concerned itself with Sunday observance before 1900. Business was not entirely separate from the churches in the nineteenth century, because many businessmen were members of Anglican synods, Methodist conferences, and Presbyterian assemblies. How much influence they wielded cannot yet be calculated, but it probably depended on the individual layman. The most well-known businessman to support his church was "Canadian millionaire," Joseph Wesley Flavelle. Among his many charities and religious activities, Flavelle occasionally advised the Alliance about the hiring of Methodist ministers. It is likely that many other businessmen did the same but, like Flavelle, played a role secondary to that of the clergy.

As for labour, Eugene Forsey has examined labour meetings and found little evidence that the workers played a role in sabbatarian movements before 1888. For the period after 1888, he and other labour historians show that labour organizations fought for a weekly rest day. The Trades and Labour Congress of Canada, especially the Hamilton and Toronto councils, increasingly supported the Alliance after 1888 and joined the denominations to denounce the Sunday business of railways, streetcars, and transportation in general.[9]

The business and politics of Canada were railways, and the churches moved to control the business of railways as well as the politics of Canada on Sunday. Although businessmen attended religious services, it seemed as if financial profits more than the biblical prophets held their loyalty. Year after year, the General Assembly of the Presbyterian Church sent resolutions against Sunday railway work to Sir John A. Macdonald, who sometimes acted as the Minister of Railways and Canals, and sometimes sent money to the Lord's Day Alliance. Railways signified rapid industrialization; street railways followed urbanization. As H.V. Nelles and Christopher Armstrong have stated, the railways were signs of rapid technological change in Canadian society, which the churches chose to combat and control. Railroads continued to operate Sundays, nonetheless, while businessmen negotiated with labour over one day's rest in seven.

In 1890, the Alliance officially denounced Sunday streetcars, visiting, pleasure driving, walking, reading secular literature, sleeping, games, fishing, skating, Salvation Army parades, mining, farming, railway activities, and secret Sunday tippling. Unfortunately for the sabbatarians, the Alliance could do nothing but fulminate. The Alliance's support for John Charlton's Sunday bills did not convince Macdonald to sponsor a federal law. The Alliance, at its inception, was obviously a ramshackle coalition created in part from older provincial societies such as a Lord's Day Observance Society (Halifax) and a Society for Promoting the Due Observance of the Lord's Day (Saint John, New Brunswick). Theological differences between Presbyterians and Anglicans, as well as Protestants and Catholics, could only weaken sabbatarian demands in the eyes of government officials. Because Christians were divided about Sunday observance, the federal government and businesses of Canada continued to ignore sabbatarians as they had in the past.

By 1897, the Dominion Lord's Day Alliance had become demoralized at yet another failure in a Toronto Sunday streetcar battle, but it was clear that Presbyterians would not abandon the field and had become the leaders in this social question. After the Toronto streetcar defeat, Methodists turned to other concerns and integrated their committees on Sabbath Observance, Temperance, Unemployment and Wages. Presbyterians, like Methodists, integrated their Committee on Sabbath Observance into an omnibus Committee on Church Life and Work. But some Presbyterians, such as Principal William Caven of

Knox College, believed that a separate Sabbath committee was needed more than ever. In 1899, at their assembly in Hamilton, the new Committee on Sabbath Observance and Legislation was founded by John Charlton and William Caven; the moving power behind the Presbyterian-dominated Ontario Alliance, John George Shearer, was named convener.

In 1899, Shearer was forty-one years old, the son of an immigrant Scottish farmer. He had been reared in southwestern Ontario, near Bright, and attended the University of Toronto where he received his BA (1889) in mental and moral science and civil polity and logic. Part of the Idealist philosophical training Canadian students received in the late nineteenth century, this general arts degree fitted him for either ministry or law. He chose the former and studied at Knox College, where the principal, old sabbatarian campaigner Caven, had an immense influence on him, as Brian Fraser ably writes. After graduation, Shearer began a pastorate in Hamilton, but volunteer work for sabbatarian causes consumed much of his energy. From 1895 to 1900, he worked directly under Caven, in the new Ontario Alliance. When Caven wrote an impressive pamphlet, *The Divine Foundations of the Lord's Day,* to show the divine command for Sunday rest (and why lenient Anglicans were wrong), Shearer, as the Dominion Alliance's field secretary, had the sermon reprinted and sent out to everyone connected with the Alliance.

At the 1899 Christian Endeavor Conference in Montreal, when organizers asked Shearer to discuss ways in which "young people may be saved from dishonoring the Sabbath by means of the bicycle,"[10] Shearer took advantage of the occasion to propose a bold move. In his speech, "How Can Organization Be Stimulated and Improved Legislation Obtained in the Dominion?" Shearer, in the Free Church Presbyterian tradition, held that the state had the power to fashion the Canadian environment and to sanctify Canada. Conservative evangelicals, Richard Allen writes, tended "to identify sin with individual acts, and taking as their social strategy legislative reform of the environment."[11] But it can be argued, as Meen has in her doctoral thesis, that all Social Gospellers, especially Shearer and Caven before him, were interested in controlling not just the morality of individuals but the morality of Canada itself.

In 1899, the Dominion Lord's Day Alliance, also meeting at the Montreal conference, took Shearer up on his proposal and hired him as the Alliance's first paid full-time field secretary and government lobbyist. By hiring Shearer, the Alliance promoted a progressive Social Gospel vision of Canada—one that attracted conservative evangelicals, too.

Shearer's appointment meant greater control of the Alliance by Ontario and by Presbyterians in Ontario. Although the original Dominion Alliance already had some provincial federates, Shearer pledged to extend the Alliance's work into all of the provinces. In a whirl of activity and travel, he quickly organized and reorganized provincial branches in Nova Scotia, New Brunswick, Quebec, Manitoba, and British Columbia according to the Ontario Lord's Day Alliance constitution. The new organizations superseded older ones which had created the Dominion Alliance. In return, new delegates from the new branches converged on Hamilton in early 1901 to reorganize the central Dominion Alliance. Headquarters were moved to Toronto and Ontario's literature was adopted for all of Canada. Ontario guaranteed financial stability and the reborn and renamed Lord's Day Alliance of Canada was debt-free. Hamilton's Presbyterians controlled the Ontario Alliance; the Ontario Alliance had successfully taken over the Lord's Day Alliance of Canada and through it the rest of Canada's sabbatarian groups.

This first Hamilton convention of the reorganized Lord's Day Alliance of Canada united young and old. In the audience were people whose names had been associated with Sunday battles of the nineteenth century: A.E. O'Meara, D.J. O'Donoghue, William Caven, and John Charlton. Sitting beside them were people as yet relatively unknown but whose names would be intimately associated with the Alliance and Protestantism in the twentieth century: Presbyterians J.G. Shearer, W.G. Hanna, R.G. MacBeth, and F.A. Cassidy, and Methodist T. Albert Moore. All were born in southwestern Ontario or had lived there for most of their lives. Caven and Shearer shared the podium, while John

Charlton, still a Member of Parliament, gave a rousing speech. He claimed enthusiastically, if simplistically, that "Christ's teaching depends upon the church and the church upon the Sabbath."[12] In a way, the older generation was passing on its sabbatarian heritage to a new generation. Everything had been said before, but at this convention the slogans were repeated by the old, while the young, with their larger and activist visions of Canada, took up their new positions in a reinvigorated Alliance.

Between 1900 and 1905, Methodists, especially those from southwestern Ontario and the Hamilton Conference, quickly allied themselves with Presbyterians and increased their coverage of Lord's Day news to several pages in their printed conference minutes. They affirmed "the validity of the Fourth Commandment, as binding on the Church" and protested against Sunday streetcars. They protested also against parades, funerals, and open Sunday post offices. They praised the Alliance and Shearer. They also arranged to keep Methodist ministers on the roll of their church (and on the pension plan) when working full-time for the Alliance. T. Albert Moore (usually known as T.A. Moore) and D.W. Snider, from Hamilton, soon travelled extensively on Alliance business. Prominent and soon-to-be prominent Methodists were enrolled. The Reverend S.D. Chown of the department of Temperance and Moral Reform was appointed a member of the executive committee of the Toronto branch in 1899. Salem Bland, later known as a radical Social Gospeller, accepted the presidency of the Ottawa branch and proved to be an active member. T.A. Moore was appointed western secretary of the Lord's Day Alliance. The Reverend J.S. Woodsworth, later the founder of the CCF (now the NDP) party, was encouraged to join William M. Rochester, a Presbyterian minister, in the Lake of the Woods branch. Woodsworth's father, the Reverend James Woodsworth, had been vice-president of the Dominion Lord's Day Alliance and member of the Northwest Territories and Manitoba branches.[13] As Shearer shifted all of the Alliance's printing jobs to the Methodist Book Room, the Methodist-controlled newspaper, the *Christian Guardian,* published articles and editorials. These praised the Alliance and promoted Sunday observance but also denounced Quebec and immigrants for their lax attitudes toward Sunday observance.[14] By such questionable means were the two churches bound closer together.

T.A. Moore, General Secretary, Lord's Day Alliance, 1907-1911. A Methodist minister, he later joined the United Church of Canada.

Methodists, however, were now embarrassed by dissent within their ranks. Many believed in the need for recreation as a legitimate expression of personal care for God's creation.[15] The personal conscience of the individual Methodist about sacred worship times and places could not be bound entirely by church rule in spite of the collective social struggle for a Christian Canada. Many examples from the Methodist circuit system of meetings, anywhere and at any time, undermined a strong belief in one time and one place for one worship activity. The greatest example of Methodist ambivalence toward Sunday was Grimsby Park, Ontario. Methodist ministers owned and ran the Ontario Methodist Camp Ground Company in Grimsby Park; gate fees, refreshment booths, and religious meetings were very successful on Sunday. Even chautauquas (open-air education and entertainment shows) were offered. A development of the Methodist camp meeting, Grimsby Park served as a permanent camp meeting. Strategically located near the Canadian border to attract American tourists, it provided entertainment, education, and religion in a wholesale and pleasant way. But paid Sunday recreation and fees to enter Sunday worship services rubbed the sabbatarians raw. In order to bring all Methodists into line behind the Alliance, Methodist Moore was delegated to write to the managers of the Methodist camp meetings. Presbyterian Shearer busied himself in protesting against the non-denominational chautauquas and studiously avoided criticizing the

Methodist camp grounds, letting Moore handle that delicate business. Methodists, such as Chown and Moore, agreed to go as far as Presbyterians on the sabbatarian path and were able to bring the rest of the Methodists along, some of them unhappily. Not wholeheartedly but at least not hypocritically, Methodists were at last able to join the Presbyterian chorus against the transportation companies.[16]

In this same period of Alliance reorganization, Anglicans were even more divided. Although Shearer encouraged Alliance members to reach out to Anglicans and reprinted the 1888 Lambeth Resolutions to impress them with the importance of the Lord's Day, he lamented that Anglican ministers ignored the Alliance.[17] Donald Akenson argues that the Ontario Anglican Church was an Irish Low Church branch of the Church of England. The Synod of Toronto, influenced perhaps by the predominantly Irish-tradition Low Church wing gathered around Wycliffe College, was almost alone in appointing a Lord's Day committee. The general Synod waited until 1902, when its Toronto members worked to appoint another committee. Although the evangelical Archbishop Bond of Montreal accepted an honorary presidency in the Alliance, Shearer found little Anglican encouragement for the Sabbath crusade outside southwestern Ontario. The General Synod, when asked by the Alliance for a strong resolution of support in 1905, deplored irreligion but did not endorse the Alliance. It stated rather backhandedly that the "characteristically sober and conservative judgment of the Church of England" should go to the assistance of the often misguided Alliance. Presbyterian principles of the Sabbath were not going to get any encouragement from Canadian Anglicans, among whom Sunday could be used for other activities as long as worship was safeguarded.

When the Alliance presented itself to the Baptist Convention for Ontario and Quebec in 1902, the Baptists quickly endorsed it and promised support for national righteousness. A new resolution of support was repeated in 1905. The Alliance was assured of Baptist support. If the replacement of the Social Gospel editor of the *Canadian Baptist* in 1904 by a more conservative person meant that social issues had become less important than doctrinal ones, then the few Baptists in Canada did not warrant more effort by the Alliance. As long as Baptists supported sabbatarian legislation, their numerical inferiority caused Shearer to consider non-attendance at meetings unimportant.[18]

In the attempt to reach all segments of Canadian society, Shearer tentatively reached out to women. For example, the Women's Christian Temperance Union busied itself in activities politically similar to those of the Alliance. Shearer's wife participated actively in the Toronto and Ontario Union branches, while Shearer wrote letters to the leaders of the movement for support. Both organizations gave each other moral support, since the leaderships were intimately intertwined in promoting Protestant values and objectives. But in the Alliance organization, there were no women. In a one-issue crusade, the Alliance had no desire to weaken its message or its drive by diverting attention to women's rights. As long as organized Christian women assured the Alliance of their support, there was no desire to bring in women who, it must be noted, could not vote at that time and did not have direct influence on national policy.

By 1899, the Lord's Day Alliance of Canada had reorganized itself on a more effective basis. But by then the railways were expanding across Canada, operating seven days every week. In southwestern Ontario, near the American border, flagrant disregard for Sunday sensibilities by the railways had roused Hamilton's Presbyterian and some of its Methodist clergy to lead the battle for a sacred Canadian Sabbath. A new and militant generation of men had risen up to seize the torch of sabbatarianism from the faltering hands of the decentralized Ottawa sabbatarians. A new, aggressive, centralized, Presbyterian-led, Toronto-based Alliance now prepared to do battle with the railways. Control was firmly centralized in the hands of a new generation of committed sabbatarians, Presbyterians first, Methodists second, and smaller sabbatarian denominations headed by Congregationalists and Baptists.

In May of 1899, the Attorney General of Ontario brought a test case to the Ontario Court of Appeal, asking if Ontario had indeed the right to enact, as it did in 1897, "An Act to prevent the Profanation of the Lord's Day," especially sections 1, 7, and 8 dealing with trade, work, street railways, tramways, and excursions for pleasure. Similar cases in Nova Scotia and in New Brunswick had been recently decided in different ways. Nova Scotia's Supreme Court had declared Sunday laws beyond provincial jurisdiction, while New Brunswick's court had decided they were within provincial jurisdiction. When Ontario's Supreme Court upheld the law, the Hamilton Street Railway appealed against the Attorney General of Ontario to the highest court in the British Empire, the Judicial Committee of the Privy Council. In London, A.B. Aylesworth, a prominent Liberal, argued the railways' case. O'Meara, the Ontario Alliance's lawyer and its former secretary, joined the Presbyterian J.A. Paterson, a sometime consultant to the Alliance and to the Ontario Government, to argue for the Attorney General. E.L. Newcombe represented the Dominion Government in favour, for once, of the provincial case. Certainly, the federal government, now Liberal, did not want to see controversial legislation of this kind given to the federal government.

On 14 July 1903, the Privy Council published its report that, "treated as a whole," the Ontario Lord's Day Act was *ultra vires* of provincial jurisdiction. The judges reasoned that Sunday legislation was indeed about religion, not just about civil or labour concerns. Religious legislation in Christendom had been classed as criminal legislation because criminal law had been based on the Ten Commandments. The commandments against killing, theft, and perjury had become part of criminal legislation, so the commandment to observe the Sabbath, if interpreted as Sunday, also placed Sunday laws within criminal jurisdiction. Under the British North America Act, the federal government was given jurisdiction over criminal law and, therefore, provincial Sunday laws passed after Confederation in 1867 were void.

Religious legislation was now exclusively a federal responsibility, whether the federal government wanted it or not. Whenever religion had appeared in federal politics—in the controversies over the Jesuit Estates, Louis Riel, or separate schools—John A. Macdonald's Conservative government tried to give it to the provinces in order not to tear apart a fragile federation with religious fanaticism. The Liberals under Laurier had gained power with the promise to satisfy the abused religious and linguistic minorities in each province, especially Manitoba. Although how they were going to satisfy everyone was a mystery, they had gained power. The government had both the legal as well as the moral right to act in the Sunday case, as they had in the Manitoba Schools Question, but the Liberals once again avoided action and began consultations.

The time between the beginning of the Hamilton Street Railway case and the decision by the Privy Council had allowed sabbatarians to organize an impressive, seemingly united force. The triennial Lord's Day Alliance convention of 1901 had recruited the Honourable Robert L. Borden of Halifax, an Anglican and, more importantly, leader of the federal Conservatives, as a vice president. A Methodist minister, John Potts, was president, while John Charlton and a labour representative from British Columbia, Ralph Smith, were vice presidents. A Congregationalist, John Copp, held the treasurer's chair. Provincial organizations displayed similar delicate balances among Presbyterians, Methodists, Congregationalists, and Anglicans. New members had been added and were organized in more branches. There were 312 branches in 1902. By 1903 there were 433; by 1904 these had grown to 510 with, the Alliance claimed, 25,000 members.

In part, the growth in membership was due to the Methodists, who were now firmly won over to the Alliance by Moore's vigorous activity. A pastor from Hamilton, like Shearer, Moore became a field secretary in early 1903. He had earlier attended the Montreal Christian Endeavor Convention as a press secretary and had been deeply impressed by Shearer's speeches. He had attended the Hamilton convention of 1901, too, as a Methodist delegate. To advance "God's Kingdom" and to preserve "for our country the holy Sabbath," Moore became Shearer's second-in-command.[19] Moore was only a year younger than Shearer, but Moore was robust where Shearer was pale and thin. This explains the phenomenal growth in membership. Moore spent weeks and months on the road, in true Methodist circuit-rider fashion, building on Shearer's Presbyterian bureaucratic foundations.

In the same period, from 1901 to 1905, the Lord's Day Alliance refined its political tactics. In 1902, Shearer re-established the fitfully published Alliance newsletter, the *Lord's Day Advocate,* on a monthly basis, expanded it, and patterned it after the popular *Presbyterian Record.*

It looked and sounded like a magazine and not just a tract. The offices of the Presbyterian Church and of the Alliance were in the same building, so that materials, typefaces, and techniques were passed from one to the other. The *Advocate*'s readership soared, since the Alliance sent it to everyone who expressed an interest in Sunday observance. Perhaps they used the *Record* mailing list to reach out to a natural sabbatarian constituency. Among articles, inspirational pieces, photographs of prominent sabbatarians, letters, and notes, the new *Advocate* published, for a religious magazine of the time, surprisingly powerful "Axioms in Sabbath Defence." Consider the following: "Ordinarily persuasion is better than coercion. But in dealing with greed—especially corporate greed—an ounce of legal restriction is worth a ton of moral suasion. Assume that an officer intends to do his duty until he demonstrates the contrary. Then get after him publicly and if necessary let his official head fall."[20] In the same mood, Presbyterian Reverend J.A. Macdonald, editor of the Toronto *Globe,* declared, "If any man among you seemeth to be religious and declineth to attend a political caucus or committee, that man's religion is vain."[21] Previously, the Deputy Attorney General of Ontario had received reports that clergymen were "willing to write letters at a long distance, but as to acting, they seemed to be afraid public opinion was too strong against them."[22] Obviously, sabbatarians were no longer afraid to use new political tactics for their crusade.

In a tremendous effort, the Alliance reached out even to Catholics. Immediately after the Privy Council's decision in the Hamilton Street Railway case, the Alliance informed Canadian Catholic archbishops of the decision. Moore summarized the argument in the following words: "We do not discuss the question of Sabbath observance, but confine our efforts to the preservation of the Weekly Rest Day."[23] Religious pluralism and mutual tolerance, Owen Chadwick has argued, are the foundation stones for secularism. The relatively youthful (forty-five in 1900) Archbishop Bruchési of Montreal, the most industrial city of Canada, was won over to the watered-down proposal for a rest day. He published a pastoral letter condemning the scandal of paid Sunday amusements. "Do you not see," he wrote, "that these amusements organized by greedy speculators lead hundreds of people to the desertion of Mass, the abandonment of the sacraments, to ignorance of the truths of faith, to the destruction of the family tie, and to the weakening, if not the complete extinction, of good morals . . . ?"[24]

Other Catholics, especially in Nova Scotia, where Catholic-Protestant relations were healthier, were sympathetic to sabbatarianism and wrote to applaud Archbishop Bruchési.[25] Throughout 1903 and into 1904, the Alliance wooed Roman Catholics by publishing statements by Leo XIII and American bishops who praised Sunday as a day of rest.[26] Eventually the *Advocate* gathered statements from several Canadian Catholic bishops in the January 1904 edition.

Not all Roman Catholic bishops were enthusiastic. When the Honourable Charles Fitzpatrick, a Montreal Roman Catholic and minister of justice in Laurier's cabinet, submitted the Alliance's proposed law to Bruchési, the archbishop conferred with his fellow bishops. One of them, the bishop of Sherbrooke, baldly stated he did not want to see the Catholic Church working with anti-Catholic John Charlton or the Lord's Day Alliance. The vicar general of Quebec declared that Catholics had less influence in Ottawa than in Quebec City and should stick to Quebec.[27] Bishop Labrecque of Chicoutimi, however, allowed his name and an anti-Sunday-work pastoral letter to appear in the April *Advocate* of 1904. He was concerned with the worker's right to Sunday rest. Some bishops had only rest for their flock at heart; others, like Bruchési, were concerned with the desecration of Sunday by theatre-going. Bruchési reported to Fitzpatrick that, in the bishops' opinions, it was not certain that the Hamilton Street Railway case left the provinces entirely without legislative authority. Moreover, the people of Quebec (mainly Catholics) differed from people in Ontario and in the Maritimes as to what was permissible. Personally, he believed the clauses against the powerful railways and theatres were too lenient, while those against small shopkeepers were too harsh. Yet he did not want railways and boats to be forbidden to carry passengers such as pilgrims to holy sites. All in all, he and his colleagues recommended to Fitzpatrick that Sunday observance legislation be left to the provinces; the provinces could make allowances for religious differences.[28] Finally,

Bruchési hinted that the Catholic bishops would be prepared to support a federal law only after it was proven that provinces could in no way make Sunday laws.

To take advantage of this Catholic fissure in the Alliance's ranks, Fitzpatrick and Laurier's federal cabinet spent time in drafting a provincial Sunday law. They hoped to place Sunday, as a civil day of rest, back within provincial jurisdiction. To test its validity, the cabinet sent the bill to the Supreme Court for an opinion. The Court handed down its decision in March of 1905, saying that the Privy Council had already decided that such laws were in federal jurisdiction. The government rushed an appeal to the Privy Council; in July the latter refused to hear the case, *The Attorney General for Canada v. The Wabash Railroad Co. and Others* on the grounds that it was hypothetical, and it was beyond the Privy Council's mandate to hear hypothetical cases. The federal government alone was still responsible for Sunday legislation. The Alliance, strengthened by delays that allowed it to grow even further, now increased its pressure on the federal government to pass a Dominion-wide law. Luckily for the Alliance, the uneasy Catholic endorsement of the Alliance's watered-down position held firm.

As usual, while one message was being given to the people in French Canada, another one was being given to those in English Canada. The Alliance promoted in English Canada the worry that Canada's English and Protestant nationalism would be weakened if a weekly rest day were not enshrined in law. Recent immigrants—white, Anglo-Saxon, and Protestant—were automatically considered good Canadians, but increased immigration from eastern Europe threatened Canada's WASP integrity. The creation of Canadian nationality meant enshrining evangelical British Protestantism in law. Shearer wrote to an Ontario politician: "No nation, therefore no Government can disregard with impunity the Lord's Day. The national welfare is bound up with the maintenance of its integrity and sanctity."[29] To help drive the national message home, Shearer published a Sabbath hymn in the *Advocate.* It was sung to the tune of "God Save the King" and loosely based on words from the American hymn "My Country 'tis of Thee."

O Sabbath, 'tis of thee,
Sweet day of liberty
And worshipping;

Type of the soul's repose
Blest at creation's close
Day when my Lord arose,
Of thee I sing.

Thou treasure house of prayer,
Thou balm for pain and care,
Thou fount of praise;

Thy mornings breathe release,
Thy evenings whisper peace,
Thy anthems never cease.
Thou psalm of days . . . .[30]

Moore himself united nationalism and the fear of foreigners by stating that the Alliance's work was "on the broadest lines of patriotism seeking to defend the rights of the people of Canada to a Weekly Rest Day against the encroachments of materialism so prominent in every part of Canada, and the influence of certain foreign elements." [31]

An evangelical Protestant coalition in English Canada, support from Catholic bishops, and a heady English Protestant nationalism united to fuel the Alliance's pressure on the federal government for a national Sunday law. If Shearer could convince Laurier that all or nearly all of Canada was behind the Alliance, then the federal government would act.

In the drive for one Sunday for all of Canada, the main Christian denominations presented a united front to the country, yet behind this facade lay traditional mistrust and deep disagreements.

Religious cooperation grew out of growing nationalism and a new generation of Social Gospellers. As in the United States, they came primarily from the ranks of Baptists, Methodists, and Presbyterians. Industrialization, epitomized by the railroads, and urbanization, compounded by immigration, brought the churches—even the Roman Catholic Church—to dedicate more time, money, and personnel to social concerns. The growing nation caused social commentators to worry about and plan for Canada's future. To civilize Canada meant, in their minds, to christianize it. The organization of Canada meant the Christian organization and reorganization of working time itself on the model of Christian sacred time. The Sunday-Sabbath was the most important model of Christian sacred time, and Christian denominations could at least agree that it was important.

A new generation of religious leaders was coming forward. Shearer and Moore from Hamilton and Bruchési in Montreal were taking over from the older generation of Caven, Charlton, and the Bishop of Sherbrooke—embittered adversaries in past battles over schools, Riel, Jesuit Estates, and countless smaller battles. The new Protestant generation was coming from southwestern Ontario and, in particular, from power bases in Toronto and Hamilton. That region of English Canada had experienced profound industrialization, as had Montreal in French Canada. Southwestern Ontario had also experienced the American Social Gospel movement. It faced, like Montreal, a growing immigrant population unfamiliar with and probably indifferent to the past compromises, past battles, and past achievements. New Christian leaders turned from the nineteenth-century preoccupation of fighting amongst themselves to, dare I say, an ecumenically minded common front in fighting the problems of the twentieth century.

These new religious leaders recognized the increasing importance of the federal government. Despite the reluctance of secular authorities, such as Laurier's Liberals, to unite church and state, court decisions and electoral pressures seemed to leave no choice. Only one opponent, the railway with the businesses it represented, favoured the separation of religion from secular life. The Hamilton Street Railway case had been able to drive sabbatarians from the provincial realm, where most business took place, into the federal realm, so now the reorganized sabbatarians confidently besieged Ottawa. The fourth commandment must be and would be enshrined in a federal law, the sabbatarians believed, for the righteousness of Canada.

Say to the people of Israel, "You shall keep my sabbaths, for this is a sign between me and you throughout your generations, that you may know that I, the LORD, *sanctify you. You shall keep the sabbath, because it is holy for you; every one who profanes it shall be put to death; whoever does any work on it, that soul shall be cut off from among his people. Six days shall work be done, but the seventh day is a sabbath of solemn rest, holy to the* LORD . . ."—EXODUS 31:12–16

Any person who violates any of the provisions of this Act shall for each offence be liable, on summary conviction, to a fine, not less than one dollar and not exceeding forty dollars, together with the cost of prosecution.—LORD'S DAY ACT, 1906

CHAPTER TWO

THE LORD'S DAY ACT

Religion in Politics, 1906

IN 1905, SHEARER APPROACHED THE ANGLICAN BISHOP of Saskatchewan to release his archdeacon for service as a western secretary with the Lord's Day Alliance. It was important to the Alliance to secure an Anglican in order to show that this important Christian denomination supported the Alliance. It was also important that this Anglican secretary be from the West so that the Alliance might bring the immigrant settlers, many of them Anglican, to observe the evangelical Sabbath. In spite of favourable Anglican pastoral letters and despite some signs of Anglican support for religious legislation to protect Sunday as a day of rest, the bishop of Saskatchewan refused Shearer's request. The Alliance was unable to agree upon any other western Anglican minister. None had the proper Sunday attitude.[1]

The eight Roman Catholic archbishops of Canada had formed a committee, which had declared that the "State cannot make its citizens

Christians, or purify their private lives, by Act of Parliament, we readily grant; but it has the power and the duty of restraining those who would force its people to forego their right to bodily rest on Sunday, with its opportunities for moral and spiritual improvements."[2] Like Anglicans, they were unconvinced of the need for legislation. If a law had to be passed, the archbishops asked that pleasure excursions, freight trains, recreations for a fee, mining, and factory work be stopped in order that churchgoing be safeguarded. Although there was no mention of Sunday's sacred character in the archbishops' letter, Shearer broadcast the accord and wrote to priests and parishioners telling them about the archbishops' support for Sunday legislation.

The people of Quebec, however, did not fall into line behind the Lord's Day Alliance. Only ten Alliance branches were formed in all of Quebec, mainly in English-speaking Protestant centres. In contrast, almost every town in Ontario had a branch. Moreover, the financial and organizational difficulties—there were never enough volunteers or donors—kept a stream of letters from the Alliance secretaries flowing to Quebec, urging more efforts and more money.[3] Shearer comforted himself with the fact that Montreal's Archbishop Paul Bruchési had written a pastoral banning Sunday theatres, political meetings, horse races, and all excursions except pilgrimages. Alliance letters went out mainly to English Catholics in Nova Scotia.[4] Perhaps the letters were more easily written in English, but more likely was the belief that English Catholics would fit more easily into the national vision of an English Protestant Canada.

Popular measures were taken to reach out to more people. An itinerant American preacher, well-known former Seventh-Day Adventist Reverend S.W. Gamble, was hired to travel the Canadian pulpit lecture circuit, "inoculate [the] people generally against the virus of the Saturday-Sabbath heresy," and "turn back to their former faith not a few of the Seventh Day perverts."[5] Seventh-Day Adventists and Seventh-Day Baptists were considered troublesome and heretical because of their insistence on the literal seventh-day Sabbath of the Hebrew scriptures. Like that of the Israelites, their Sabbath began at sunset on Friday and lasted until sunset on Saturday. To avoid a public conflict highlighting how the Christians themselves were divided as to which day was the actual Lord's Day, newspapers were pressed for neutrality or even silence on this issue, while the American preacher roamed to convert more literalistic Christians.[6]

Jews were not ignored but were labelled an insignificant, hostile, foreign minority along with Muslims and Buddhists. The Alliance's *Advocate* asked a nativist question: "Why should aliens be encouraged and tolerated, who trample upon our rights and institutions, when we make them sharers in our heritage of law, liberty, and equality?"[7] T.A. Moore wrote: "Something should be done at once to prevent our Sunday from being so openly desecrated: our law from being so flagrantly broken; and our country from being degraded by the vicious practices of foreigners."[8] Nationalism became the secular form of the sabbatarian creed. Nationalistic arguments were brought out against many who, as David Rome drily observed, were several generations from their immigrant ancestors. At least, one might add, many Jews were hardly more recent immigrants than the people Moore was addressing. Mormons, who were believed not to be Christian and were often American immigrants, were treated with softer words, since they and their *Book of Mormon* supported Sunday observance.[9]

As the Alliance moved towards legislative reform, it did not forget the effective pressure that prosecutions under the pre-Confederation laws afforded, but these efforts—in prosecutions, newspaper battles, and in preaching—were sometimes wasted. The differences and exceptions from one provincial law to another made Canadian Sabbath observance a patchwork and unacceptable to the righteous and unity-minded nationalism of sabbatarians. So, public pressure through the Alliance branches was brought to bear on the government. Even members of Parliament were elected in absentia to Alliance committees and were then strongly invited to attend Alliance meetings or have their constituents informed that their member of Parliament had declined the honour.[10]

By 1905, the Alliance was ready to carry its crusade to Ottawa. Since 1902, the *Advocate* had grown to a circulation of over 30,000 and theoretically reached 100,000 people, according to Alliance estimates.[11] Using the *Advocate,* Shearer and his friends arranged to flood Parliament

Hill with petitions demanding legislation. Each and every one of them, Shearer reminded Laurier, was signed *"only* by *Electors."* Furthermore, although "there will no doubt be a small counter petition from the Seventh-Day Adventists, who number less than fifteen hundred members in Canada, led almost exclusively by American preachers, and while there will be strenuous opposition by certain interested corporations, there can be no doubt that the great mass of Electors are with us in seeking this law."[12]

This combination of nativist arguments, force of numbers, supposed Catholic and pan-Protestant support, some western and some labour support, and petitions convinced Laurier's government that the elusive will-o-the-wisp, public opinion, demanded action. The Alliance kindly provided a draft Dominion Lord's Day Act signed by its prominent church and parliamentary members.[13]

"An Act respecting the Lord's Day" was announced in the Speech from the Throne on 8 March 1906, along with the Laurier government's self-congratulations for the entry of the western provinces, Alberta and Saskatchewan, into Confederation. Significantly, another national concern reported in the Speech from the Throne was an extension of the National Transcontinental Railway. The government's agenda delicately balanced diverse Canadian issues of the Social Gospel, the growing nation, and industry. The Lord's Day Alliance would soon be struggling on the floor of the House of Commons with the railways for a different vision of the Canadian nation.

Four days later, Charles Fitzpatrick, minister of justice, introduced the Lord's Day bill. Except for works of necessity or mercy on Sunday, the bill prohibited "sales, the prosecution of ordinary work or business, excursions, games for prizes, the opening of places of public amusement for which an admission fee is charged, to advertise any performance or other thing prohibited by this Act." The stricter pre-Confederation provincial laws were untouched. Public response to the first reading was mixed. While the Alliance rejoiced, a growing number of counter-petitions were sent to Ottawa.

The *Advocate* commented enthusiastically on efforts by Catholics such as Charles Fitzpatrick and Archbishop Bruchési to curb Sunday activities. Bruchési had written a letter to Laurier approving the proposed law in principle. He stated that although some sections of the proposed bill were too severe, the state had the right to legislate in matters of custom.[14] On 30 March 1906, the largest circulation French-Canadian newspaper, *La Presse,* commented favourably on the proposed law as it was interpreted by Bruchési. But who was to decide what was custom and what was truth? Laurier decided that Sunday was indeed a matter of custom and wrote to Bruchési that he would protect both French and Jewish minorities.[15]

At the second reading on 3 April 1906, Fitzpatrick felt compelled "by the criticism offered by some public bodies, by the press, by anonymous correspondents" to offer an explanation "that the Act respecting the Lord's Day did not intend to affect the religious observance of the Sabbath." It promoted the custom of a weekly rest day and, if the worker desired it, allowed him a time for worship. Sunday rest or Sunday work was a matter of custom, this Catholic cabinet minister stated. In explaining the provisions of this bill, the minister dealt with Quebec customs, special religious practices, and business interests. He quickly allowed Quebec customs, such as notarizing deeds for those who could not go to town on work days or the sale of articles at the church for charitable purposes. Two Conservatives from Hamilton, George E. Foster, a Free-Christian Baptist, and Samuel Barker, an Anglican, urged business exemptions for trains and continuous manufacturing processes, which a Catholic, Fitzpatrick, just as quickly admitted.

As for "the religious convictions of some elements in our community," in the House of Commons, Fitzpatrick parroted the Alliance's arguments against Jews: "It is not desirable for us to be too considerate of the wishes of alien immigrants who . . . while they are obtaining the benefits which this country is affording them, will not be subjected to undue hardship if they are obliged . . . to obey any rules which we, as a Christian community, find it necessary to lay down for the observance of the Sunday."[16] In the name of nationalism, Sunday sabbatarianism would beat down Saturday sabbatarianism. The bill was hastily sent to a select committee for modification.

While the bill was in committee, the Alliance stepped up its pressure campaign by instituting a Lord's Day Week from 22 April to 29 April. Ministers and lay people were encouraged to contact their members of Parliament. This, too, visibly helped as "Several individual members . . . who were opposing the bill, experienced very speedy conversions to our side, as a result of communications received from our Branches in their constituencies," reported Shearer.[17] Shearer also planned an unprecedented series of pamphlets in French to send to Quebec and to other parts of Canada. Nonetheless, indifference in Quebec to Alliance claims continued, and a lack of donations stifled the Alliance's efforts in that province. Only the Roman Catholic hierarchy within Quebec continued its already qualified support of the Alliance.

When Jews visited the committee, a Montreal group led by Harris Vineburg argued that the repeated statement about the necessity to maintain Christianity in the nation did not automatically lead to Sunday laws. England and the United States did not have such restrictive laws. The bill was likely to become law, so Rabbi Goldstein of Holy Blossom Temple asked the committee for an amendment. It was to become known as the Jewish exemption clause, although it could apply equally to Seventh-Day people who were also in attendance.

> [W]hoever conscientiously and habitually observes the seventh day of the week as the Sabbath and actually refrains from work and labour on that day, shall not be subject to prosecution for performing work or labour on the first day of the week, provided that such work or labour does not disturb other persons in the observance of the first day of the week as holy time, and that the place where the same is performed be not open for traffic on that day.[18]

It embodied a common practice among many Jews in Christian countries, but Alliance sabbatarians jumped on the amendment as one "so cunningly worded that a Jew or Adventist could open and run his factory on Saturday with Lord's Day observing employees, and on Sunday with Saturday observing employees."[19]

In the middle of this debate, A.B. Aylesworth, the Methodist lawyer who had argued before the Privy Council in the Hamilton Street Railway case that the Ontario Sunday law was outside provincial jurisdiction and so opened Pandora's box, became the new Minister of Justice. The former Minister, Fitzpatrick, escaped to the Supreme Court. Now, on 6 June, Aylesworth introduced the bill but publicly despaired of reconciling business and religious interests. He might have worried more about French Catholics.

In the House of Commons, major opposition came first from Henri Bourassa. Indebted to Laurier, who had originally fostered his career, and finding it impossible to support a mainly Protestant and English Conservative Party, he was a Liberal fellow-traveller. His uncompromising bi-cultural nationalism, his stance against Canadian participation in the Boer War, and his arguments for separate schools in the Manitoba schools controversy made him the Liberal Party's gadfly and an implacable foe of any narrowly defined nationalism. In 1906, he attacked both Liberal and Conservative members of the Alliance:

> [T]here has been no more absurd piece of legislation ever introduced into this parliament not only since confederation, but since the existence of parliaments in Canada. There is no more antiquated, medieval, or absurd legislation than this Bill which takes as its basis the assumption of the fact that the people must be deprived of their liberties [on Sundays] and then be granted piecemeal a few of them.[20]

He denounced the government for attempting to coerce morality and therefore "putting a premium on hypocrisy, drunkenness, idleness and the vices that develop in any country where the attempt is made to make people virtuous by law, instead of relying on the individual conscience and the moral quality of the church." On this high road of reasoning, Bourassa also indulged in a few low digs by asking if the bill would "allow farmers to clean cattle. I am told that in some of the holiest parts of Ontario some farmers refrain from cleaning their cattle on Sunday, they think that it does not come within the meaning of the words 'necessity or mercy.'"

Others rapidly joined Bourassa. His familiar nationalist lieutenants, Camille Piché and Armand Lavergne, and the Labour candidate from Montreal, Alphonse Verville, defended French-Canadian customs. They were as quickly followed by Conservative opposition members, such as Sam Hughes, who always enjoyed a chance to harass Liberals. The "thing is wrong side up," Hughes complained, "because it says what one may do instead of saying what one may not do."

To the Alliance's prayerful thanks, Laurier rose to lend his influence to the bill. His statement was a frank avowal that if "Sunday legislation has any meaning at all, and if it can have any basis at all, it is to give sanction to the divine precept that Sunday shall be made a day of rest and that there shall be no work on that day. If it has not that basis, what basis can it have?"[21] With this telling point, Laurier defended the traditional Judeo-Christian union of natural rest and divine worship, but he then weakened his position by explaining that many exemptions were needed in the new and growing country. New circumstances, unknown to the Israelites, demanded exceptions; the huge spaces of Canada needed the transportation technologies and certainly needed trains and boats to operate on Sundays.

In the debate that followed, Presbyterian David Henderson, a member of the Liberal-Conservatives, saw any amendment as an attempt to amend the fourth commandment. John Barr, a Methodist and Conservative, opposed the bill with Henderson, but because there was an amendment for Jews. Bourassa jumped in to give vent to his own anti-Semitism. To make the bill logical, he asked that no special privileges be given to anyone, least of all "to pander to the Jewish vote."

> Is it because they are the least remunerative class that we can get—that class which sucks the most from other people and gives back the least? Is it because they are the most undesirable class that can be brought into the country? . . . They do not adapt themselves to the customs of the people among whom they live, but on the contrary they conduct themselves in such a way that they are vampires on the community instead of being contributors to the general welfare of the people.[22]

If there were to be exceptions, everyone should be allowed exceptions.

Amid the jeers and catcalls throughout that night and the next day, Bourassa realized the implications of what he had just said. Suddenly, dramatically, he turned his back on his own bigotry and on the anti-Semitism mixed with Christian nationalism in the House of Commons. He began to argue that if the Jewish minority was to be safeguarded, then distinct Catholic customs in Quebec, which he had been preparing to sacrifice for a greater degree of common Canadian nationality, should be allowed as well. Bourassa wished that law and justice be extended to both the Jews and the French. He reintroduced the Jewish exemption clause.

The Conservative John Barr rose again to point out the difference between the Catholic hierarchy and the majority of the Catholic parliamentarians. Bourassa answered the Methodist that Bruchési, as his archbishop, was to be followed in matters of faith and morals. But Bourassa had not renounced the right to express his opinion about mere customs. Catholics believed Sunday observance to be only a custom, even if some Presbyterians believed it to be the law of God.

A torrent of words continued to shower on Bourassa as the Jewish exemption clause divided the House. Parties fractured as each member followed his own conscience. Methodists and Presbyterians, for the most part, spoke in favour of the bill and against the clause; Anglicans and Roman Catholics spoke against the bill and for the clause. Liberals debated with each other and voted with some Conservatives over and over again. The climax of the debate came with the discussion of the Jewish exemption clause itself.

George Smith, a Presbyterian and a Liberal, reiterated that Canada was a Christian country "running things on Christian lines;" Jews were voluntary strangers. Frank Carvell, a Methodist, believed that although the Seventh-Day Adventist is "so far ahead of the Jew that he ought not to be mentioned in the same class . . . both should be prohibited. There is only room in this country for one Sabbath. . . . I feel that we should have simply one law for every class of people in Canada and if these people do not like it they need not come here."[23] Aylesworth, his co-religionist, agreed and fought against any exception. Henry Miller, a Methodist member of the select committee in charge of examining the bill in its details, stated that if "we adopt the amendment we shall have to provide for a choice of Sabbath by the Mohammedans."[24] There were objections to the bill, because Jews would be forced by conscience not to work on their Sabbath as well as on Sunday. But James Kennedy, a Presbyterian elder, believed that "Jews can earn as much in five days as any of us can earn in six."[25] Besides, whether Jews had any respect for either conscience or their own Sabbath was an open question for many in the House of Commons![26]

Lonely voices objected; Jews were British subjects, as were Seventh-Day Adventists, and one right of a subject was liberty of conscience. They were not "strangers in the land" and, if they were, Christianity was "to do unto another as you would like another to do unto you."[27] If Canada was truly a Christian country, the Christian spirit would make room for conscientious convictions.[28] Armand Lavergne pleaded for consideration of the "Mahommedans or Chinese" who might have another Sabbath entirely. (He really did not know, but it made a good argument.) Anglican Charles Parmelee warned that if no exceptions were made, the law would create martyrs and, quoting the third century Christian writer, Tertullian, "from the very foundation of the Christian religion the blood of the martyr has been the seed of the church."[29] One member, Anglican William Cockshutt, explained the ferocity of the Sunday debate by saying that most Protestants put all of their religion "on the first day of the week and have very little left for the other six days."[30] There was so little sacred in the new Canadian nation that evangelical Protestants were fighting hard to safeguard what little they had. Late at night, tempers were short and chairs were emptying. Seeing support slipping away, the government forced the Jewish exemption clause to a vote. It was defeated 79 to 57.

Alliance sabbatarians were relieved that the Jewish exemption clause was defeated, but they did not have long to rejoice. Another amendment was introduced. It allowed the bill to be restricted by any provincial bills "[n]ow or hereafter in force regarding matters coming within the exclusive powers of provincial legislatures." It afforded the means by which the bill could be "if not more acceptable at least less disagreeable to the people of the province of Quebec."[31] Edward

Macdonald, Liberal and Presbyterian, objected and accused the French of sowing seeds of discord, but the amendment passed, demonstrating that members from provinces other than Quebec wanted it. In effect, this amendment gave the law back to the provinces and defeated the purpose of having a uniform federal, criminal law to regulate the Sabbath. Regional nationalisms had won a major battle over the proposed uniform federal nationalism. In effect, a notwithstanding clause (long before the end of the twentieth century popularized the phrase) had been introduced.

Once the outline of the law was decided, more economic amendments sprang up like mushrooms. Continuous processes needing Sunday work were broadly defined. Sunday trains were defended, as was the hiring of horses or carriages—especially when used to court women. Aylesworth valiantly tried to defend the bill; he criticized the Grimsby Park Methodist Camp Ground Company run by members of his denomination. He also attacked the broad definition of necessity many businesses used to justify Sunday work. After maple syrup manufacturing was considered a work of necessity by Prime Minister Laurier himself, however, Aylesworth gave up and the bill was read a second time.

Presbyterian Thomas Martin exploded and scoffingly described the government's purpose, not unjustly, as to start "at the first clause, go right through the Bill and emasculate it out of useful existence."[32] Only greed, he said, was destroying the bill. Bourassa responded by reading letters from his constituents condemning the Alliance people as narrow-minded bigots. They were "animated by the spirit of another age, a spirit which should not exist in a Christian, civilized, modern country."[33] This, of course, made a sensation in a House of Commons packed with volunteer Alliance members convinced of the progressive nature of the proposed law. Borden, quietly ignoring his own vice presidency in the Alliance, hammered away at the breaches in Liberal ranks until Fielding pointedly reminded him that Conservatives were as hopelessly divided. Amendment after amendment was proposed, debated and accepted. The talking went on in order to have the bill die with the end of the session, but on Saturday 7 July, at 3:25 a.m., third reading was forced.

The Senate speeches were pithy summaries. The bill was introduced by the Senate leader, Sir Richard Scott, a Catholic who had drafted the Scott local option Temperance Act (1878) and was probably trusted to have the experience to engineer some sort of compromise between Protestants and Catholics. He warned the Senate that he had "come to the conclusion that Acts of Parliament are of very little use where they encroach on the habits and customs of the people." So, he begged for compromise, safeguarding provincial rights, and cooperation between the two races of Canada.

His fellow senator, Liberal James McMullen, was soon on his feet to disillusion Scott. Calling the bill "one of the most important . . . that has been placed before the Senate since confederation," he expressed surprise that Quebeckers could reconcile God's Sabbath law with gambling, horse racing and amusements. Crudely confusing the Lord's Day bill with the fourth commandment, he challenged the French and the Catholics of Canada to judge themselves by the standard God had set up and Queen Victoria had exemplified!

This challenge was answered by Henry Joseph Cloran, another Liberal but a Roman Catholic. He admired the intent of the bill, but he protested that it was the product of excessive zeal. No compromise was possible, because each person's conscience had to decide how to carry out the commandment. Echoing Bourassa and the Roman Catholic archbishops, Cloran insisted that people could not be forced to be good or virtuous by fines or punishment. As for McMullen's insinuations about Quebec's moral laxity, Cloran retorted that Catholics were slaves to the whole gospel. They were in peril for their souls when they missed Sunday mass; this Protestant bill fined people one dollar for failing to observe the Sabbath. Above all, he was against the bill for religious reasons. After the religious, ethnic, and national arguments between the two Liberal Irishmen were on the record, the round of amendments went on as merrily as in the House of Commons. In recognition that the bill had very little to do with the Lord's Day and that Christians, Adventists, and Jews did not agree on which day actually was the Lord's Day, the Senate even tried to change "Lord's Day" to "Sunday" in the title. Would Catholics and Anglicans in the Upper House succeed in removing all traces of sabbatarianism from the bill?

The House of Commons turned down this last suggestion but accepted most of the other amendments. Royal Assent was given to the "Act respecting the Lord's Day," and Parliament was prorogued on 13 July. "It is far from perfect," Shearer admitted in the *Advocate*, "but it is probably the best Lord's Day Act on the statute books of any country. And it can and no doubt will be improved in future years." Moore summed up the result by saying that "throughout all Canada, there is no Sunday trading, no Sunday work, except in cases of necessity or mercy, no Sunday theatres, no Sunday entertainments where an admission fee is charged, no Sunday games for prizes or reward, no Sunday shooting at targets, no Sunday Newspapers, and a great reduction in labor and business in many other regards."[34] Perhaps.

Laurier tried to recognize Christianity without alienating minorities and special interests ("money and the ethnic vote"). A.M.C. Waterman believes that by the end of the debate, Christianity had been buried under an avalanche of exceptions. Secularism was on the rise in 1906, he states, because Christians did not influence public economic policy or progress. Waterman argues that the law was a dead letter even in 1906. The lack of strict Sunday sabbatarianism in the 1906 legislation has been equated with a decline in religion and with a rise in secularism. Waterman's analysis cannot be accepted, however, unless one also accepts his narrow economic definition of secularism and of religion. Must Christianity adversely affect the economy of the nation? In 1906, only a strict sabbatarian form of Christianity would have curtailed railway profits. The fact that enough exceptions were introduced to satisfy most businesses does not mean that Christians everywhere were dissatisfied. Only sabbatarians objected. Or was this, as sabbatarians often complained, "the thin edge of the wedge"?

More importantly, Waterman concludes that the "only live religious issue sustained throughout the entire debate was the question of the strict Sabbatarians ('Saturdarian' as the *Advocate* sneeringly called them), the Jews and the Seventh Day Adventists."[35] Yet there was a lively religious debate among Christians, too. Only Methodists and Presbyterians spoke in favour of the bill and against the Jewish exemption clause. Even among these two evangelical Protestant groups, some Methodist clergymen wanted to keep Grimsby Park open for Sunday camp meetings. Mainly Catholics and Anglicans spoke against the bill and for the Jewish exemption clause. This forcefully shows the conflict between two broad forms of Christianity. The seventh-day controversy was only one of the controversies that split the Christian community. Others were based on differing conceptions of religion and, specifically, of sacred time. Was Sunday rest a custom or a divine commandment still in force today?

What of the fact that the sabbatarians had gone into politics? Presbyterians and Methodists, dissenters in England, might have been expected to skirt legislative control of religious matters. At second glance, however, one remembers the strong theocratic impulse within the puritanical circles that had fought for control in England, in Knox's Scotland, in Calvin's Geneva, as well as in the New World. The term "Blue Laws" was coined from the Massachusetts' Puritan-inspired laws bound in blue and famous throughout New England for their severity. Evangelicals were looking for ways to make their own beliefs manifest in Canada.

One might have thought that Anglicans and Catholics, with long traditions of close church-state cooperation in other countries as well as in Canada, might have favoured the Lord's Day bill in its strictest form. Some Catholic and Anglican clergy were ready to co-operate with the state, but their theological conception of time did not invest one particular day of the week with sacred power. Catholic and Anglican church-state cooperation for a national holy day remained divided and unenthusiastic at best.

Lay Anglicans and Catholics, such as Bourassa, did not reject compromise between the claims of church and state, but they retained a vivid appreciation of healthy cultural restraints on the totalitarian demands of religious enthusiasm expressed in evangelical denominations. Their traditions allowed a much greater importance to be accorded to custom. Both hierarchies and their parliamentarians worked on the assumption that the choice of Sunday as the Christian day of commemoration was one of church discipline and of culture. The day itself could be discarded in favour of other religious principles—including tolerance for Jews.

The Catholic hierarchy supported the law, as Sharon Patricia Meen states "for reasons of its own." And those reasons were substantially different from sabbatarian ones. Similarly, Catholic parliamentarians—Bourassa and Laurier—realized that religious minorities such as French-speaking Catholics needed protection against the crusading and nationalistic sabbatarianism, the English-speaking Protestants.

More simply still, Roman Catholics, many of them French-Canadians, might have had a greater sense of belonging and of indigenous nationalism, which would have conferred an equal sense of identity and security. In this case, there was no pressure to create a Christian Canada in their own image. They were already Canadian and already Christian. Their spaces and their times had already settled into sacred and secular patterns. There were already sacred pilgrimage sites and sacred holiday times. There was no great need to institute new ones to civilize Canada. Canada, outside of Quebec's borders, was lost to French-Canadian national hopes; why should Quebec's elites help the English Protestants fashion the rest of Canada in an English and Protestant image?

Anglicans had also been courted by the Alliance, yet they did not accept sabbatarian presuppositions about the need to consecrate the expanding Canadian West. Many Anglicans opposing the Lord's Day bill were from the West, specifically from British Columbia, and their conception of western needs had little to do with the homogenization of all westerners into the evangelical Protestantism of southern Ontario. Anglicans seemed to have less concern for Canadian national life; they protected their British-inherited, English-language advantages. Edward Pulker believes that the Lord's Day Act of 1906 was the first Canadian Anglican involvement in social activism. Yet never again in his work does Pulker refer to the Sunday question. For the majority of Anglicans after 1906, many other theological debates were of greater importance. And Anglican England held greater significance than an evangelical Canada.

Presbyterians, Methodists, and Congregationalists had confused Christian custom with the biblical Sabbath and invested Sunday with

This cartoon is adapted from one appearing in a New York paper. The male figure is Father Knickerbocker who personifies the city of N.Y. It strikingly illustrates the value of a good Lord's Day Act such as ours. Of course the cartoonist had not seen Montreal or certain parts of B.C. on the Lord's Day.

From the Lord's Day Advocate, *1906. Canada was usually portrayed as a young and virtuous woman compared to an older Uncle Sam.*

divine sanction. For them, therefore, no cultural variations could be allowed, without the risk of trespassing on God's law. The Sunday-Sabbath was doubly important in that it was a sign of how a Christian ideal could become a concrete practice. Actual passage of the Lord's Day Act signalled the arrival of a new crusading vision of Christendom, that of Shearer, Moore, and other sabbatarians who would later move into other social-reform areas.

In 1906, religious fragmentation contributed to the rise of what is popularly known as "secularism." Religious authorities, Presbyterian and Methodist, with the qualified support of some Catholics and Anglicans, had enough power to bring their desires to Parliament but not enough to enforce their evangelical will. The separation of Canadian religious and secular realms appeared to have widened another degree. Yet it was religion among Catholic and Anglican parliamentarians, supported by Jews and Seventh-Day Adventists, which allowed the "Act respecting the Lord's Day" to be gutted by amendments. In 1906, Canadian Christendom clearly showed two factions: reforming Methodist and Presbyterian churches versus conservative Catholic and Anglican churches with support from Jews. The latter coalition safeguarded the economic growth of Canadian industry and helped the rise of "secularism," but it did so on religious grounds: tolerance.

Secularism, as R.C. Tucker has suggested, also means "the displacement of religious emotion into other areas, particularly the political."[36] In Protestant Canada, Christian civilization encouraged the consecration of the Canadian nation and ultimately the world. In 1906, one form of Canadian Christianity tried to legislate the Kingdom of God. There was to be no place for religious dissent. Other forms of Christianity fought to safeguard their religious differences through the tools of provincial dissent and broad definitions of natural necessity. Sabbatarians succeeded in bringing Christian moral authority to the political arena for a law embodying sabbatarian principles. This movement into the political arena in exchange for a religious law was the real secularization of 1906.

Religious fragmentation weakened the sabbatarian demand. When held up to scrutiny in Parliament by politicians, and not just religious leaders, divisions and fissures among sabbatarians were evident, and Parliament was able to assess sabbatarianism's true power on secular grounds. Power there was, so Laurier and the other parliamentarians agreed to pass a law. Shearer and Moore were overjoyed by the fact that some type of sabbatarianism had been able to influence the government of Canada. They would push for more concessions at some other time, but Shearer realized that sabbatarians received in law the equivalent of what the many different Alliance elements had demanded in common: very little. Sabbatarians implemented some of their theocratic vision of a righteous Canada, but religious fragmentation prevented them from winning a complete victory in the political arena. This very secular political arena found itself to be the final court of appeal for religious groups of Canada. The true secularization present in 1906 was the fact that a religious problem was being debated and decided not by religious authorities but by political authorities. Throughout 1905 and into 1906, the Lord's Day Alliance secularized its sabbatarian message by translating it into the language of nationalism. Nationalism helped to unite most Protestant churches behind the Sabbath crusade, but English Protestant nationalism alienated both French Catholics and Jews.

For six years you shall sow your land and gather in its yield; but the seventh year you shall let it rest and lie fallow, that the poor of your people may eat. . . . Six days you shall do your work, but on the seventh day you shall rest; that your ox and your ass may have rest, and the son of your bond maid, and the alien, may be refreshed.—EXODUS 23:10–12

If a manufacturer wants to keep his shop open seven days a week, and can get people to work for him, let him do it.
—RATIONAL SUNDAY LEAGUE DECLARATION, 1907

CHAPTER THREE

PYRRHIC VICTORY?

Sunday and Regionalism, 1907–1914

TO SABBATARIAN REJOICING, THE LORD'S DAY ACT came into force on 1 March 1907. It forbade excursions on any transportation system, newspaper work and sales, unnecessary railway and steamship work, paid sports, and most other types of work. The more severe pre-Confederation laws in the Maritimes and in Ontario prohibiting amusements, hunting, shooting, and fishing were untouched and could be used to prosecute Sabbath breakers. For the first time, corporations, such as the great railways, could be fined like individuals. As John G. Shearer, the general secretary of the Alliance crowed: The "railway men are about the maddest crowd you could find in this Dominion. It is something new for them to be beaten and to be beaten by preachers and their like is too humiliating altogether."[1]

Alliance success brought Canadian sabbatarians into world prominence. Alliance secretaries were invited to serve on executive positions of the Sunday Rest Associations of America. As in the United States, the successes of Canadian sabbatarians promoted greater cooperation among Protestant denominations, which led to the Moral and Social Reform Council of Canada, organized in 1907, with Shearer at its head. The Canadian Alliance became an inspiration for Britain, the United States, and Presbyterians everywhere. The entire world seemed to be adopting the Canadian model. Switzerland, France, Spain, Belgium, China, and Japan passed Sunday laws.[2]

In Canada, however, the Sunday battle was far from finished. Federal law gave administration of the 1906 Lord's Day Act to the provincial Attorneys General. This meant that a national Sunday was still not guaranteed. Roman Catholics in Quebec and in northern Ontario, Seventh-Day Adventists in the Prairies, and Anglicans in British Columbia found that they could lead effective regional oppositions against sabbatarians, who were in the majority probably only in Ontario. As immigrants swelled Canada's population, power ebbed from sabbatarians. Questions about whether a Christian nation must have a Sabbath were heard across Canada from 1907 to 1914. Religious fragmentation reasserted itself and gave the railways a second chance to impose their own economic vision of Canadian nationalism. Had it not been for the prominent and mainly Presbyterian or Methodist sabbatarians guarding Canada's Sunday, other religious groups and the railways would have had their way.

IMMEDIATELY AFTER PASSAGE OF THE LORD'S DAY ACT, the leadership of the Alliance disintegrated. Members, once they believed there was no longer any need of their services or no longer any political power in a spent crusade, left to join other organizations. For example, Conservative leader Robert Borden resigned in late 1906. Enthusiasm became a memory, and the Alliance transformed itself into a political watchdog. Membership peaked at 40,000 in 1907 and began a slow decline. The second triennial meeting, a gala affair held in late November 1907, united the who's who of English Canada to celebrate not only the federal law but also the honorary doctorate that the Presbyterian Church's Knox College gave to Shearer. At the same time, reports were trickling in from around the country of deaths, resignations, and non-attendance. The dead: Archbishop Bond, Primate of the Church of England and honorary president of the Alliance; President John Potts, the Methodist minister; Maurice Baldwin, the Low Church Anglican Bishop of Huron and long-time supporter; William Caven, principal of Knox College; and D.J. O'Donoghue, the Labour representative. Shearer retired officially at the triennial meeting to work for the Presbyterian Church as general secretary of its new department of Moral and Social Reform. Moore, who took Shearer's place as the Alliance's general secretary, had been rewarded with the secretaryship of the Methodist Church's General Conference, so his vigorous work for the Alliance declined as work in Methodist administration took up more of his time. By 1908, Moore's nagging worry was how to "electrify" and inspire the provincial Alliance meetings.[3]

W.M. Rochester, General Secretary, Lord's Day Alliance, 1911–1927, and a Presbyterian minister.

One way to increase enthusiasm and continue the Sabbath crusade was to increase paid, full-time staff. At the height of the 1906 controversy, when the Alliance's efforts to secure an Anglican or a Baptist secretary failed, the executive committee turned to another Presbyterian to act as its western secretary. Born in southwestern Ontario, the Reverend William Marshall Rochester had impeccable academic credentials and had been on the Presbyterian Church's Sabbath Observance Committee since 1893. Moreover, he had actually served in western pastorates. When Moore resigned in 1910, Rochester took over the general secretaryship. Another Presbyterian, the Reverend W.G. Hanna, former secretary of the Ontario Alliance and a well-known moral reformer from Toronto, succeeded Moore as eastern secretary and then was transferred back to Ontario when Rochester became general secretary. A Presbyterian, George Mingie, was chosen for Quebec and the Maritimes, while another Presbyterian, J.S. Watson, was hired for Manitoba and Saskatchewan. Only British Columbia and Alberta, when Rochester left that field for the head office in Toronto, enjoyed the services of someone other than a Presbyterian. Charles H. Huestis, a Methodist minister, was a well-known pacifist writer and psychology lecturer at Alberta College and, later, at the Alberta School of Religion. He started full-time work for the Alliance in 1911. The Sabbath crusade was still led by Presbyterians and followed closely by Methodists. As in the United States, Presbyterians were firmly in the vanguard of the continuing Canadian Sunday controversy.

Although older faces were disappearing—John Charlton died in 1910—other Presbyterians took their places, and so the Alliance was able to continue its work. A victory had been won; the crusaders had gone on to other crusades. But the Alliance's religious leadership had been largely renewed with new Presbyterians; it could now continue as a political lobby and watchdog. Many denominations disagreed with the Alliance about the need for a national Sabbath. After 1906, they would have their say wherever they formed an important percentage of the community.

IN THE 1907 TO 1914 PERIOD, five regions of Canada disagreed with Presbyterians about the need for a national day of rest. In Ontario itself, two regions could be found. Persistent anti-sabbatarian feeling was found near the American border in southwestern Ontario, despite the evangelical tradition or perhaps in reaction to it, and influenced by the United States. Northern Ontario provided another opponent to Toronto's Lord's Day Alliance. Quebec, British Columbia, and the Prairies also presented the Alliance with persistent anti-sabbatarian campaigns. These regions were religiously different. Quebec, Windsor in southern Ontario, and northern Ontario held high numbers of Roman Catholics. British Columbia had a relatively higher percentage of Anglicans, Americans, and non-Anglo-Saxon immigrants than Canada as a whole. The Prairies were filling up with American,

Seventh-Day Adventist, and eastern European immigrants with no knowledge of and no sympathy for the Sunday-Sabbath of Canada's English Protestants.

First and foremost among the opponents to the Alliance was Quebec. Henri Bourassa's final Commons speech in the 1906 Lord's Day bill debate stated that the people of Quebec "will regard this law as some Americans said they regarded Indians. The saying there was that the only good Indian was a dead Indian. I think the people of Quebec will regard this as a good law because it is a dead law." In the reorganization of the Alliance from an irresistible national crusade into a watchdog, the Quebec Alliance had almost completely fallen apart, leaving behind an annoying debt. Alliance contacts withered and Shearer's successor, Moore, really did not know what was going on in Quebec.[4] Into this void, on 28 February 1907, one day before the federal law came into force, Quebec rushed a provincial Lord's Day Act through its Legislative Assembly to take precedence over the federal law. It incorporated a Jewish exemption clause and also allowed everyone to "be and remain entitled to do on Sunday any act not forbidden" by the laws of Quebec. This law mildly forbade pleasure excursions and theatrical performances, but its intent was to avoid the federal Lord's Day Act with its far-reaching prohibitions.

Lomer Gouin, the Attorney General and Premier of Quebec, granted authorizations only for prosecutions under the provincial law; Moore's insistent requests to have the more stringent federal law observed were ignored. To the surprise of Montreal's English Protestant press, Archbishop Bruchési exhibited a puritanical strain and continued to send out letters denouncing Sunday amusements, cinemas, horse races, and theatres. The frequency of Bruchési's reminders shows how little he was heeded. The Roman Catholic population of Montreal believed, as Henri Bourassa, that Sunday activities were matters of custom and best left to the discretion of each individual. Once religious obligations had been fulfilled, Sunday was the same as any other day.

The Alliance tried to reorganize its Quebec branch in 1909 by hiring another Presbyterian. Like Rochester, George W. Mingie had been an academic whirlwind at McGill University and at Presbyterian College. His bilingualism and later legal studies made him an obvious choice for the Alliance in Quebec. Mingie's first assignment was to close the theatres. Moore, since 1907, had been urging Quebec's Attorney General to close the moving-picture houses. But the Ouimetoscope, Montreal's popular movie house, hid behind a Montreal license to operate on Sundays. Since Montreal's charter predated the Quebec and the Dominion Lord's Day Acts, L.E. Ouimet claimed to be exempt from the Sunday laws.[5] The *Montreal Herald* of 20 May 1913 reported that the feisty "Picture Men" were "Ready to Fight to Finish Attempt of Alliance to Put 'Lid' On." This controversy convulsed the Quebec political scene and involved everyone; even the young Louis St. Laurent briefly took on three theatre cases.[6] The decision from the Quebec Supreme Court came in February 1911. It declared that showing moving pictures had never been declared a crime by the federal government, so they were a civil matter under the control of the Montreal charter. The lawyers' fees mounted higher, but the Alliance contested the decision in the Supreme Court of Canada.

In May of 1912, the moving-picture case of *Ouimet v. Bazin* was decided by the Canadian Supreme Court chief justice, Sir Charles Fitzpatrick. Fitzpatrick referred to the now famous Hamilton Street Railway case of 1903, and repeated the same arguments he had given when he had introduced the federal Lord's Day Act into Parliament as Minister of Justice in 1906. He declared that Christianity formed the basis of law in Canada, and Sunday legislation formed part of its criminal legislation. Restrictive sections of the Quebec Lord's Day Act were part of criminal law and thus were beyond provincial jurisdiction. He then stated that the federal government had delegated power to the provinces to permit acts forbidden by the federal statute. This unexpected landmark decision allowed provinces to dispense with provisions in the federal law but did not allow them to pass stricter Sunday laws. Happy with this decision, the Attorney General of Quebec, Gouin, refused to pursue the case to the Judicial Committee of the Privy Council. The federal Lord's Day Act became a dead letter in Quebec.

The Alliance refused to accept defeat. Roller skating in the Montreal Forum bothered people attending the Douglas Methodist Church services a block away, so the Alliance field secretary, Mingie, instituted *Mingie v. Forum.* In 1913, relying on the federal law, the court ordered the Forum to close on Sundays.[7] The General Assembly of the Presbyterian Church reported proudly on the Alliance's success. Montreal's Presbyterian College bestowed a Doctorate of Divinity on Rochester for his role in getting Quebec to recognize that there was only one Sunday law in Canada. The rejoicing came too soon. *The Montreal Herald* encouraged Forum lawyers to appeal the decision. In early 1914, the Forum won by arguing that it held a provincial charter allowing Sunday sports. Clearly, Quebec could allow on Sunday that which was forbidden by Ottawa.

Relations between Ontario's Protestant sabbatarians and Catholics soured. The E.B. Eddy Company in Hull, Quebec, lent French-Canadian workers to the Booth Company across the river in Ottawa for Sunday work in the Ontario pulp-and-paper industry. When ministers complained, Booth explained that it was doing the workers a favour by giving them wages for Sunday work, which they needed to support themselves. Besides, the work itself was necessary and continuous. Certainly, the company claimed, there was no profit in it. To Alliance complaints that newspapers were being sold on trains in Ontario, the Canadian Railway News Company explained that many of its news agents worked out of Montreal; the boys needed the money. Certainly, it also claimed, the company did not make any money.[8]

An extreme example of the Protestant-Catholic Sunday struggle came about in Rockland, Ontario, in the Ottawa valley. In 1910, a Baptist minister, C.G. Dunlop, complained to Moore that the local Catholic priest had organized an excursion to Montreal on Sunday. Moore reluctantly told Dunlop that religious excursions to the Eucharistic Congress being held there were not illegal.[9] The following year, a Jew in Rockland refused to close his store. After all, the French store did not close. The French storekeeper claimed that his Catholic priest permitted Sunday sales. This brought a Protestant townsman to say that "The fact that . . . the Parish priest . . . authorizes selling is all

Montreal's Herald *ran a series of cartoons comparing Toronto unfavourably to Montreal and predicting financial disaster should the "lid" be clamped down in 1913.*

Making Montreal As Good As Toronto—By "FITZ"

THE MONTREAL HERALD.
102ND YEAR. NO. 183.
SATURDAY, MAY 24, 1913.
ONE CENT.
The Half Million--If Sunday "Lid" is Clamped Down in Montreal,
It Will Affect Manner in Which Half the Population Spends Its Day Off
No Ice Cream, No Cigars,
No Sunday Ball, No Parks
7,000. ATTEND THE BASBALL GAMES
1,600 ASCEND THE INCLINE RY.
200,000 VISIT ICE CREAM PARLORS
THE LID
MONTREAL

the more reason for stopping it as we surely do not recognize priest law to dominate British law." Father P.S. Hudon denied having given any permission, but he implied that he did not know how selling candies and cigars could be against the law.[10] The area's crown attorney explained to the outraged Alliance field secretary that Rockland's population was principally French, mainly from Quebec, which was separated from Rockland only by the Ottawa River and, he told Hanna, "they differ somewhat materially from the Protestant communities as to the observance of the day."[11] He therefore refused to institute prosecutions. In 1912, the Superintendent of Baptist Home Missions complained to Hanna about the St. Jean Baptiste Society's Sunday picnic. There were hundred-yard races, potato races, a fat man's race, sack races, long and high jumps, and lacrosse games. The new Baptist pastor at Rockland declared that "we want to see those *criminals* brought to justice. The priests teach & the people believe, that the Roman clergy are above the law, & break it if they please . . . All day long the Papal flag flew from the steeple of the Catholic church, & the Union Jack far below it on the flag-staff. Such conditions are bad enough in R[oman] C[atholic] Quebec."[12] More complaints went up from Rockland to the Attorney General's department in the following year with as few results. There was nothing illegal about the picnic.

Religious conflict took on a more commercial form in southwestern Ontario, which had been in the midst of a prolonged fight for Sunday streetcars when the Lord's Day Act was passed. A major battle came with the London and Lake Erie Electric Railway. In 1909, the provincial government amended Sunday clauses in the Ontario Railway Act to allow municipalities with at least 50,000 people to have Sunday streetcars if a majority vote called for it. The size of the municipality would indicate that it had grown large enough to require a seven-day transportation system. To save money on a census and to avoid defeat, London ludicrously asked the Ontario government for an order-in-council proclaiming London to have more than 50,000 people. The London and Lake Erie Electric Railway Company then applied to the Ontario legislature for permission to operate on Sunday in Port Stanley and in St. Thomas. When that was refused, the company applied to the federal government for a charter on the basis of a proposed international link to Cleveland. This charter was granted.[13] It allowed the railway to bypass the Sunday law on the plea that the railway did business for the good of Canada. Business ties with the United States were important enough to override the Lord's Day Act.

Nonetheless, the London railway battle was not just a clear contest of corporate greed against religious principles. This controversy spawned the Canadian Rational Sunday League. Before the 1906 law was passed, a prominent businessman and flamboyant public figure, J. Enoch Thompson, who represented the Spanish government in his spare time, wrote to the *Toronto World* against the modern "Inquisition." By the beginning of 1907, Thompson had assembled an impressive group: the consul of the German Empire (a like-minded Canadian businessman); Victor Cawthra, then acting as president of the Royal Canadian Academy; ubiquitous Toronto scholar Goldwin Smith; radical suffragette Flora McDonald Denison; and Unitarian Reverend Victor Gilpin of London. These and others founded a Rational Sunday League to combat the Lord's Day Alliance. Their first broadside was a four-page magazine lambasting the clerical tyranny that stopped Sunday liquor sales, streetcars, newspapers, golf, trains, steamers, amusements, and everything else. Thompson wrote that the "The formation of this League has been forced upon us by the tyrannical Sunday Laws recently enacted at Ottawa. This legislation was secured by professional agitators in the name of religion, and under sanction of this iniquitous law a religious persecution has commenced. Those who do not agree with the Lord's Day Alliance are to be converted to their views by fines and imprisonment."[14]

The League tried to arrange band concerts in Toronto's Queen's Park but was refused permission by the municipal government.[15] Its first public meeting at the King Edward Hotel on the evening of 21 August 1907 was not well-attended, but the annual meeting of October 1907 passed resolutions demanding repeal of the Lord's Day Act on the grounds that it interfered with transportation, mercantile, and manufacturing industries. One delegate stated: "If a manufacturer

Saturday Night *published this commentary 29 February 1912 on Toronto's quiet Sunday. Note the padlocked library.*

wants to keep his shop open seven days a week, and can get people to work for him, let him do it."[16] The London *Free Press* reported the League's every move, and the London *Advertiser* ran letters against the League.[17] While the London and Lake Erie Railway Company case made its way through the courts, the Rational Sunday League continued to argue for personal freedoms on Sunday and was endorsed by the Alliance's implacable foe, *Saturday Night,* in the issue of 16 December 1907. Money was certainly at the root of London's struggle, but religious leaders, naive or not, could be found on both sides of the debate. The League counted on support from the *Catholic Record* of London, which asked on 21 August 1909, in the middle of the streetcar battles, by what authority the Lord's Day Alliance interpreted the scriptures to confuse the Sabbath with Sunday. "Having no power to oblige religious service, they call in the aid of the state to exclude recreations." The Unitarian Reverend Mr. Gilpin, secretary of the League, left London shortly afterward and successfully formed a new branch in congenial and Catholic Montreal.

From the very start of the Sunday struggle, Windsor presented a problem for sabbatarians. Shearer received a letter from the Windsor Alliance in 1900 that stated, "Every form of Sabbath breaking is carried on to perfection in Windsor."[18] Since 1904, the Windsor newspapers protested the Alliance attempts to block the Windsor, Walkerville, and Chatham railway. Even the Windsor Alliance secretary had trouble getting ministers interested enough to attend a meeting.[19] Ultimately, the Windsor struggle settled into a protracted squabble over American Sunday newspapers. The Sunday newspaper business, clearly forbidden by law, was closely related to the business of railways. Railways carried the papers to their customers. The first prosecution under the federal Lord's Day Act was *Rex v. Birk* (1907) of a Hamilton news vendor selling, on a Sunday, American Sunday newspapers brought in by train. Everywhere else in Canada, except for Vancouver, the sale of newspapers on Sunday had stopped. Work on the Monday paper could pass unnoticed if it were hidden from view behind drawn curtains. In Windsor, however, the Sunday sale of newspapers went on openly. Moore complained to the Attorney General of Ontario that "Sunday newspapers are distributed all over the city, and sold to all who care to buy; in fact, the newsboys (most of whom are Italians, Jews and other foreigners) loudly cry their papers, often even in the near proximity of a church, while Divine worship is being conducted."[20] Foreigners and American tourists, he stoutly claimed, were degrading Canadian moral standards. The Attorney General admitted that Moore was right, but in practice the Attorney General's department refused to stop the importation of American goods, such as the *Detroit Sunday Free Press,* because international trade was a federal matter. Moreover, the solicitor for the Ontario Attorney General was not sure the Lord's Day Act forbade the mere importation of newspapers.[21] To outraged Windsor sabbatarians, the Attorney General's solicitor explained that the importation of newspapers and other items stopped the Windsor people from continually rushing the bridge and ferries every Sunday! Allowing American newspapers into Windsor controlled transportation chaos, encouraged Americans to visit, increased tourist revenue in Canada, and decreased hardship to Canadians formerly forced to travel to Detroit to buy their papers. When Moore found evidence that Canadian Railway News Company's president, T.P. Phelan, was a friend of the Attorney General and that both were Roman Catholics, he wrote the Attorney General to confront him with the situation. J.J. Foy declared he had the authority to decide how to prevent people from endangering their lives by overloading the Windsor ferries each Sunday.[22] The Alliance's branch secretary in Windsor commented in disgust, *"Lord deliver us from dirty Politicians* . . . Politics are Rotten and about the only men who have any influence now are the men with the Cash to buy these backboneless excuses."[23]

The area known as "New Ontario," recently incorporated into the province, showed a tendency to flout sabbatarians. From 1906 to 1914, the Alliance and Protestant ministers in Cobalt complained about labour, construction, newspapers on trains, mining, claim-staking, small retail sales, smelters, baseball games, and all of the activities of a booming frontier area. "Cobalt", the Alliance claimed, "is the heart of the conflict."[24] Cobalt and much of the surrounding area are closer to the Quebec border than to Toronto. Its population was growing with recent European immigrants and French Canadians. In 1911, over 35% of the Cobalt and Windsor populations was Catholic. Although this percentage was only slightly higher than in Canada as a whole, it was 15% higher than in Ontario as a whole. Cobalt and Windsor were considered wide-open towns by Ontario standards, but they were also, almost, Catholic towns. One minister in Amherstburg blamed Catholics for allowing American Sunday newspapers. "The Magistrate," he wrote, "a Roman Catholic, buys his Sunday paper and is sympathetic with law violation. We get no favors from him . . . The Chief of Police is a Roman Catholic and is counted as indifferent in the matter of the enforcement of the Lord's Day Act."[25]

One of the noisiest Sunday campaigns in the prewar period involved the closing of Toronto's winter slides in 1912. The City of

Toronto worked employees on Sunday to maintain security and the functioning of snow slides and ice rinks. When the Protestant ministerial association requested that these parks be closed, the opposition was immediate and immense. The fact that these parks were named in newspapers brought them more publicity and more patronage. As the *Toronto World* trumpeted on 15 January "Ministers Boom Sunday Sliding. All Records Broken at Hills Yesterday." The *News* made the same point one week later: "Thousands Used Slides on Sunday. Agitation to Close Them Proved a Big Advertisement." The ministers, organized by the Alliance, urged the city to close its slides in order to give their workers a day of rest. The opposition wanted to keep them open to accommodate the leisure time of off-duty workers. In the chorus against the Alliance could be found the remnants of the Rational Sunday League, some Catholics, Jews, Quakers, newspaper owners, and alcohol manufacturers. As one excited female preacher shouted at a meeting called in support of keeping the slides open, "Who are in this meeting, anyway?" she screamed. "Only a lot of heathens, Jew Anarchists, Socialists and Catholics, who would tear down the holy institution of the Lord's Sabbath! They are nothing but a lot of smokers, chewers and drinkers!"[26] The Alliance won a small victory, and the Toronto slides were closed—in spite of the opposition of smokers, chewers, and drinkers.

Like Quebec, British Columbia had early shown itself to be at odds with the sabbatarian ideal. Shearer once observed that the 1906 Lord's Day bill met opposition "at times vigorous, coming mainly from the Provinces of Quebec and British Columbia as well as transportation interests."[27] After passage of the law, every Attorney General in Canada agreed to enforce it—all but the Attorneys General of Quebec and British Columbia. The Alliance then blamed the controversy on "large numbers of Orientals, British remittance men and western Americans, of by no means the highest order."[28] In the campaign leading up to passage of the Lord's Day Act, Shearer had anxiously kept in touch with his Methodist and Presbyterian colleagues in British Columbia, yet there were constant problems of financing and staffing Alliance branches in British Columbia. British Columbian members of

Parliament had to be stampeded into support for the Lord's Day Act by well-timed letters from their sabbatarian constituents.[29]

Opposition in British Columbia came, as Shearer shrewdly knew, from Anglicans, from Americans, and from non-Christian groups.[30] The population of British Columbia in 1911 was 25% Anglican, up from 22% in 1901, and the total would continue to grow. In 1911, the proportion of Anglicans was over 10% higher than in the country as a whole. "Oriental" religions formed over 6% of the British Columbian population, and British Columbian "Orientals" formed over 90% of Canada's total. Anglicans and Anglican clergy, many of them recent immigrants to British Columbia, like Americans, were not caught up in the planned evangelical Christian recreation of the Canadian nation. How could they be? English loyalties were to the British Empire; American loyalties were to America. Neither group's self-identity could be restricted to a narrower evangelical Protestant Canada. Of course, those classed among the "Orientals" were considered beyond the pale of Christian Canada.

British Columbian opposition to Sunday laws took many forms. Railway work, hunting, and Sunday recreations in golf, football, and baseball were going strong in 1906. In Vancouver, local papers had always been sold on Sundays but not on Mondays, so employees worked on Saturday to produce the Sunday paper but did not work on Sunday. Newsagents worked on Sundays. Drink, a major Methodist concern, and Sunday, a Presbyterian obsession, combined in a powerful campaign against Sunday drinking. British Columbian newspapers carried items about the anti-Sunday drinking campaign, while the rest of the country watched closely. By 1907, the police chief of Victoria announced to the Attorney General that the law "is being totally disregarded throughout the City." The Attorney General, weighing the pros and cons of the political situation, decided not to issue any consents to prosecute.[31]

William Marshall Rochester, the Alliance's western secretary at the time, vigorously pushed for compliance with the federal law and convinced several organizations to shut down Sunday recreational activities. Proponents of British Columbia's Sunday activities, however, held one potent legal weapon. Pre-Confederation Sunday laws in British

HUSH! HUSH! HUSH!
The "Sawbeth" in Winnipeg—if the Lord's Day Alliance should have its way.

Opposition to the Lord's Day Alliance in western Canada was captured by the Winnipeg Saturday Post *in February 1908.*

Columbia were even more muddled than in Ontario. Since Vancouver Island and continental British Columbia had been separate colonies, they had developed slightly different legal systems. In 1906, a judge dismissed a charge against a Victoria merchant on the grounds that the Dominion Act did not apply to British Columbia as a whole, which had an 1888 provincial law, and in particular did not apply to Vancouver Island, which was exempted by the same 1888 provincial law. On an appeal that dragged on until 1913, the 1888 Lord's Day Act of British Columbia was finally thrown out on the same grounds as the Ontario post-Confederation Sunday laws. So, British Columbia had successfully avoided the Dominion Lord's Day Act until this 1913 decision! Without Rochester and other Alliance secretaries pushing the legal cases, British Columbia would have evaded the federal law even longer.[32]

As for the Prairies, on 4 May 1901, the Hamilton *Spectator* had optimistically reported Shearer's speech on "Regeneration From the West." Evidently, no one told people living in the West that they were to be the shining lights of Sunday civilization for the East. Winnipeg and Edmonton wanted Sunday streetcars. Saskatchewan insisted that the Sunday construction of its parliament buildings was a work of necessity; the weather was fine and work had to go forward. All across the Prairies the Canadian Pacific Railway and the grain elevators were operating on Sundays. In 1910, when the CPR won its case that railway work was necessary, the Alliance turned to prosecuting entertainments in the West. As in Quebec, moving pictures bedevilled the Alliance. Sunday evening entertainments, run by Catholics, Jews, Anglicans, or charitable organizations were regularly held in Saskatchewan. Band concerts on the Prairies cost expensive legal and private investigators' fees. But in 1913, the Alberta Supreme Court case of *Rex v. Thompson* decided that only shows with voluntary collections were legal. Paid admissions were not. This small victory consoled the Alliance after the railway loss, but once again big businesses were working on Sundays, while smaller businesses were not. The Alliance came to be seen as persecuting the little guy and letting the big bosses get away.

William Rochester blamed western agitation on newly arrived Russians and other immigrants of differing religious beliefs. The end of pioneer conditions on the Prairies, which made railways necessary and entertainments possible and profitable, also meant that many non-Anglo-Saxon-Protestant immigrants had arrived. The Reverend Charles Huestis, living in Red Deer, Alberta, wrote in the *Annual Report of the Alberta Lord's Day Alliance 1912–13* that: "The population of Western Canada is becoming more and more cosmopolitan; and with the influx of immigration come many who have not been accustomed to a quiet Sunday free from business." The influx of Americans, Germans, Italians, Greeks, Jews, Czechs, Ukrainians, and Russians was impressive. For example, from 1901 to 1911, the Ukrainian population jumped from 5,682 to 75,432. There were ten-fold increases in Romanians and Hungarians, five-fold increases in most other European immigrants, and many groups appeared for the first time in the census. Complaints about foreigners in the western provinces as well as in northern Ontario and Windsor multiplied. Moore and the Protestant churches insisted on "canadianizing" and "christianizing" these strangers. This often meant converting Christian immigrants to Protestant sabbatarianism.

Although the Maritimes were generally quiet economically and, for lack of anything else to do, observant of the Lord's Day Act, religious fragmentation delayed the Sunday campaign beyond Canada's borders into Newfoundland. Moore, through his contacts with Methodists in Newfoundland, tried to organize Lord's Day Alliance branches there to combat Seventh-Day Adventists. Newfoundland, however, was not entirely impressed. On 12 August 1908, the *Newfoundland Plaindealer* published letters denouncing religious persecution of Adventists. Adventists argued that the Bible commanded work six days out of every seven as well as rest on the seventh. The legal requirement to rest on Sunday would take away a second work day, if they observed Saturday, and would also be against their conscience. More important as an argument, about one-third of Newfoundland's population was Catholic. Few Catholics, if any, believed that Sunday was sacred. In Newfoundland as in Ontario, the Attorneys General undoubtedly took these real political considerations into account and regularly refused to prosecute anyone under any Sunday law. Until it entered Confederation, Newfoundland ignored Canada's Sunday law.

Progressive secularization of the Sunday-Sabbath was the result in great part of religious fragmentation. Shearer understood this. He hired the Reverend S.W. Gamble as a travelling lecturer against Seventh-Day Adventists who were organizing the Religious Liberty Association to fight Sunday sabbatarians. These Adventists grouped themselves behind the Canadian Publishing Association, The Southern

Publishing Association, The Pacific Press Association, The Religious Liberty Association, and *The Canadian Union Messenger* in order to fight the "evil religious legislation" of 1906. Catholics in Ontario, Jews and Catholics in Quebec, Seventh-Day Adventists in Newfoundland and on the Prairies, and Anglicans in British Columbia fought against the Protestant Sabbath.

Nonetheless, between 1907 and 1914, sabbatarians were sometimes successful in enforcing the Lord's Day Act. Alliance lawyers won important court battles. To the astonishment of later lawyers, a highly respected Ontario judge, William Middleton, a Presbyterian, ruled in 1911 that for the Sunday sale of food to be an act of necessity or mercy, and therefore exempt from prosecution, the purchaser had to eat the food on the spot and thus demonstrate need. No one could carry ice cream, cigars, or any food out of a store on Sunday. The "Middleton" decision was widely publicized by the Alliance and it figured in retail prosecutions, especially in the West where Ontario models were closely monitored. The relative lack of Sunday activities in the Maritimes delighted the Alliance. Laws in Quebec and in British Columbia were challenged, and the uniform federal law prevailed. Alliance secretaries continued to shuttle back and forth from Ottawa in the hopes of obtaining stricter amendments to the law. The Attorney General of Canada was also that of the Yukon; in 1908, he agreed to enforce the Lord's Day Act in that region. Early in the Canada-wide campaign, the Alliance asked for the closing of post offices. The Deputy Postmaster General stalled by telling Shearer that public opinion would have to be behind the Alliance before these offices would close. As the Alliance whipped up support, Winnipeg, Calgary, and Victoria newspapers labelled them "Officious Busy-bodies," "an idiotic outfit," "reactionary," "medieval," and "fanatical." The Alliance organization had enough public support to have this question raised in the House of Commons and force the Postmaster General to close the post offices on Sundays as of 1 February 1910. Henceforth, immigrant farmers in the West would have to pick up their mail during the week. It was declared in court case after court case, as in the 1906 House of Commons debates, that Canada was a

Christian nation, Sunday was a moral issue, and Canada could try to make people moral by act of Parliament.

The Alliance organization successfully attacked Canadian leisure habits as well as state power. "With rapid increase of wealth there has developed a widespread desire for pleasuring on the Lord's Day" the Ontario Alliance complained.[33] To stop "pleasuring," pool rooms were closed, fishing was prohibited, and baseball playing was prosecuted. The Alliance campaigned against golf, which required the hiring of caddies, grounds keepers, and other employees. Swimming races were condemned, especially if people were called on to bet or pay to watch. In Ontario and the Maritimes, older pre-Confederation statutes forbade baseball, football, racquet, tennis, or any other noisy game. The official Alliance position stated that Sunday golf, tennis, and any such "pleasuring" were not against the law as long as they did not become part of a business transaction or the employment of servants. Unofficially, Alliance sabbatarians disapproved "for the reason that they are not necessary on Sunday, there being ample opportunity, for the most people, to secure sufficient recreation of this character during the week; and, further, there is nothing that so tends to secularize the day, robbing it entirely of its sacredness, as games of this and similar character."[34]

Sports, Howell writes, require a concentration on this world and the physical skill of the human body, and appeared to be a crass separation from God.[35] Sabbatarians believed that God's creation was sinful or turned away from God, so that glorying in nature, or in sports, or in creation was a fundamental turning away from God's transcendent holiness. Whether sport was caused by sin, or sin by sport, sabbatarians were against sport. In their eyes, playing games was a secular, ungodly activity. From 1907 to 1914, the Alliance often imposed its viewpoint that God's creation and entertainments in it were fundamentally sinful, especially on Sunday.

The many sabbatarian successes that the Alliance acquired were direct results of the survival of the Alliance itself as an organization that had first transformed itself from a crusade into a quasi-official interchurch watchdog and political lobby. If it were not for the many paid Alliance secretaries active in all parts of the country, many court cases would not have been undertaken, many businesses would not have been closed down on Sundays, many entertainments would not have been stopped. For these successes, each general secretary, Presbyterian and Methodist, had been rewarded by his church with recognition, an honorary doctorate, prestige, and a voice in the councils of the church. For closing the post offices in 1910, Moore received his doctorate of divinity and resigned from active Alliance work to replace Chown as the powerful general secretary of the Methodist department of Temperance, Prohibition and Moral Reform. Rochester, the western field secretary, took over as leader of the Alliance and received a doctorate of divinity in 1913 after his successes in the West and in Quebec. He turned down the Presbyterian Church's repeated calls to higher service in its administration in order to stay with the satisfying work of sabbatarianism. Secretaries such as Rochester, Mingie, and Moore organized sabbatarians everywhere so that their numbers would influence the governments of Canada.

Roman Catholics, Anglicans, Seventh-Day Adventists, Jews, Hindus, Buddhists, Muslims, and other religious groups, in British Columbia, in Quebec, in the north and along the borders of Ontario, as immigrants or as native-born Canadians, found themselves in opposition to the creation of a sabbatarian Canada. "To Canadianize our Immigrants" in cleanliness, schooling, housing, the English language, and citizenship had been an important theme in the Alliance and in Protestant church writings of the first decade of the twentieth century. The "strangers" or "aliens" within the gates, from the King James version of the biblical commandment to have sojourners observe the Sabbath, became a stock Alliance, indeed a standard Canadian Protestant phrase, even before J.S. Woodsworth published his plea for immigrant assimilation titled *Strangers Within Our Gates* in 1909. Ethnic and religious organizations, Seventh-Day Adventist groups, and the Rational Sunday League obtained only small successes. But religious opposition to sabbatarianism gave moral legitimacy and power to the railway, newspaper, and recreational businesses. Without Catholics throughout Canada, without Anglicans and non-Christians in British Columbia, without Jews, without Seventh-Day Adventists, and without immigrants—whether Orthodox, Eastern Rite Catholic, Seventh-Day Adventist, Catholic or Jewish—there can be little doubt that the Lord's Day Alliance would have quickly succeeded in recreating Canada in its own image. But besides Methodists and Presbyterians, who would there have been in Canada? Before the Great War, religious diversity just held its own against the Lord's Day Alliance of Presbyterians and Methodists creating a sabbatarian Canada. Nonetheless, whole areas of Canada—the Maritimes, the Yukon, most of the West, and Ontario—seemed to be building a Protestant Kingdom of God, dragging the rest of Canada—Quebec, British Columbia, and Northern Ontario—along. To organized sabbatarians in the Lord's Day Alliance, during its heady days from 1907 to 1914, it appeared at times as if the world itself, as well as Canada, must and would bow down to the fourth commandment.

But if you do not listen to me, to keep the sabbath day holy . . . then I will kindle a fire in its gates, and it shall devour the palaces of Jerusalem and shall not be quenched.
—Jeremiah 17:27

We are working every man we can possibly get on Sundays as well as nights, and we believe under the present conditions that it is a case of dire necessity . . . It is not our Companies' principle to recklessly violate the laws of the country, but we feel in this case that our small efforts are equal in effect to those who are enlisting and fighting in the battles at the front.
—Canada Explosives Ltd, 1915

CHAPTER FOUR

The Great War

The State versus Sunday, 1915–1919

When Canada found itself in the Great War on 4 August 1914, one newspaper announced that the Governor General (who was a Lord's Day Alliance patron during the war), "Will Review Canadian Army On Sunday."[1] The military ran, jumped, trained, and entrained on Sundays. When military men were piled together in training camps prior to overseas duty, sports served to improve fitness, create camaraderie, and release extra energy. Team sports became more visible on Sundays. William Rochester once assured a minister that noisy Sunday rifle practice and troop movements could be stopped on appeal to the minister of militia, Sam Hughes. But Sunday troop activities escalated throughout 1914. Military camps needed transportation and food, and local businesses, restaurants, photographers, trains, and theatres catered to the military and to their families on every day of the week.

Canadian governments actually encouraged the escalating Sunday war work. Originally, the federal Lord's Day Act allowed works of necessity or mercy and, significantly, work done on government orders. The military took immediate advantage of these exemptions. Businesses, too, hastened or were forced to take advantage of them. When the federal government passed the War Measures Act (1914), its orders-in-council now overrode Parliament and many Canadian statutes supposedly hampering the war effort. Rochester admitted to one irate Hamilton sabbatarian, "As a matter of law we can do nothing in these cases of Sunday work involving Government contracts."[2] Metal works for engines, guns, portable kitchens and utensils, shoes, clothing, blankets, and all types of leather were in short supply. The Just Wright Shoe Company of London, Ontario, claimed it had a government contract and must work on Sundays to fulfil its obligation. Tanneries in Nova Scotia, filling the government boot orders, were working Sundays for the first time in their history. The militia department required the Hamilton Steel Works to work Sundays. The nationalized Canadian Government Railways ordered Sunday work because "of the National importance and urgency." On the Prairies, farmers, grain handlers, and shippers worked on Sundays, sending food to the troops in Great Britain. One official of the federal government, T.K. Doherty, Canadian Commissioner of the International Agricultural Institute, actually proposed the suspension specifically of the Lord's Day Act to encourage more farming to offset the food shortage.[3] In Moncton, New Brunswick, a senator contacted the minister of militia for permission to hold an excursion and a parade to help recruiting.[4] Across the country, in Ontario, in Nova Scotia, in British Columbia, and on the Prairies, Sunday work grew on the order of or, at least, with government permission.

The government business of war affected every part of Canada, and southwestern Ontario, the industrial centre of Canada, was most affected. Wherever business used the definition of Sunday necessity, the government gave permission. More hydro-electric lines, bridges, railway tracks, canals, grain elevators and ports were built. Domestic, restaurant, railway, dairy, and flour mill employers took advantage of the government's wartime definitions of "necessity or mercy." The militarization of transportation allowed railways to increase their activities "for the general advantage" of Canada. Excursions to and from military camps for men and their families stretched the definition of mercy. As the war persisted, the Canadian Manufacturers' Association, meeting in Hamilton in June of 1916, petitioned the Minister of Justice to suspend sections of the Lord's Day Act.[5] It was found unnecessary to suspend an act that the state had already gutted, but the Canadian Manufacturer's Association tried to establish Sunday work even in industries where mercy, necessity, or government could not be argued. War, as business in almost every country and time has learned, is good for business.

For sabbatarians, one moral danger to Canada's Sunday, like work or drink, was frivolous, time-wasting, leisurely entertainment. Whether this took the form of sports, fishing, hunting, excursions, movies, or musical concerts, sabbatarians objected to any activity that took the mind away from God and the body away from church. Before the war, the lines dividing supporters of Sunday activities from sabbatarians were clear. Catholics, Anglicans, and immigrants, many of them Catholic or Anglican, thought that nothing was wrong with leisure.

But now government sponsored charity drives to raise men and money for the expeditionary forces. Toronto newspapers throughout January and February of 1916 traced the rise of Sunday recruiting in theatres by the Citizen's Recruiting League. Sporting associations introduced professional Sunday baseball "in the pretence to aid the Red Cross."[6] The Sportsmen's Patriotic Association of Toronto also introduced filmed fight matches during recruiting drives and organized branches in London and Hamilton to do the same.[7]

The state had decided that leisure was useful for the war effort. Restless soldiers in isolated camps required Sunday movies for entertainment. When the Lord's Day Alliance objected, the set response was that soldiers fought on Sunday and so were allowed recreation on Sunday when possible.[8] Many Canadians supported the military by organizing entertainments. In Niagara Falls, young Anglican ladies organized a Sunday patriotic musical tea to help the Red Cross.[9] Elsewhere in the city, a theatre ("run by a Catholic-American of not very estimable character," a sabbatarian wrote) had tried for years to get any church to locate some of its services in the theatre on Sunday. With the advent of war, the theatre promptly offered Sunday concerts for the Patriotic Fund.[10] The Imperial Theatre of Saint John, New Brunswick, offered a "classical," "religious," and "patriotic," fundraising concert, which many people believed to be so "high-toned" that it could not possibly be illegal.[11] The Sons of England (many of them Anglican) supported it; money was sent to the Red Cross. One sabbatarian complained of these concerts that the "religious tone of the music, and the getting of some clergyman to act as a chairman was only a means to an end."[12] The chairman was, of course, an Anglican minister. When recruiting drives were held in theatres, after a concert and some prayers, one could watch movies, all in the interests of recruiting and charity.[13] Perhaps some entrepreneurs were more interested in making money than in making money for charity. Still, the end was profit, for the entrepreneur, the charity, or the government. Luckily for the Alliance, the Red Cross refused to accept the money. Interestingly, the Moose Jaw concerts, after expenses and wages had been deducted, would have netted the charity only five dollars and forty cents.[14] In most cases, it is impossible to know how much money went to charitable organizations from such events. The truth that recruiting meetings in theatres had more to do with theatre and "Yankee Sunday movies" than with recruiting could not be denied, but the meetings went on. During the war, the governments of Canada refused to prosecute anyone under the Sunday laws for showing movies. Government officials, military recruiting officers, and their volunteers used Sunday, Sunday theatres, and Sunday movies for recruiting and fundraising.

War also excited a defensive patriotism. Businesses working on government orders on Sundays were able to paint the sabbatarians as less than patriotic. Had not the *Advocate* once praised the German Emperor, the grandson of Queen Victoria, for his sabbatarianism?[15] In the prewar years, members of the Lord's Day Alliance had regularly denounced Canadian military parades, Sunday camps, drills, band practice, sports, entertainments, and excursions. Now these complaints seemed traitorous. Windsor newspapers, when they were refused the privilege of Sunday sales, concentrated their criticisms on the most visible sabbatarian: William Rochester, the general secretary of the Alliance. They wondered aloud if he were a Prussian sympathizer trying to bring the Kaiser's authoritarian methods into Canada.[16] As a matter of fact, Rochester had two sons in khaki and a third was on his way to the front; by war's end, two would be dead and the third wounded. Rochester himself donated time to speak in favour of war recruiting and war charities but not on Sundays.[17] Nonetheless, the army and the business of war claimed a higher and more pressing patriotism, "equal to the sacrifices at the front."[18] No one wanted to work their employees on Sundays "unless it was of the utmost importance," but they all thought that it was absolutely necessary, so employees in factories, in theatres, and in concert halls worked on Sundays. Should someone complain, he was labelled "one of those pro-German persons, who would be well pleased to see this factory closed."[19] Healthy, fundraising sports were patriotic and Canadian, claimed the Sportsmen's Patriotic Association and the Great War Veterans Association.

The Alliance argued, as it had done in the past, that true patriotism was in law-abiding Christianity, not in a pagan—now described as a German—Sunday. Causing a fury in Toronto's newspapers in January and February 1916, the Alliance announced that the "Churches Provide Best Field for Securing Army Recruits" and that, in war, Canada needed the moral advantage that Sunday righteousness gave. Pointing to the Prince of Wales, who refused to attend Sunday patriotic concerts, sabbatarians tried to fight war patriotism with Christian patriotism. Sabbatarians, who had relied heavily on the patriotic argument before the war, suddenly found the argument used against them. Sunday work had become part of the war effort.

Sabbatarian attitudes and activities did not change during the war. In delegations from warring countries, including Germany, Belgium, France, and Canada, they travelled to the Fourteenth International Lord's Day Congress in the still-neutral United States to hear Booker T. Washington on "The Sabbath and the Uplift of a Race."[20] Prominent ministers of the Presbyterian, Methodist, and Baptist churches continued to meet in Alliance branches to discuss the decline of the Sabbath. Presbyterians in Canada continued to print the Alliance's denunciations of Sunday activities. Saving paper temporarily ended the printed reports of the Methodists, which makes it difficult to assess their official views, yet a study of the Alliance and Attorneys General correspondence shows that Methodists were still firmly committed to Sunday observance despite their vocal support of the war. Anglicans continued to waver between criticism and support of the Alliance.

Predictably, sabbatarians claimed that "[w]ithout a doubt one of the great underlying causes of the war raging in Europe to-day, and one of the most apparent reasons for the Divine chastisement of the nations is that Europe had, to a shocking degree flung away the Christian Sabbath."[21] They doubted whether the war in Europe really needed Sunday activities in Canada. One correspondent pointed out that the Nobel explosives company, which now claimed necessity, had worked on Sundays even before the war.[22] Money, the Lord's Day Alliance suspected, was the root of Sunday activities, before and during the war. Essentially, the war reinforced the sabbatarian interpretation of the world. Aside from patriotically saving paper by cutting back its own newspaper, the *Advocate*, the Alliance did not change its views about Sunday activities during the war. In fact, the Alliance thought that the sabbatarian crusade could be renewed.

Canadian sabbatarians feared that the war's "moral tone" would demoralize the nation's youth. Happily, the governments of Canada worried, too, about the decline in moral standards. Without moral standards, such as the Ten Commandments, which included the commandment to observe the Lord's Day, much of Canadian civilization and law, everyone believed, could not and would not survive. The president of the Collingwood Citizen's Temperance and Moral Reform League lamented the influence Sunday work would have on "our soldier boys, many of them who have left good homes and good positions . . . to grub and pile up old pine stumps on the Sabbath."[23] Rochester wrote about these parental qualms to Sam Hughes that "the best families of the country who have given their sons in response to the call of the Empire sorely lament the fostering of conditions that are inimical to the finer sensibilities and to that high moral tone so necessary for the soldier and so coveted for their sons and brothers by these families."[24] Protestant morality and Canadian patriotism were interchangeable.

The greatest moral danger—or at least the one moral danger that could be freely mentioned in mixed company—was alcohol. Methodist and Presbyterian clergy, after the successful 1906 Sabbath crusade, joined with the Women's Christian Temperance Union to press for prohibition of Sunday liquor sales.[25] By the outbreak of war, the Women's Christian Temperance Union had moved to second the Alliance in all of its activities, so that Rochester became amazed at how much Alliance literature the WCTU requested and circulated.[26] From a committee, the Canadian WCTU formed a Sabbath Observance department, which reported every two years, starting in 1916.

The personnel of the Lord's Day Alliance and the Dominion Alliance for the Total Suppression of the Liquor Traffic were almost identical. For example, Shearer and Moore headed their respective Presbyterian and Methodist committees and boards examining the liquor trade. Many ministers would belong to the Alliance; their spouses, such as Mrs. Shearer, would belong to the WCTU. All of these groups, religious, sabbatarian, and prohibitionist, lobbied the government for legislative control of morality. All of these organizations were essentially English and Protestant organizations building a righteous, English, Protestant nation.

Faced with a powerful, interlocking lobbying network composed of the Dominion Alliance (for Temperance), the Lord's Day Alliance, and the WCTU, government officials were forced to acquiesce at least in the prohibition of alcohol on Sundays. Ontario's Attorney General assured the sabbatarians that Sunday liquor sales would not be tolerated.[27] The chairman of police commissioners of British Columbia wrote to British Columbia's Attorney General that drunkenness caused by a mild ginger beer could be tolerated normally but not on Sundays.[28] By 1916, at the peak of prohibition's power across Canada, all provincial governments (except that of Quebec) passed temperance acts as a patriotic measure. An ad hoc opposition to the combined Lord's Day-Dominion Alliance sprang up in "The Personal Liberty League" to fight for liquor-licensed restaurants open on Sundays.[29] The League originated and had its greatest strength in Windsor, London, and wherever the percentage of Roman Catholics and the proximity of the international border offered a different example of Sunday drinking. Interestingly, these were the same towns that supported the Rational Sunday League which had opposed the Alliance before the war. The Lord's Day Alliance, having helped to stop Sunday drinking and being, in many cases, the same people as the Dominion Alliance for the Total Suppression of the Liquor Traffic, took heart from the success of prohibition and hoped to pressure governments on the Sabbath question.

Canadian Protestant patriotism was exercised against foreigners, but a new xenophobic element was introduced into the Sunday question when the Hochelaga, Caughnawaga (Kahnawake), Six Nations, St. Regis, and Hogansburg reserves organized Sunday sports with paid admission during the war. Ministers wrote to Ottawa, noting that many of these aboriginals were from Quebec and, unfortunately, Catholic. But they found it difficult to ask aboriginals to live up to Canadian patriotism, because other Canadians could not claim to be the original Canadians. Canadian aboriginals, however, like Canadian blacks and other visible minorities, were systematically excluded from participation in the war. Both aboriginal and black Canadians, like immigrants and French-Canadian Catholics, were not expected to be patriotic or to help build the Canadian (and Protestant) Kingdom of God. Sabbatarians successfully prosecuted aboriginals. The Sunday crusade had not entirely died during the war.

THE STRESS OF WAR diminished what little tolerance there had been among Canadians in four ways: religiously, ethnically, regionally, and nationally. Firstly, religious rivalries, as before, played a role in the Sunday controversies. For example, in Ontario, a Baptist minister complained of Sunday work in a tannery run by Jews.[30] The Great War, it goes almost without saying among historians who have studied the conscription crisis, intensified French-English and Catholic-Protestant tensions. Complaints about enemy Austrians were new, but most Austrians were also Catholic.

During the war, a familiar complaint came from one resident of Prince Albert, Saskatchewan, who wrote that local Catholic priests encouraged "the peasants to disregard Sunday as a day of rest and make into a day of amusement, cardplaying and dancing" to raise money.[31] Complaints about Rockland, Ontario, on the Quebec border, common before the war, became so heavy after the war's outbreak that its Catholic priest began to believe that the Sunday law was used just to persecute French Canadians. In Grand Falls, New Brunswick, a Presbyterian minister complained that the high number of French people had contaminated his flock into thinking that Sunday military band practice was acceptable. In Smithers, British Columbia, a Protestant minister complained about Catholic stores opening on Sunday. The prevalence of Sunday sales in a predominantly French-Canadian town in the interior of New Brunswick led one Anglican minister to label it a "Godless hole."[32] Whether the events were Corpus Christi celebrations or Knights of Columbus fundraising concerts for an orphanage, whether in eastern or northern Ontario, northern Alberta, Saskatchewan, Manitoba or in New Brunswick, wherever Catholics or French Canadians gathered, English Protestants protested their neglect of the Canadian Protestant Sabbath. Toronto's Archbishop Neil McNeil was the only Catholic to warn his people against Sunday war greed. Living in the heart of Canadian Protestantism (and being of Scottish descent), could he have done otherwise?[33] The stresses of war gave sabbatarians more opportunities to single out those religious groups that did not share English Protestant mores.

Secondly, xenophobic complaints across Canada increased against Greeks, Italians, Austrians, Bulgarians, Finns, Chinese, and, of course, Jews. Ethnic groups came under attack. A Methodist minister in Cobalt in northern Ontario asked that all stores be closed so that "husky foreigners" working in shops could be put to "work of national importance." The Finnish population, he believed, consisted of immoral anarchist Bolshevik free lovers who played baseball and read newspapers on Sundays. They needed "close watching."[34] These complaints were the same as those before the war, but the war helped single out the Finnish immigrants. They might have wanted Russia to lose the war so that Finland could gain its independence.

Thirdly, the wartime sabbatarian crusade reinforced provincial and regional anti-sabbatarianism. In Quebec, where French Canadians had early become disillusioned with the war because of English-Canadian imperialism and federal mismanagement of the war effort, the provincial government reversed its prewar stand against the federal law. Before the war, when the federal government had promoted the Lord's Day Act, the Quebec government, responding to its Catholic majority, had promoted Sunday activities. During the war, when the federal government decided that federal military necessity justified all Sunday work, Quebec decided that a rest-day law was useful. So, in 1915, the Attorney General announced in the press that prosecutions would begin under the federal Lord's Day Act. In 1917, the Donnacona Paper Company was successfully prosecuted; its childish argument—that everyone else was doing it—was dismissed.[35] It was perhaps no coincidence that companies prosecuted under the federal Sunday law worked in English. English and Protestant residents of Montreal protested that Sunday amusements were still allowed. One woman asked the Alliance what it was doing to prevent the "Devil's work."[36] Not much; the Alliance refused to pay for staff who could work in French.[37] So, Quebec went its own way. The provincial government's erratic support of the Lord's Day Act had very little to do with sabbatarianism and a great deal more to do with sour federal-provincial and English-French relations during the war.

Western provincial governments showed the same indifference to Alliance claims. Moore, now president of the Alliance as well as general secretary of the department of Temperance and Moral Reform of the Methodist Church, alerted the Alliance to a Sunday retail business in Derrick, Saskatchewan. Because the store belonged to a member of the Saskatchewan legislature, nothing was done.[38] In 1914, only one-tenth of Alliance investigations in Alberta resulted in government prosecutions—which is to say that over three hundred cases out of three thousand complaints were prosecuted in Alberta. For the same period in British Columbia, just over 100 cases were prosecuted and the small number was "not due to improved conditions."[39] The Alliance had been able to convince the Alberta government to hire a special Lord's Day police force, similar to prohibition inspectors; British Columbia did not. But in both provinces, most complaints were ignored by their governments.

British Columbia's government had bowed to substantial sabbatarian pressure and enforced the federal Lord's Day Act before the war. By 1914, however, few prosecutions had been started. Victoria's authorities refused to ask for prosecutions from the province's Attorney General, claiming that everyone in Victoria would be in court. The province was willing to accept this reasoning, claiming that municipalities could better distinguish which person to prosecute in order to safeguard the spirit of the law. Some people in British Columbia were obviously above the law. The Attorney General, furthermore, really did not believe there was anything criminally wrong with Sunday activities and did not need much argument to ignore the Lord's Day Act.[40] When sabbatarian pressure became too great in Victoria, the mayor asked for consents to prosecute an avalanche of cases that then clogged the courts for months. The judicial system could not deal with these cases; many were tossed out, because they went beyond the prosecution's time limit. As the war went on, the British Columbia government authorised Vancouver Sunday trains and government work in the province with the excuse that it was necessary to win the war. In effect, Sunday activities continued in British Columbia throughout the war—as they had before the war.[41]

Before the war, Maritime ministers had been as active as Protestant ministers elsewhere in complaining about the railways, quarrying, Catholics, American work crew superintendents, and immigrant labourers. But the relative lack of any Sunday (or weekday, for that matter) economic activities had made the Maritimes seem like a sabbatarian delight. The war changed this. Geographically closer to the war, being the natural embarkation point for troops going overseas, Nova Scotia began to flout the Sunday laws. Halifax's heterogeneous population and vigorous trade had sometimes troubled sabbatarians in the Halifax Ministerial Association before the war, but in 1913, Nova Scotia decided that Sunday sales in Halifax would not be prosecuted.[42] Although the Lord's Day Alliance triumphed in the courts, the onset of war allowed Nova Scotia's government to plead wartime necessity. Sunday sales were thereafter tolerated. Sunday recruiting began in Maritime theatres, too, with some entertaining intermissions. After the Halifax disaster struck on the morning of 6 December 1917, patriotic charity concerts broke out in full force throughout the Maritimes to raise money for survivors of the munitions-ship explosion. Sabbatarian ministers and lay people who protested the breaking of the Sunday law, even for charity, lost credibility in ravaged Halifax and in the Maritimes. Nova Scotia's government used the war to permit on Sunday what had been forbidden in peacetime.

Fourthly, and lastly, English Protestant patriotism and xenophobia across the country, usually directed against immigrants and Catholics, was now directed also against the United States. With war's outbreak, Canada's perennial anti-Americanism increased among sabbatarians, especially while the United States remained neutral. Rochester denounced charities that organized "American sports" or "alien" field meets on Sunday in Canada.[43] Complaints came in about American railway contractors, American branch plants, American Mormons holding revivals, and the American Panama-Pacific Exposition.

During the war, the strongest anti-Americanism was aroused by American Sunday papers. These newspapers' lucrative advertising of Canadian events tempted Canadian newspapers to flout the Lord's Day Act. At the outbreak of war, the *Toronto World* trumpeted so-called news in a Sunday war extra; other papers, such as the Halifax *Morning Chronicle,* followed the next weekend. By September, the Alliance fought back by blanketing Canadians with leaflets denouncing the American-style Sunday papers. Sabbatarian clergymen denounced these money-making, ad-carrying, fake-news newspapers. The time was right, one wrote, "to do something about Sunday newspapers, as some of the American newspapers have published some rather disagreeable letters to some Britishers."[44] One Alliance secretary helped to convince the Attorney General of Ontario to prosecute newspapers by sending him a clever little poem. American-style Sunday newspapers, he wrote, were:

Sixty-nine pages of rubbish,
Twenty-two pages of rot,
Forty-six pages of scandal vile
Served to us piping hot.

Seventeen hundred pictures—
Death, Disease and Despair—
Lies and fakes and fakes and lies
Stuck in most everywhere.

Thirty-four comic pages
Printed in reds, greens and blues:
Thousands of items we don't care to read
But only two columns of news.[45]

The *Toronto World* was prosecuted. This case demonstrated that the newspaper published more than war news (and news contradicted the next day), that it was for profit, and that it was unnecessary. As a result, many Canadian newspapers returned to the six-day week, to the joy of sabbatarians, who ignored the fact that the Monday paper was prepared on Sunday.[46] Xenophobic and nationalistic arguments seemed to work.

The sabbatarian crusade then moved against imported American Sunday newspapers in southwestern Ontario. Windsor united all three strands of anti-sabbatarianism: It held a high number of Roman Catholics; it held many French Canadians and recent immigrants; and it was near the United States. Moreover, Windsor proved to be a tenacious exception to the law that American newspapers were not to be imported into Canada and sold on Sunday. Transgressions were overlooked by the Ontario government for electoral reasons.[47] Windsor ministers were outraged and again turned to hyper-nationalism during the war. Detroit newspapers contained, one said, "the most rabid Pro-German and Anti-British sentiment."[48] Nonetheless, the Conservatives were in power in Ottawa, in Ontario, and in Windsor, and an Anglican minister had written from Windsor to Toronto in favour of the newspapers. The wartime loyalty of the Conservative government and of an

CHASSONS LES HYPOCRITES DE LA "LORD'S DAY ALLIANCE"

BAPTISTE — Mon v'limeux, tu veux faire du dimanche un cimetière? Tu veux tout fermer, nous empêcher de fumer, rire, lire, manger, et... d'aimer, le dimanche? Eh! bien, tiens; attrappe ça, pour te fermer la g...le.

"Let's Kick Out The Lord's Day Alliance Hypocrites" *The French language humorists were even more hostile to the Alliance, as the 5 March 1922* Le Canard *shows: Baptist: "You scoundrel, you want to make Sunday as quiet as the grave? You want to close everything, stop us from smoking, laughing, reading, eating, and ... loving on Sunday? Well! So, then, take this, to keep your trap shut!"*

Anglican minister could not be questioned. A Port Lambton Methodist minister cried out against the *American curse.*[49] Municipal and provincial governments, however, decided to turn a blind eye to the importation and sale of American newspapers on Sunday.[50] Canadian sabbatarians could control Canadian newspapers, but they could not control either American newspapers or Canadian politicians.

When the United States entered the war, anti-Yankee sentiment was suddenly transformed into gratitude for the substantially English and Protestant help that Americans were giving to Christian civilization. President Woodrow Wilson became an Allied hero for his lofty war aims. Canadian sabbatarians applauded his decision to have the American forces observe the Sabbath.[51] Surely, the sale of American newspapers on Sundays in Canada could not be so bad? The Sunday newspaper business in Windsor, like business in general, Rochester sadly commented, "has been going on long before we had war, but the war makes a convenient plea."[52] The American war effort, however, did not end anti-Americanism. Complaints continued. At the end of the war, the Alberta Alliance secretary pointed out to the provincial government that most Sunday offenders were Americans who had recently emigrated to Canada.[53] America's entry into the war, however, ended wartime prosecutions of American-style activities in Canada.

There were small sabbatarian successes against French Canadians, Catholics, Americans, and immigrants, but governments of the day had decided that, in the effort to preserve a Christian Canada, the Sabbath was not essential. The Sunday law was abandoned. Nova Scotia ignored Sunday sales. Municipal workers in Halifax worked on Sundays. Vancouver and Victoria clogged the court system with Lord's Day cases. The Prairies saw farm work, sports, and dances held on Sundays. Ontario and Maritime businesses claimed wartime necessity and worked their employees seven days each week. Quebec occasionally prosecuted English-language businesses that overworked French Canadians; otherwise, Quebec ignored the Lord's Day Act. Northern and western regions, Ontario, and the Prairies, claimed pioneer hardships. Ethnocentric fanaticism grew in the hothouse atmosphere of wartime Canada, so all non-believers in the absolute necessity of a righteous, sabbatarian, Christian Canada were under constant criticism. But the state did not prosecute them, and Sunday activities continued.

Note that the government constantly demonstrated its power over religious questions. It stopped Sunday activities only when it was convinced that the war required an end to those activities. For example, to sabbatarian relief, gasless Sundays were instituted in 1918 by the government to save gas for essential war services.[54] With no gas to fuel cars, many holiday excursions stopped. Unfortunately for the Alliance, the gasless experiment lasted only six weeks, because enough gas was soon found for the army. When theatre recruiting declined, Sunday theatre entertainments were no longer sponsored by recruiting leagues. Even the prosecution of newspapers or the prohibition of alcohol could be directly traced to the state's demand that news be controlled by the state or that people be sober for war work. Behind all official or voluntary Sunday activities or inactivities lay the state. Sabbatarians had turned to the state to reform the rest of society by acts of Parliament, because the churches did not agree on the common denominator of a Christian Canada. The state then placed itself as a judge above all of the churches and transcended its own Sunday law. In 1919, the *Presbyterian Witness* printed a missionary's letter that compared Canada's 1919 Sunday with the 1900 Sunday. Everything, he complained, had changed.[55]

So, the First World War saw an accelerated movement of moral authority from traditional religious authorities to state authorities. The importance of the political arena to secular power became clearer to sabbatarians with each passing year. Shearer resigned from the Presbyterian Board of Social Service and Evangelism which had been amalgamated with Home Missions to work for the interdenominational Social Service Council of Canada. Moore headed a renewed Board of Evangelism and Social Service, which had swallowed up the Sabbath Observance Committee. Each reorganization was dedicated to bringing the clergy further into political life in order to control the nation's morality. Sunday was no less important to Presbyterians and to Methodists than it had been before the war, but direct political action—not sermons—seemed the best way to institute their kind of Christianity.

Sunday seemed irrelevant during the struggle for Christian civilization itself. On the personal level, some Canadians joined the war effort as well as they could by enlisting or by working in factories on Sunday. Others escaped from the horrors of war by turning to movies, theatres, and sports on Sunday. A third response to the war united the first two in charity. A person could donate to a war charity or pay a war tax for a Sunday movie, concert, game, or other entertainment. For many people, this was practical religion. With Sunday work and charity drives and self-sacrificing prohibition laws, the war kept a macabre balance between the sacred and the secular. Moral authority, it would seem, had not disappeared but had been transferred more firmly from the churches to the state.

While the people of Israel were in the wilderness, they found a man gathering sticks on the sabbath day. . . . And the Lord said to Moses, "The man shall be put to death; all the congregation shall stone him with stones outside the camp."—NUMBERS 15:32–5

Undoubtedly the Lord's Day Alliance thinks there is a moral lapse somewhere about a Sunday Excursion train; and it seeks to save morality by the legal weapon. But where the Alliance loses out is in the difficulty which the average intelligent mind has in seeing where the moral lapse comes in. How the visit of a few trainloads of citizens and their children to the sands of Lake Winnipeg on a Sunday can sap the morals of the state is hard to make out.—WINNIPEG FREE PRESS, 29 MAY 1923

CHAPTER FIVE

THE LOST CRUSADE

Sunday in the West, 1919–1929

PEACE AND THE SUCCESS OF THE SUPPOSEDLY CHRISTIAN cause gave Canadian sabbatarians pause to hope for better things. William Rochester, still the general secretary of the Lord's Day Alliance of Canada and now also chairman of the World Commission on the Christian Sabbath, favourably compared Canada to the rest of the English-speaking world. To the international Christian Citizenship Conference meeting in Pittsburgh, he proudly said: "Perhaps no nation in history has come through such an experience of war and retained in such measure the integrity and sanctity of her Sabbath as Canada."[1] Charles Huestis, Alliance secretary for Alberta and British Columbia, wrote confidently to the Attorney General of British Columbia: "We are starting out to make a new world." He assumed the war had been fought for Christianity and that the Lord's Day would be part of the postwar world.[2] The *Lord's Day Advocate* of 1922 proclaimed again and again to its convinced readers that, "If the Sabbath goes, we can have no hope of salvaging civilization" in the postwar world.

Sabbatarians were emboldened by the fact that those who survived the Great War demanded a better Canada purified by self-sacrifice. Required to work Sundays in a depressed economy, outraged veterans clamoured for stronger Sunday laws.[3] Seven-day work weeks bred strikes in the Cape Breton Steel Industry and in 1919 Winnipeg. Prime Minister Robert Borden suggested to the Paris Peace Conference "The adoption of a weekly rest of at least twenty-four hours, which should include Sunday wherever practicable." To the Alliance's joy, the Conference accepted this suggestion. The Canadian government immediately set up a royal commission to recommend the Sunday rest day and passed an order-in-council using the rest-day terms of the League of Nations.[4] The immediate postwar period gave sabbatarians much hope.

Initial postwar enthusiasm, especially in Canada's West, allowed the Lord's Day Alliance to increase its finances, expand its staff, and improve its contacts with all Canadians. Immediately after the war, British Columbia and Alberta distinguished themselves for their financial support of the Alliance. Western regeneration of Canada's entire moral fibre seemed assured. The expansive mood was reflected in the Alliance administration. The Reverend Wesley Spencer, a Baptist, was hired for New Ontario. The Rev. A.I. Terryberry, another Hamilton Conference Methodist like T.A. Moore, began work in southern Ontario in 1923. Speakers filled Toronto's Massey Hall in 1921 to praise the "Blue Sunday" over the "Yellow Press" and the "Red Blasphemy." No attempt had been made to establish the Alliance in Newfoundland since Moore's brush with Seventh-Day Adventists before the war. Now, another attempt was made to have Newfoundland adopt the Canadian Sabbath and the Lord's Day Alliance.

The volume of letters sent to the Alliance from both churches and individuals increased substantially, a sure sign that people were more sensitive to Sunday's claim as a special day and more aware of the Alliance's role in securing it. The readers of the *Advocate* sent in donations; the newspaper returned to monthly publication and increased its prewar twelve-page format to sixteen pages. As might be expected, Methodist conferences and the Presbyterian General Assembly commended "the splendid service of the Lord's Day Alliance," but even

Anglicans were increasingly visible in the social-reform movements of the period. The Salvation Army, fresh from its wartime service, also entered fully into mainstream Canadian national Protestantism by joining the Alliance. Support for a better and a sabbatarian Canada reached a crescendo on 6 June 1920, when many pastors attending Methodist conferences and the Presbyterian General Assembly turned their pulpits over to Alliance topics. Rochester conservatively estimated that, at the very least, seventy talks or sermons were given to congregations on that one day. In a time when each pastor used to preach on subjects dear to his own heart or the hearts of his immediate congregation and when someone could go to a dozen services in one day and never hear the same thing twice, this level of coordination was unusual. The number of people who heard a sabbatarian message on that day and every day that Alliance ministers or other sabbatarian ministers preached is incalculable.

Ironically, the Lord's Day Alliance was unable to sustain this postwar momentum. R.U. McPherson, legal advisor and original drafter of the Lord's Day Act, died in 1924. D.W. Snider, the Ontario secretary and one of the original Lord's Day Hamilton Methodists, also died in 1924. The greatest blow came when the first real leader and constant advocate of a sabbatarian Christian Canada, John Shearer, dropped dead of a heart attack in March 1925, while on a preaching tour of the Maritimes. The sudden resignation of Wesley Spencer and changes in personnel, especially in the important Ontario fields, left the Alliance seriously weakened and unsure of itself just before the church union of 1925, which was meant to bring Presbyterians, Methodists, and Congregationalists together, and just before a crucial legal case in Manitoba.

Immediately after church union, William Rochester, the last secretary to have served with the founding members of the Alliance, resigned after twenty years to become editor of the continuing Presbyterian Church's monthly *Record.* Although in a different office, Rochester still wrote almost one editorial a year in support of the Alliance and kept it in the forefront of Presbyterian consciousness. But his influence on all of Canada was that much diminished, since two-thirds of the Presbyterian Church had gone into the United Church of Canada.

The loss of his expertise was keenly felt, and his successors occasionally found it necessary to consult him.

The Reverend A.I. Terryberry of Ontario resigned in 1928, because of ill health. The Quebec representative, George Mingie, refused to pay Alliance debts out of his salary, clamoured for his salary arrears and, finally, passed bad cheques to the Alliance to pay his expenses. These peccadillos were forgiven, since the Alliance had been equally casual about Mingie's salary. In a few short years after the war, the Alliance had lost almost all of its field secretaries through death, illness, and lack of funds. The whole organization was in a shambles. Even the *Advocate* suspended publication in April 1927. The work of twenty years had crumbled. Why?

Churches interested in the Sunday-Sabbath were more interested in the cause of church union than in an interdenominational group. Before 1906, to save time and money, Shearer encouraged united or union meetings in the West, so that he would not have to address each group separately. The desire for a Christian nation led to movements that promoted not only sabbatarianism but also the creation of an omnibus Protestant United Church. Recognizing this, the *Montreal Daily Star* humorously stated in an editorial cartoon, "Church Union Will Never Be Successful Until the *Fordites,* and—The Sabbath *Recreationists,* and—The Seventh Day *Golfites* and Similar Denominations Come Into the Union."[5] Mingie, the Quebec secretary, reported more practically that the Alliance was no longer able to appeal for funds from the churches, because the church union debate took up all of the pulpits.[6] Methodists, Presbyterians, and Congregationalists—the Alliance pillars—were busy fighting to salvage their members and their funds. When Rochester elected to go with the continuing Presbyterians, Mingie plaintively reminded him that it would not help anywhere but in Ontario, where the bulk of the continuing Presbyterians were clustered. Mingie, too, stayed with the Presbyterians but found it as difficult to collect money from them because the remaining congregations were disorganized. Even in Ontario, however, the Alliance fell into greater debt. The "animosities are very bitter," Mingie wrote after church union, "Nearly all the Presbyterian Churches are so

The Montreal Daily Star, *12 January 1924.*

weakened that they do not welcome interdenominational work and the United Churches are not yet sure of their position or relation to the others and their finances."[7] Ironically, church union did not strengthen the sabbatarian cause. How many other interdenominational Protestant causes were similarly affected by union?

A cleavage between the United Church and the Lord's Day Alliance began when some Presbyterian congregations protested that the union vote had been taken on a Sunday—further proof of worldly motives.[8] The split deepened, moreover, when Rochester remained with the continuing Presbyterians. Nonetheless, in the newly formed United Church, where Moore became the general secretary and George Pidgeon the moderator, the General Conference immediately welcomed a delegation from the Lord's Day Alliance. The United Church, however, was undergoing a revaluation of its social priorities before moving on to the long-sought creation of a Christian Canada. The new church actually wavered before endorsing the Alliance. Its newspaper, the *New Outlook,* daringly reported that there was some doubt whether the biblical Sabbath commandment was a permanent Christian obligation.[9] Eventually, the United Church General Conference officially commended the Alliance. But the welcome for Rochester was certainly warmer at the rival Presbyterian Church General Assembly. Meanwhile, former Methodists, Moore in Hamilton and Webber in British Columbia, worked on regional United Church conferences to put pressure on the General Conference to throw its entire weight behind the Sunday-Sabbath. For several years, nothing materialized; the churches were too busy rebuilding. Only in 1928 did Hugh Dobson of the United Church Board of Evangelism and Social Service begin reporting on the nation's Sabbath observance.

While church union passed through the legislatures of Canada, "blue laws" were going down to defeat in plebiscites and referenda. Prohibition, one of the hard-won signs of God's Kingdom during the Great War and one of the reasons for church union, came under severe attack. Across Canada, 1925 was the pivotal point in the temperance crusades. Before 1925, prohibition seemed possible. After 1925, the churches were in disarray. Prohibition was only grudgingly accepted by the Canadian populace even as a war measure. With peace, as in the Sunday controversies, newspapers, returning veterans, and the proximity of the American border brought cries for personal liberty. Quebec and British Columbia, which meant Catholics and Anglicans, both abandoned prohibition in 1921. Newfoundland followed in 1925. Ontario's Temperance Act was defeated in 1926. New Brunswick and

Nova Scotia fell off the wagon in 1927. Throughout the decade, the Prairies gradually slipped into the government sale of alcohol and then the public sale of beer. By 1928, prohibition was defeated across Canada, except in Prince Edward Island.

As a result of these changes, the Lord's Day Alliance had been forced out of the mainstream of Canadian Protestant life. By hiring a Baptist minister, Alvin S. McGrath, president of the Baptist Ministers Conference for Ontario and Quebec, the Alliance tried to show that it could still reach out to denominations other than the Presbyterian Church and the United Church. Since both churches were exhausted from the legal and financial wrangling of church union, it made good sense to approach Baptist churches. Nonetheless, it was a sign. Presbyterians, once the driving force of Sunday social reform, had dropped behind. And the United Church had not yet taken control of Canadian moral-reform movements. Methodists and Congregationalists had disappeared into the United Church. Unfortunately for the Alliance, fundamentalist Baptist pastor T.T. Shields split the Baptists in 1927, and Baptists were once again embroiled in questions of orthodoxy. Years passed before that denomination took another united stand. In stark contrast to the enthusiasm at war's end in 1919, by 1929, a mere decade after the war, the Lord's Day Alliance found itself pushed to the edges of Canadian church work.

Throughout that bleak decade, the Alliance again turned to the West for inspiration and regeneration. After Rochester left to run the *Presbyterian Record,* the Alliance recognized the growing power of the western provinces and appointed Charles H. Huestis, who had completed sixteen years as western secretary in Alberta and British Columbia, to the post of general secretary. Huestis immediately busied himself in rewriting the Alliance constitution to increase western representation on the executive. Ontario kept the same numbers, while Quebec's small contingent was cut in half to make way for western delegates.

The Social Gospel, Richard Allen writes in *The Social Passion,* had originally been more popular in the West than in the East. In the

Canadian West, the growing population threw itself into the taming of a secular world. Food and shelter were essential. Only a religion that helped them conquer the secular world could survive. To reach western farmers, ministers secularized or increased the social content of the Christian message. In the 1920s, the Social Gospel of Protestant churches reached its apogee. Sundays were "formal occasions" when the United Farmers of Alberta or the Grain Growers' Association would gather their followers to talk politics, talk wheat, and if a minister were present, which was likely, talk religion. Westerners, Gerald Friesen has shown in *The Canadian Prairies,* used religious symbols to describe their land, their crops, and their hopes. The subjects melted easily, perhaps naturally, into each other. Since everything was secularized, the "line between the sacred and the secular is being rubbed out," Allen wrote. For Christian ministers, he also claimed, that meant an increase in religion, since in their perspective, "everything is becoming sacred."[10] For the worldly minded, however, everything was becoming secular. The use of religious language to discuss secular topics could have been a convenient way of using available language to refer to treasured possessions. Whether the Social Gospel's Kingdom of God referred to the here-and-now or to the hereafter probably depended on the farmer. In either case, the social forms of Christianity were uppermost in western minds as settlers built a new society. The secular and the sacred, severely and perhaps artificially divided into church and state in the East, rejoined each other in the West as settlers tried to build their own secular Kingdom of God.

C.H. Huestis, General Secretary, Lord's Day Alliance, 1927–1937, and a formerly Methodist minister who joined the United Church.

Although the Social Gospel was more popular in the West than in the East, Sunday laws were increasingly less popular. They interfered with the inseparable cycles of weather and work. The Canadian national Sabbath had been developed for an industrializing, clock-watching East and imposed on the West, just as eastern dreams for a western empire made in the East's image had been shaped in post-Confederation Canada. The western elite struggled to live up to eastern standards; western immigrant farmers, closer to the weather, farmed on Sundays. Sunday farming was marginally legal if necessity could be proven.

Yet eastern Canada and the Lord's Day Alliance based in the East still controlled western Canada's activities. Court cases about the eastern and federal law clogged the judicial system throughout the West. Western requests for exceptions or dispensations from the Lord's Day Act routinely arrived in the office of the Minister of Justice. For example, the Saskatchewan Grain Growers' Association asked for a suspension of the Lord's Day Act so that grain could be moved.[11] Pastors at Estevan, Saskatchewan, complained of a garage open near a church; nothing was done by the local authorities, who considered the garage more important than the ministers' Sunday.[12] Letters from the Prairies about Sunday shooting, municipal bylaws, sales of food or of gas, all went to the Minister of Justice in Ottawa. Unlike the former colonies of British Columbia, Ontario, or even Prince Edward Island, the recently formed Prairie Provinces did not have pre-Confederation laws to govern themselves differently from the federal law.

In British Columbia, the Anti-Blue Sunday League (friends called it the Anti-B.S. League, others simply the A.B.S. League) sprang into existence in April 1922, after the British Columbia Liberty League's successful anti-prohibition campaign.[13] In May, the Anti-Blue Sunday League held a plebiscite in Victoria, asking people whether they favoured rigorous enforcement of the Lord's Day Act. Alliance supporters boycotted the informal straw vote, and under 4000 out of an eligible 13,500 voters turned out. When the votes showed that most favoured a more open Sunday, the league claimed victory and put greater pressure on politicians to abandon the Lord's Day Act. Victoria's Board of Police Commissioners refused to recommend any more prosecutions to the Attorney General.[14] One writer to the *Victoria Colonist* reported that Rochester

> hastened out . . . from the sanctum sanctorum of Canada (Toronto) to rescue us from eternal perdition as the penalty of purchasing a bottle of ginger beer or a bag of peanuts on Sunday.
>
> Apparently Mr. Rochester's moral olfactory organs have been offended, at a distance of three thousand miles, by something which emanated from sinful Victoria and permeated the entire atmosphere of Canada. How horrible that anything should happen to disturb the pure and sanctified air of that holy place, Toronto![15]

Rochester protested against the province for using an unofficial city plebiscite to ignore Canada's Lord's Day Act. The Attorney General replied that he had to abide by the recommendations of the Victoria Police Commissioners, who were the legal representatives in Victoria. When Rochester and the president of the Anti-Blue Sunday League met to come to an agreement, the president stated that he did not advocate an "open" Sunday but resented "any interference with the customs" of British Columbia on the part of central Canada and the central government.[16] In an apparent compromise, British Columbia's government upheld the Lord's Day Act by prosecuting mainly the Chinese and Japanese, not the majority white population, to the Alliance's dismay.[17]

Manitoba's discontent, frustration, and problems were brutally suppressed, partly by the federal government, in the 1919 Winnipeg General Strike. Business and professional intransigence during the strike weakened even relatively progressive Social Gospel labour gains such as the Lord's Day Act. Although the provincial Lord's Day Act had been tossed out by the courts in 1921 for the familiar reason that Sunday laws were in federal jurisdiction, harassed authorities did not enforce the federal law. Instead, Manitoba sacrificed Sunday for entertainment. Theatres, band concerts, and sports for veterans crept in across the province. The Manitoba debate centred around Winnipeg's demands. Complaints had been heard about the unfairness of the wealthy being able to drive out of the city, while the poor had to swelter in the unhealthy Winnipeg humidity. Resorts remained elite preserves, the newspapers stated, because working people, free to travel only on Sunday, were prevented by the Lord's Day Act, which prohibited excursion trains. The rich were not allowed to use trains either, but this logic did not faze the excursion promoters and the newspapers. "Public opinion" convinced legislators that peace in the tense city of Winnipeg demanded Sunday trains to smooth away differences between rich and poor. It was easier to convince legislators to allow the poor to pay to leave Winnipeg by Sunday train than to convince employers to pay their workers more or work them less so that workers could leave on another day by some other way.

From 1922 to 1923, Manitoba court appeals multiplied. The Alliance fought a rear-guard action against the combined influence of movies, concerts, and railways, while other western provinces waited for the outcome.[18] The government of Manitoba amended the supposedly dead Manitoba Lord's Day Act to allow Sunday excursion trains "to summer resorts, beaches or camping grounds within the province"—which meant near Winnipeg. The Manitoba Supreme Court obligingly ignored the issue of whether this provincial law could even exist. It decided instead to allow excursions on the basis of Manitoba's common law, which had been established before the Lord's Day Act of 1906. On the theory that what was not forbidden was allowed, the court argued that although no statutory law had been passed allowing excursions, as the federal act required, common law allowed Sunday excursions. Excursions were still legal, because federal law allowed exceptions by laws in force prior to the federal law. In magnificent legal legerdemain, the court confused Manitoba's undefined common law with statutory law. The 1906 law forbade excursions, but the clause "[e]xcept as provided in any provincial Act or law now or hereafter in force" conveniently did not exclude common law. The federal lawmakers of 1906 had expected that clause to allow stricter provincial statutory law, as in Ontario, to control Sunday activities even further than the federal law. The Manitoba legislators of 1922 found that the federal clause gave provinces Sunday freedom not restriction. In an aside, the Manitoba Supreme Court also declared that while the provincial Lord's Day Act had been out of line for prohibiting activities, it was definitely allowed to permit them. The Alliance warned the country that this meant that the entire Lord's Day Act of 1906 was "an empty shell." Any province could permit anything.

This debate convulsed the country. When Saskatchewan's Supreme Court refused to follow Manitoba's unusual confusion of common and statutory law in similar cases, upholding the federal law, the Alliance, for the second time since 1903, appealed to the Judicial Committee of the Privy Council for a ruling.[19] In twenty years, much had changed in Canada's attitudes toward Christianity as the religion of the state. For example, J.S. Woodsworth, a former member of the Alliance and former Methodist minister, now represented another section of Canada's population by suggesting that the Alliance drop its petty prosecutions of the people's pleasures and concentrate on securing a rest day from work. The Alliance pointed out to the Manitoba Independent Labour Party member, who would move on to become the CCF leader, that pleasure usually meant someone working to provide the ice cream, sell the candy, or conduct the trains. After the death of R.U. McPherson, Alliance lawyer and original drafter of the Lord's Day Act, the Alliance turned to Newton Wesley Rowell. A prominent Toronto Methodist, an active Ontario Alliance member, former leader of the Ontario Liberal party, and former minister in both Laurier's and Borden's cabinets, Rowell went to Westminster in England to argue for the Lord's Day Alliance. Unfortunately, he was inexperienced in Alliance cases.

To safeguard its jurisdiction, the federal government sent its Deputy Minister of Justice to argue on behalf of the Alliance that Manitoba had not existed prior to Confederation; therefore pre-Confederation common law could not be applied to Manitoba. Conflicts over provincial and federal powers, civil, common, and criminal laws, and religion and state formed a knotty puzzle for the Judicial Committee. So complicated were the issues that "Lord Carson of the Judicial Committee remarked that he had been busy throughout the week-end writing a long judgment and therefore had not had an opportunity to make himself familiar with the merits of the present appeal." Lord Dunedin enlightened him by remarking, "I think it is connected with a question whether Lord Carson, if he lived in Manitoba, would be permitted to write long judgments during the week-end." At the end of 1924, the Privy Council dismissed the case against Manitoba.

Manitoba, and ultimately the West, had won the right to run excursion trains. London had accepted Manitoba's secondary argument: Permissive provincial legislation, under federal clauses that granted exemptions under a "provincial Act or law now or hereafter in force," was legal. From 1923, with its excursions amendment, Manitoba had thrown over the federal Lord's Day Act and had stopped enforcing its provisions. Manitoba became the second province (after Quebec) since the Alliance's successful Hamilton Street Railway appeal to the Privy Council in 1903, to bring parts of Sunday—and religion—back into provincial, local and, ultimately, individual control. Both Quebec and Manitoba had won Privy Council Sunday decisions giving them the power to allow on Sunday what was prohibited in federal law. Alberta followed Manitoba in asking for exemptions and passed its own law to regulate theatres opening on Sundays. The federal Lord's Day Act and the power of Ontario sabbatarians were weakened across the country.

These appeals bankrupted the Alliance. Luckily, the federal government agreed to pay the costs of going to the Privy Council, but that still left the Alliance several thousand dollars in debt for the appeals to the Manitoba Supreme Court, the Saskatchewan Supreme Court, and to all of the lower courts. Although Rowell was a staunch sabbatarian and an excellent lawyer, his services in his brief and unsuccessful appearance in London alone cost $4622.06. When the Alliance wanted to visit the Supreme Court and argue that the Manitoba decision defining common law was an invalid point, they could not pay for their appeal.[20] The Alliance lost this round in the Sunday battle for Canada.

Post-war peace brought relaxation of self-imposed war discipline. Sports, movies, concerts, tourism, and entertainments of all kinds were promoted by and for the returning soldiers, not just in a desire to escape the memory of the war but also to make money in a depressed economy and, perhaps, to escape the increasingly disappointing postwar world itself. The war had popularized new technologies, moreover, which brought on Sunday car and plane tours managed by veterans. Tourism boomed, and this required garages, gas stations, more restaurants, and more petty Sunday sales. One man claimed that he had been wounded as a Scottish piper going "over the top" and could do no other work than sales.[21] The churches' postwar demands for a better Christian society seemed too much like more of the same wartime self-sacrifice, although the immediate reason for heroic self-denial had gone. Only returned soldiers, who were assured of work, demanded one day off each week; they had survived the war to enter a growing, salaried, middle class with its rest-day morality. Those veterans who suffered from unemployment or poor wages were only too willing to work on Sundays to make some money. Strikes and walkouts in Cape Breton or Winnipeg over seven-day work weeks were for those who had jobs, no matter how badly paid. People, many of them immigrants to the West, began to decide for themselves how they were going to spend their Sundays.

Patriotic Canadians, sabbatarians reasoned, would not be spending their Sundays in such a way. The Alliance looked to the Prairies, but no help for the Christian nation came; the Alliance again began to see "Strangers Within Our Gates." These were American settlers on the Canadian plains. American chautauquas, travelling variety shows that included sermons, lectures, music, and magic shows on Sundays, set up their tents in Canada just as they had before the First World War. American Sunday radio programs reached into each Canadian home that had a wireless. Symphony-concert associations in Saskatchewan, British Columbia, Manitoba, and Alberta met on Sundays to practise, give concerts, distribute tickets, and finally take in money. Some of them imported musical talent from the United States. The United States, so admired when it promoted goals similar to those of Canada's elite, so feared and hated when it did not, haunted the sabbatarian imagination in postwar Canada. The American return to a more relaxed Sunday after the war affected Canada, because Canada's elite had publicly admitted during the war that the United States—associated with conscription, war enthusiasm, and success—was an example to

Canada. The United States had abandoned many of its Sunday laws a generation earlier than Canada, however, so that Sunday theatres, concerts, and sports flourished openly in the republic. When the Canadian public looked for models of entertainment, it looked to the United States. One correspondent to the Toronto Star stated,

> as the war is now over and as everybody apparently has made up his or her mind that this world is going to be a better and more enjoyable place to live in, and as an antidote to the present unrest and tendency to Bolshevism, we must have a relaxation of the blue laws which prevent the people from enjoying themselves in an orderly manner on Sunday, witnessing clean, manly sports, and I think it's time we followed the action of New York State in opening the baseball parks.[22]

Sunday "Quality Burlesque," "Beautiful Women and Social Follies," "Merry, Good-to-look-upon Show Girls," or "20—Wiggling, Giggling Girlies—20" captured the Windsor and, undoubtedly, the Detroit tourist imagination more readily than the sabbatarian vision of a purified Canada.[23] Even while running burlesque ads, the irrepressible *Windsor Border Cities Star* of 28 January 1925 reported that the Anglican primate condemned Sunday dancing and tea parties. To the Canadian population, familiar with alcohol-smuggling and burlesque, Archbishop Matheson's Sunday sorrows were irrelevant or even funny.

The Lord's Day Alliance nervously watched public enthusiasm for American entertainment and even more nervously followed the American cinema's fight for Sunday openings. Webber examined the Canadian entertainment and film industry and discovered, not for the last time, that it was controlled by American syndicates. The American example hit home when books by the popular Canadian writer Ralph Connor, some of them praising the Sabbath ideal, were made into American movies and shown on Sundays. When news of Connor's Sunday royalties appeared in Toronto newspapers, the retiring moderator of the Presbyterian Church was Charles Gordon, whose pen name was none other than Ralph Connor. Gordon had dedicated his book,

The Man From Glengarry, with its Protestant themes including sabbatarianism, to the men who were "helping to build the empire of The Canadian West." In anger against the burgeoning American film industry muscling into Canadian markets, the Social Service Council of Canada demanded and received the right to censor movies coming into Canada. Not surprisingly, the general secretary of the Social Service Council at the time was John G. Shearer. The recording secretary was T. Albert Moore. Charlotte Whitton was assistant secretary. And the president was an Anglican Dean, Norman Tucker. All of these officials attended meetings of the Lord's Day Alliance of Canada.[24] The Alliance and the Social Service Council pressured provincial governments to pass stricter provincial laws against Sunday films. Many movies and concerts, however, were shown for charity, which made them exempt from Sunday laws. The organizers justified concert receipts by declaring that they were for poor churches, poor veterans, and poor western farmers who were deprived of urban advantages. In Ontario, meanwhile, a perhaps typical Alliance Sunday meeting featured five speeches, three hymns, two prayers, two solos, and a duet.[25] Canadians were starved for entertainment, and American films could not be kept from them.

Another form of entertainment, sports, continued to grow. In peacetime, soldiers and militia participated in Sunday sports to keep fit. At the close of war, the Liberty League revived and requested Sunday slides in Toronto. Windsor officials requested that Sunday sports even be legalized.[26] At first, the civilian debate referred to Sunday golf and baseball. The quiet game of golf was legal on Sundays. Unfortunately, the cost of clubs, grounds fees, caddies, and other paraphernalia—all illegal when charged on Sundays—made golf too expensive for most people. Thus, Sunday golf became a red flag to the fans of cheaper but illegal forms of sport such as spectator baseball, which required paid professional players and tickets for entry to baseball parks.[27] An ordinary game of pickup or municipal baseball was legal in the western provinces, but selling tickets, hotdogs, or pennants to spectators was not. Furthermore, noisy games such as baseball and tennis were illegal in the older, eastern provinces ruled by pre-Confederation laws. Professional baseball promoters lamented the fact that the masses were deprived of this healthy, innocent game, while others enjoyed golf. This line of reasoning, not surprisingly, gained the support of the less-than-sabbatarian Anglican and Roman Catholic clergy and their people. Other noisy sports that shocked sabbatarians were Sunday shooting, swimming, Indian (or pagan, as they were called) lacrosse games, and dancing.

The one bright spot among the Sunday sporting events was Eric Liddell, the Scottish track star who refused to participate in Sunday preliminary heats for the 100 metres race at the Paris Olympic Games of 1924. When Liddell unexpectedly won the 400 metres gold medal, Canadian sabbatarians went wild with joy. Liddell went on to become a Presbyterian missionary and martyr in China and an inspiration to Canadian Presbyterians for several years. He was later immortalized in the popular movie, *Chariots of Fire.* But the Sunday sporting movement had advanced so far in Canadian popular culture, one writer claimed, that there was "no need to go to China for heathen."[28]

Sabbatarians again turned to the government for help in the purification of Canada. The state was the great hope of the church. Only the state could put teeth into the Lord's Day Act and the Temperance Act, and only it could pass the United Church of Canada Act. Rochester stated the case best, when he told the World's Christian Citizen Conference: "We are all a little chary about the relation of Church and State. . . . [W]e stand absolutely for the independence of Church and State. The Church is an organization, the Sabbath is an institution—there is that difference. From the first day of its mention to us, in social relationship, the Sabbath has been identified with the State, and the State with the Sabbath; and what God hath joined together, let no man put asunder."[29]

And if the state would not help, then the Ku Klux Klan might.[30] The *Vancouver Sun* and other newspapers still argued that law and force would not make the world any better.[31] This struck at the basis of the Lord's Day Alliance and state control of society. Neither the Alliance nor the state believed journalistic rhetoric. In passing the Privy Council order for one day's rest in seven, the federal government had decided that moral questions were questions of state. Provincial governments in Alberta, British Columbia, Saskatchewan, Manitoba, and Ontario, too, decided that moral questions were questions better solved by their governments. Alberta and British Columbia decided to empower municipalities such as Victoria to decide who would be prosecuted. Ontario used its own pre-Confederation act to avoid using federal law. Saskatchewan avoided prosecuting farmers. And Manitoba's struggle with the federal act was an example to the entire West. In battles over Sunday observance, the provinces were able to weaken federal power and increase their own authority.

The creation of the Prairie Provinces in 1905 had once nurtured Christian hopes of building a sabbatarian nation. Instead, prodded by veterans demanding rest and recreation, western provincial governments seized control of Sunday from both the federal government and sabbatarian leaders. The reorganization of Protestant members and their money was taken up by the Methodist and Presbyterian churches partly to control the secular authorities. And this time church union was pushed through. Ironically, the effort shattered Protestant unity throughout the decade. Interchurch movements such as the Alliance were bled of support and money. Finally, many older sabbatarians died or faded away into other crusades. New members took up the work, but they were inexperienced and had yet to prove that they could lead the nation into the paths of righteousness. The changeover in religious leadership and the increase in western provincial government power made the 1920s a time of western secularization.

Sunday was a test case of provincial and federal jurisdictions. Once again, the transfer of authority from one centre of power to another—first from the sabbatarians, then from the central government—meant increased secularization. In the fine balancing between sacred and secular, there had occurred another transfer of power from the church to the state.

A religious vacuum had appeared during the reorganization of the churches. Preoccupied by church union, Protestant churches granted their authority over such moral issues as Sunday observance and prohibition to governments. The secular power dealt with national morality according to state interests. The churches temporarily allowed their creation, the Alliance, to starve. After the death of key people in the organization and in the country, little was left of the original crusade. Western Canadians and their governments had at the same time, in an agrarian revolt, taken power from the federal government and ultimately from the Alliance which had relied upon the central government to safeguard the national Sabbath. The Social Gospel, Allen wrote, can "be termed the religion of the agrarian revolt" against the colonial power of the East. Looking at the West gaining control over the Lord's Day Act from the federal government, there was more social than gospel apparent. In the postwar years, Canadians were determined to make money or to work very hard at their secular recreation in concerts, theatres, movies, baseball, tourism, and all the sales that these activities meant. The Sunday holy day was rapidly becoming a holiday.

And this is why the Jews persecuted Jesus, because he did this on the sabbath.—JOHN 5:16

[Jews] are vampires on the community instead of being contributors to the general welfare of the people.
—HENRI BOURASSA, HOUSE OF COMMONS, 1906

CHAPTER SIX

SUNDAY IN QUEBEC

1907–1937

BEFORE THE GREAT WAR, THERE HAD BEEN SOME signs that French Canada had been interested in a strict observance of the fourth commandment. Indeed, there had been complaints by clergy in New France, and later in Lower Canada, about the pleasuring done on Sundays in the colony. But whether dancing or the fact it was being done on Sunday was the main point is not yet known.

Like Protestant Social Gospel sabbatarianism, modern Catholic sabbatarianism grew in answer to industrialization and urbanization. Unlike Protestant sabbatarianism, Catholic sabbatarianism did not base itself entirely on a literal biblical interpretation. In 1891, Pope Leo XIII's encyclical *Rerum novarum* set out the Roman Catholic vision of harmonious relations between workers and employers; this inspired Catholic Action movements in the early twentieth century. *Rerum novarum*'s importance for the reconstruction of capitalist society at first seemed unappreciated in Quebec, since no practical steps had been taken to apply its teachings until industrial problems brought the cardinal archbishop of Quebec to intervene in a shoemakers' strike in 1900. The same year saw Leo XIII's encyclical *Tametsi* (1 November 1900), which mentioned the fourth commandment. In 1905, Pius X encouraged prayers to Saint Joseph, patron saint of workers, so that Sunday would become holier.[1] Catholic sabbatarianism depended less on the Bible than the Protestant version and more on the teaching authority of the papacy.

So, when representatives of the Alliance visited the bishops of Quebec, the latter for once were disposed to listen favourably. They agreed in principle with the Lord's Day bill, as noted above. Archbishop Paul Bruchési wrote pastorals to Montreal's Roman Catholics reminding them of their duty to refrain from work on Sunday in order to free themselves for mass and prayer. Religious differences nonetheless triumphed over a uniform nationalism in 1906. Henri Bourassa brought many Canadians to believe that Roman Catholics were in no way sympathetic to sabbatarianism. The amendment giving administration of the 1906 Lord's Day Act to the Attorney General of each province guaranteed that, henceforth, national Sabbath observance would be defined by provincial majorities and would be circumscribed by provincial boundaries. Protestants could well try to build their version of a Christian Canada in the other provinces, but Roman Catholics would control Quebec.

Outside of Quebec, there were some stirrings of French Catholic sabbatarianism, but these attempts to apply a culturally French and Catholic version of the national religion were hampered by French Catholics' minority status.[2] As a minority in Ontario and elsewhere, French Catholics were more interested in sabotaging the English Protestant version of the Sunday-Sabbath than in establishing a French Catholic Sunday.

Within Quebec, however, an active and majority French Catholicism meant that Catholicism would be as vigorously applied to the secular realm of politics and citizenship as Protestantism was in other provinces. In 1909, the ecclesiastical hierarchy of Canada met in Quebec City for the First Plenary Council of Quebec. Out of 380 pages of decrees organizing the United Church of Canada, three were dedicated to feast days and Sunday observance. The decrees stated that Sunday was a matter of choice by the Church and was not, in itself, sacred. Rest was prized, and menial work was forbidden, but pious and charitable works of mercy and necessity, even if menial, were encouraged. None of these statements, however, went into the joint English and French pastoral letters summarizing the decrees. Sabbatarianism was a relatively unimportant topic in the Canadian Catholic world. Shortly after the decrees were published in 1912, Bishop Labrecque of Chicoutimi, faced with severe labour conflicts in the pulp-and-paper industry, wrote pastoral letters commending Leo XIII's labour encyclicals. He vigorously argued for the cessation of all unnecessary work in the pulp-and-paper industry, rest periods for the workers, and their attendance at religious services. His vicar general, founder and chaplain of the first Quebec Catholic Union, pressured the Quebec legislative assembly to examine Sunday work in the Price Brothers Paper Company. These Catholic sabbatarian efforts were few and disjointed, because the two types of sabbatarianism—the first pre-industrial and biblically based, the second post-industrial and based on the need for a day of rest—did not join forces until later in the twentieth century.

A new generation of Catholics began to transform weak Catholic sabbatarian arguments into a secular force. In 1910, Jesuit priest Léonidas Hudon reformed the League of the Sacred Heart, a pious organization for prayer, and linked it with other Catholic societies to become a fighting social force in Quebec society.[3] Hudon's successor as chaplain to the League of the Sacred Heart was another Jesuit, Joseph-Papin Archambault. A short, slim person, Archambault's voice was nasally high pitched and, when preaching, monotonous. Yet his energy and his intellect were undoubted. On taking over the League of the Sacred Heart, Archambault insisted on the need for more education of the Catholic laity in the practical application of the teachings of the Roman Catholic Church in the Canadian context. Using Belgian and Dutch Jesuit examples, Archambault educated League of the Sacred Heart Catholics during the war by promoting intense, closed, monastic retreats. During these retreats, where his knowledge and small intimate talks offset the deficiencies of his speaking voice, periods of prayer, fasting, and Bible readings alternated with the study of European Catholic Action principles, authors, and techniques.

After the First World War, highly educated elite groups crept out from self-imposed, monastic, wartime silence to propose an articulate Catholic critique of Quebec society. Archambault emerged as the pre-eminent theorist of Catholic Action and went on to organize the *Semaines sociales* (social weeks) in 1920. These almost annual conferences brought together the Catholic elite—bishops, priests, religious, and laity—to renew the intense educational experiences of the monastic retreats and to spread these teachings. As president, Archambault himself spoke little, but he did choose many of the speakers and topics. The 1920 conference studied *Rerum novarum* and touched on problems that would occupy conferences for the next forty years. Even in 1920, speakers called for the six-day and the forty-eight-hour work week.

At Bishop Labrecque's urging, two of the 1922 social week talks dealt with Sunday. The first discussed the biblical and church texts, from Genesis to Leo XIII, establishing Sunday as a day of physical and social rest for divine worship. The second talk, by the vicar general of Chicoutimi, Eugène Lapointe, claimed that Sunday work in Quebec's factories and the pulp-and-paper industry destroyed workers' health, their home lives, and their spiritual lives. Immediately, the social week executive approached the episcopate of Quebec for its opinion on the Sunday problem.

On 18 April 1922, Cardinal Bégin, archbishop of Quebec, and the bishops of the ecclesiastical province of Quebec published a joint pastoral letter on Sunday's importance. The letter had three sections. The first set out the theory of Catholic Sunday observance. It emphasized attendance at religious services—as opposed to the strict Sabbath rest of Jews and Protestants—and argued this position from the Bible, Thomas Aquinas, the Plenary Council of Quebec and, naturally, Leo XIII's *Rerum novarum.*

The second section spoke to employers in general and argued that Sunday desecration was a wilful social sickness that tempts God's punishment. On a practical note, the letter also stated that Sunday rest could be useful in keeping workers content while allowing time for worship. The bishops warned employers that if workers were not given the chance to rest and go to religious services, God's punishment would come from revolutionary, dechristianized workers breaking down the social order. Although communism was not mentioned, the recent Russian Revolution and the Winnipeg General Strike brought the fear of socialist revolution to Canada. The bishops recommended to employers a strict observance of rest from midnight Saturday to midnight Sunday. In an oblique reference to Jews, the bishops called upon the civil power to ensure that non-Christians did not require work from Christians.

The third section of the pastoral was directed mainly to lay people. It declared that all those who missed Sunday mass were in mortal sin, especially those who missed mass for excursions, theatrical shows, and professional sports. Excursions, innocent entertainments, and sports in themselves were not sinful, the bishops pointed out; they were permissible on Sundays but only after all obligations to God had been fulfilled. The bishops concluded that Sunday observance brought honour to the parish, strength to the family, and blessings to the nation. Comments on the permissibility of innocent amusements and the appeal to the Roman Catholic Church's authority as well as to the authority of the Bible marked the main differences from the Protestant Lord's Day Alliance of Canada.

The bishops had also given the social-week executive a signal that the time for study was over. The Catholic elite was ready; the bishops had spoken; it was time to move from theory to practice. At Monseigneur Lapointe's urging, an ad hoc committee headed by Quebec's chief justice, Sir F.-X. Lemieux, in the city of Quebec successfully prosecuted Sunday theatres. Six months later, Lapointe proposed a league to co-ordinate ad hoc local prosecution committees. On 16 April 1923, Archambault brought fifty people together in the Union catholique Hall in the basement of the Gesù, the Jesuit Church in downtown Montreal. Representatives of the main Montreal Catholic societies attended, many of them former retreatants. For example, the Union catholique, the Saint Vincent de Paul Society, the Association catholique des Voyageurs de Commerce, Catholic unions, the Association catholique de la jeunesse canadienne-française, the Ligue d'Action française, *Le Devoir*, and the Saint-Jean-Baptiste Society were represented. It seemed as if the who's who of Quebec's Catholic lay people had come. A constitution for the new Ligue du Dimanche, drafted by Archambault, was approved and the Ligue du Dimanche was born.

The Ligue accepted individuals and organizations as members. Each signed a pledge not to work on Sundays, not to employ anyone on Sundays, not to go to theatres on Sundays, to fight Sunday work by any means, and to follow instructions given out by the Ligue. Only practising Catholics were allowed to join, and the Ligue restricted itself to Quebec, where the majority of practising Catholics lived. Its goal was to have Sunday laws enforced and Sunday observed according to church law and teachings. To do this, the Ligue studied Sunday work, educated lay people through conferences, tracts, newspaper articles, congresses, and local committees, and lobbied the government through petitions and prosecutions. Its central organization was divided into three major urban and ecclesiastical committees: Montreal (including Sherbrooke, Valleyfield, St-Hyacinthe, Joliette, and Ottawa areas); Trois-Rivières (including Nicolet and LaTuque); and Quebec City (including Chicoutimi, Rimouski, and the Gaspé). Montreal, the largest city of French Canada, was the seat of its central committee. Montreal's regional committee sent three representatives to the central committee, Quebec only two, and Trois-Rivières two. The central committee named a secretary-general in charge of correspondence, statistics, and archives. Regional committees were formed with a minimum of ten members and local committees with five, three of whom were executive members. In practice, Montreal provided the secretary, most of the executive officers, and the chaplain, Joseph-Papin Archambault. A new religious elite, formed by Archambault, had begun the work of bringing Christian sacred time into secular and national practice.

The first targets of the Ligue du Dimanche's Catholic Action crusade were the pulp-and-paper mills. Cardinal Bégin wrote a pastoral letter to workers on May Day of 1923, a traditional labour holiday and the feast of St. Joseph the worker, advising all workers to quit their jobs when forced to work on Sundays. This was stupidly impractical, given most people's economic situations, and easily ignored. Montreal's Archbishop Gauthier directed his clergy to instruct the faithful in their Sunday duties. But if they worked, Sunday duties went unfulfilled. Monseigneur Lapointe, however, urged immediate political action against the Price Paper Company. Surviving documents show that the Quebec committee alone amassed over 6700 members and gathered resolutions against Sunday work from 211 municipalities. The pressure from so many Catholic organizations culminated in a visit by a delegation from the Ligue du Dimanche to Premier Taschereau, who agreed to enforce the Sunday laws.[4] In alarm, the pulp, flour, and glass mills appealed to Taschereau to recognize that their particular industries required Sunday work and were thus able to gain a brief reprieve as the government studied the situation.

Throughout 1924, the pressure on Taschereau mounted higher. *Le Soleil, Le Droit, Le Devoir, Le Colon, La Patrie, La Presse, Le Canada, Le Bien Public, L'Action Catholique, L'Etoile Du Nord,* and *Le Nouvelliste* published articles, editorials, and letters in June and July about the Ligue du Dimanche and Sunday rest-day resolutions sent to the federal as well as provincial governments. Also in 1924, Archambault published a pamphlet *Contre le travail du dimanche* (Against Sunday Work) in the Catholic Action series, *L'Oeuvre des Tracts.* In it, he affirmed that the Ligue was founded to prevent people from becoming industrial serfs. Why did the transportation industry insist on working Sundays? Why did factories run until 4 a.m. or 6 a.m. on Sunday and start again at 4 p.m. or 6 p.m.? Money, he answered in disgust. At the 1925 social week, one speaker lamented that provincial law did not allow the full severity of the Mosaic law to fall upon Sunday transgressors: death. Public opinion became so insistent that Premier Taschereau finally wrote to the pulp-and-paper companies that the law would be enforced in future.

Each company promised to stop work on Sundays, but each had its own way of interpreting the law. The Saint-Maurice Pulp and Paper Company cleaned machines for six hours after shutting down at midnight on Saturday and spent six hours in preparation for the week before midnight on Sunday. The International Paper Company spent the morning in repairs and began work again at 4 p.m. The St. Lawrence Paper Company began repair work at 8 a.m. The Wayagamack shut down from 8 a.m. to 3 p.m. The same half-hearted attempt to comply with the law could be seen at Laurentide, Price Brothers, Eddy, Booth, International, and Canada Cement. A 1926 provincial commission of inquiry into Sunday observance in the pulp-and-paper industry exerted additional pressure on companies but unsuccessfully. The mills were too powerful and isolated in regions of Quebec where their rule was law. The Ligue du Dimanche published a book, *Le repos dominical* (Montreal 1927) reviewing sabbatarian arguments in religion, law, morality, society, industry, and labour. Archambault, of course, wrote the introduction and emphasized the problems in the pulp-and-paper industry; he concluded by insisting on government intervention. Finally, Taschereau began to prosecute. It had been almost five years since the *semaine sociale* and the pastoral letter of 1922.

Now, Quebec's Catholic elite turned its attention toward movies. Cases against Sherbrooke theatres, instigated by English residents, had periodically dragged through reluctant courts.[5] To the surprise of the Lord's Day Alliance, Taschereau suddenly advised the provincial police to crack down on offenders. He had to act; an election was near, and he had to move against something that would raise the party's popularity without hurting its income from larger companies. Movies, long condemned by the clergy for their portrayal and glorification of passionate immorality, were vigorously prosecuted. Sherbrooke movie houses, nonetheless, continued to present Sunday movies and vaudeville shows to so many paying customers that fines were ineffective. Even the Montreal branch of the Syndicats catholiques nationaux (National Catholic Unions) recognized popular sentiment and crossed out the clause forbidding attendance at theatres before sending in its own Sunday pledge to the Ligue du Dimanche. Popular opinion temporarily stalled the creation of a uniform French Catholic Sunday.

Ligue sabbatarians were not frustrated long. Between four and five o'clock on Sunday afternoon on 9 January 1927, a fire broke out in the Laurier Palace Theatre in Montreal's poorer Hochelaga district. Seventy-eight children between the ages of five and sixteen years of age suffocated or were trampled to death. More were injured. Little coffins lined St. Catherine Street. The shock forced a provincial commission of inquiry. All Catholic organizations, unions, and newspapers that were affiliated with the Ligue du Dimanche asked for Sunday theatre closings. From the moment the fire cooled until the commission's final report, Montreal's diocesan newspaper, *La Semaine Religieuse,* called for the closing of all theatres on Sundays and the exclusion of children at all times. The fire, said militant Catholics, was a punishment from God for desecrating Sunday.[6] The Retail Merchants Association and international labour organizations protested, the former for profitable motives and the latter for entertainment reasons.

In a compromise, the Laurier Palace Theatre Commission examined the reasons why films were so popular that people would ignore their priests' anathemas. Judge Boyer concluded that immorality, free love, adultery, divorce, thefts, murders, suicides, and, more importantly, the depiction of people flouting legal and religious authority attracted people.[7] Although the federal law of 1906 forbade Sunday theatrical shows entirely, the Alliance's request that the federal law be enforced was not discussed. The government realized that it could not stop people from watching movies; too many votes and profits were involved. Yet the Roman Catholic Church insisted that the portrayal of successful immorality promoted disrespect for authority. Since both church and state were able to agree that children's respect for authority was important, on 30 August after the 1927 provincial elections were safely won, the judge recommended only that children be denied entry into theatres. Although the Laurier Palace Theatre had been overcrowded, badly ventilated, and had lacked enough exits, building safety standards were never discussed in the report. The Taschereau government introduced a law forbidding entry into theatres to children under the age of sixteen. This legislation implied that Sunday shows were legal for everyone over fifteen in spite of the 1906 federal Lord's Day Act, which outlawed all Sunday shows. If someone aged sixteen or older died in a theatre, then it was obviously his or her own fault.

This half-hearted measure angered the bishops so much that their sabbatarianism took an extreme direction. Every bishop and archbishop of Quebec signed another pastoral letter to denounce all Sunday activities—even those that raised money for charity. Furthermore, they encouraged people to go to court and into politics. "If need be," the bishops wrote, "use the civil law, and if it is again successfully avoided, we are sure our legislators will dutifully amend, refine, strengthen, and give the law effective penalties."[8] Clearly, if Taschereau's Liberals were slow to close the theatres, the bishops were prepared to support another set of legislators who would do so quickly. Taschereau began a new series of prosecutions. One prosecution, *Marin v. United Amusement Corporation,* forced a theatre to close in 1929 under the federal Lord's Day Act; others followed. It seemed as if the Christian gospel could indeed be secularized successfully and applied directly to politics in Quebec.

There remained only one clause in Quebec's Sunday law that made Quebec substantially different from the rest of Canada. The Quebec one allowed Jews to do business on Sunday if, from conscience's sake, they did not do business on Saturday and did not disturb anyone's Sunday rest. In practice, Jews were allowed to work on Saturday or Sunday but not both. And they were not allowed to have non-Jews working for them on Sunday. Catholics were caught up in the rising anti-Jewish hysteria of the post-1918 economic recession. As conspiracy theories and publication of the outrageously anti-Semitic *Protocols of the Elders of Zion* flourished, Ligue members saw Jews behind every evil. A Ligue investigation showed that many small Jewish businesses were open both Saturdays and Sundays. The Ligue thought that it saw Jews owning the pulp-and-paper mills and forcing good French-Canadian Christians to work on the holy day of Sunday. Looking closely at the theatres on 1 September 1926, the Ligue and *La Semaine Religieuse de Montréal* saw Jewish owners or filmmakers corrupting the morals of Canadian youth. Finally, spy squads of Catholic Action members could see the same Jews working both Saturdays and Sundays in little shops on Boulevard St-Laurent and Sherbrooke Street in Montreal. This put stores owned by French Canadians, supposedly working only six days in the week, at an economic disadvantage. Montreal's courts began to condemn Jew after Jew for petty Sunday offences.

In 1929, Archambault instituted *le mois du dimanche* and dedicated the entire month of April to Sunday observance. Every Catholic liturgical celebration on every day in April was taken up with the Sunday question. Schools were asked to set assignments and exams with Sunday as their topic. Songs were composed, poems and stories were written, prayers were said. Every papal pronouncement was brought out; every episcopal pastoral was studied again; every saint who had ever said anything about Sunday was brought forward for veneration. Over sixty monthly magazines and over fifty weekly and daily newspapers participated. This was in the middle of a provincial election. Both political parties promised to do their utmost to enforce the provincial and the federal Sunday laws. The month's campaign was a resounding success. Once re-elected, the Taschereau government named two Sunday-law inspectors, upon the Ligue's recommendations, to travel the province. Ironically, the inspectors worked only on Sundays and needed other jobs for the rest of the week. In memory of this outpouring of public opinion, the Ligue promoted a *Semaine du dimanche* every year from 1930 to 1960, similar to the Alliance's Lord's Day Week. How could Jews continue to work on Sundays?

The Jewish exemption from French Catholic control over the national Sunday came under increased attack. In *Rex v. Poyaners Inc.* (1925), the judge decided that a corporation owned by Jews could not take advantage of the Jewish exemption clause. Since corporations had no soul and no religion, the court ruled, they could not conscientiously observe the Jewish Sabbath day. Nor could they employ Christians on Saturday and Jews on Sunday and thus keep open seven days each week. This success against companies owned by Jews still did not satisfy the French Catholic sabbatarians. There remained the individual Jew, who persisted in working on Sunday.

An avalanche of complaints about Jews and of support for the Ligue poured into its offices. The president of the Fédération Nationale Saint-Jean-Baptiste, Marie Gérin-Lajoie, well-known for her position on votes for women, wrote to the Ligue. She pledged her personal support and that of her organization.[9] The Ligue's secretary, Alphonse de la Rochelle, was also on the executive of the Société Saint-Jean-Baptiste and was able to bring that organization to support the Ligue. Complaints from the local and central committees of religious and nationalistic Quebec organizations flowed into the Ligue and into the executive committee of Montreal. Newspapers as diverse as the right-wing religious *L'Action Catholique,* the liberal *Le Progrès du Saguenay,* and Adrien Arcand's fascist *Le Miroir* published articles against the Jewish exemption clause.

The flash point occurred when Allan Bray, president of the City of Montreal's executive committee, decreed that since the Jews celebrated New Year's on Saturday, 21 September 1930, and closed their stores on that day, they could open their stores on the following Sunday.[10] The campaign against Jews, fuelled by the increasing anti-Semitism in western societies and promoted by the Catholic sabbatarian elite, took on new dimensions. The harassed Mr. Bray reassured de la Rochelle that Montreal had been busy with over 148 Sunday cases in the preceding six months, most of them involving Jews. De la Rochelle complained that the number of cases against Jews was not high enough; Catholic Action squads had discovered 134 more cases in one day in only one area of Montreal.[11] The Confédération des Travailleurs Catholiques du Canada (Confederation of Catholic Workers of Canada), the Knights of Columbus, the Fédération des Ouvriers du Canada (Labourers Federation of Canada), and other organizations called for repeal of the provincial exemption clause. Maurice Duplessis, the Conservative Member for Trois-Rivières, pledged his support to the Ligue and was duly enrolled as an honorary member. When a Catholic youth group, Jeune Canada, complained that the federal Lord's Day Act was used to persecute French Canadians while English-speaking Jews were left alone, the provincial government felt such strong pressure that it decided to prepare a confidential study about recent prosecutions.

The study found that only 3% of all cases in Quebec involved French Canadians. The others involved "foreigners," the vast majority of whom were Jews. The rest were Italians, Greeks, and English-speaking Canadians. The government commissioned this secret report in order to prove that it was not party to an anti-French federal campaign; it proved instead that the provincial and municipal governments of Quebec condoned an anti-Jewish campaign; equality before the law was overlooked.[12] The government never needed to make the secret report public; Montreal court records from 1930 to 1932 were a public roll call of Montreal Jews and proof enough of persecution. Jews were allowed to open stores on Sunday; but if they sold on both Saturday and Sunday, they were prosecuted. If they sold to non-Jews on Sundays, they were prosecuted. If they did anything besides selling to Jews on Sundays, they were prosecuted—making a criminal of almost every Jewish storekeeper in Montreal. Although there was evidence that many French-Canadian shops kept open, too, very few of these were prosecuted. After 1933, comparing Montreal to Nazi Germany, Jewish storekeepers said nothing, paid their fines, and often closed their doors. Lita-Rose Betcherman states that the Ligue so often promoted and participated in anti-Semitic campaigns that she considered it a fascist organization. French Catholic organizations still demanded repeal of the Jewish exemption clause.

Archambault asked Alphonse de la Rochelle, secretary of the Ligue du Dimanche, to write to the premier of Quebec and formally ask that the Jewish exemption clause be stricken from Quebec's Sunday law. The idea of Jews working on Sunday was "against the spirit of our legislation based on Christian principles and contrary to good order."[13] A hidden threat of unforeseen consequences, of civil disorder, and of riots underlay the demand. Adrien Arcand had written that his fascist followers were prepared to beat up Jews who opened on Sundays, and some members of the Catholic elite were inclined to turn a blind eye to any fascist wrongdoing in retaliation for what they believed was a greater moral wrong perpetrated by Jews.[14] Taschereau bargained for time by replying that the provincial government could not repeal a statutory clause recognized by the federal government. The provincial Sunday law had been passed before the federal law had come into effect and could not be changed, since any action on the part of the province would infringe federal power.[15] Jews were being prosecuted under the provincial act if they were open to the general public for business, moreover, or if they kept anyone else from observing Quebec's Catholic Sunday. When the Ligue turned to federal authorities, the latter strongly and unhesitatingly argued that Quebec had a right to repeal the clause without asking federal permission.[16] Quebec had been the first, in *Ouimet v. Bazin,* to demonstrate that provinces could exempt classes of its population from criminal prosecution. Logically, a province could repeal its own exemption clause. The federal government obviously did not want to bring a touchy religious issue back into the federal arena.

In May 1935, Duplessis and his colleague, Jean-Paul Sauvé, again brought the Jewish exemption clause into the Quebec legislature. Taschereau outflanked the demand by staging a successful majority vote to submit the question to Quebec's Court of Appeal. This move bought Taschereau the chance to hold another election during which he could promise to repeal the clause if the courts decided that he could. He obviously preferred not to abolish civil and provincial rights so hard-won by Bourassa and Quebec's Liberals many years before, while he had been a young parliamentarian. By going to the courts, he probably thought that there was some chance of avoiding the decision. The Ligue's lawyer, Antonio Perrault, a professor of civil law at the University of Montreal who had practised his Sunday arguments in Archambault's 1927 book, *Le Repos Dominical,* claimed that the Attorney General of Quebec (in this case, Premier Taschereau) had absolute control over the provincial law and administrative authority over the federal law. It was Taschereau's right to repeal the Jewish exemption. The provincial court agreed. Although the case was heard in October, the ruling was postponed until 3 December, conveniently after the 25 November elections. Taschereau returned to power with a slim six-seat majority.

The Union Nationale had insisted throughout its campaign on immediate repeal of the clause. This, among other issues, had helped to win the clergy's endorsement of the Union Nationale. Taschereau bowed to the politically inevitable. By declaring that he really had no objections to repealing the exemption, he hung on to those of his nervous followers who were ready to defect to the growing Union Nationale. The legislature voted, and the Jewish exemption clause was repealed on 10 June 1936, thirty years after Bourassa's successful fight for individual conscience and Quebec autonomy. The disintegration of the Quebec Liberal Party, the stress of a declining majority in the legislature, and perhaps the abandonment of principles for which he had previously fought led Taschereau to resign the next day. Catholic Action members in the Ligue du Dimanche found, as had Social Gospellers in the Lord's Day Alliance, that entering the political realm was the most powerful way of applying Christianity to society.

During the Ligue du Dimanche campaign, the Alliance bitterly insisted that "Had the Lord's Day Alliance secured from the people of Quebec any reasonable measure of support, the condition of affairs which they now deplore and attempt to correct would never have existed."[17] Although George Mingie, the Alliance's field secretary for eastern Canada took credit for helping to form the first Quebec City committee of the Ligue, his presence was of minimal importance, since he was often working in eastern Ontario and the Maritimes. The new general secretary in 1927, Dr. Charles H. Huestis, a United Church minister who had long been a successful field secretary in British Columbia and Alberta, wrote for more information about Quebec. What had happened in the motion-picture controversy? Why were there so many letters from English Montrealers complaining that the Alliance was not doing anything? Who were the Alliance officers in Quebec? The answers boiled down to the bald fact that the Alliance organization had shrunk to Mingie in Montreal. Unfortunately, during the Laurier Palace inquiry, Mingie declared that he was busy with health and family problems. Huestis had to go to Montreal to collect from the local financiers: Birks, Holland, Dawson, and McConnell, so that the entire financial year would not be lost. On his return, Huestis reviewed Mingie's worth to the organization. In the rest of Canada, donations were declining, court cases were being lost, and postwar Canadian confidence was being ground away in western revolts. Mingie seemed to be doing nothing in a part of Canada that promised so much hope to the Alliance. On 12 July 1927, in the middle of the Laurier Palace Theatre inquiry, Huestis informed Mingie that a new secretary had been appointed for eastern Canada and that Mingie would no longer be needed.

When Montreal's Protestants revived the Montreal Alliance Branch in early 1928, they independently hired Mingie as their secretary. Huestis protested that this meant that the Quebec organization had unilaterally seceded from the Alliance.[18] For the rest of that frustrating year, Huestis tried to convince the Quebec "separatists" that Mingie had been an Alliance employee dismissed for dereliction of duty and was now disrupting the Alliance's national organization in revenge. Mingie, in return, argued that "Quebec has its own special position in the Dominion of Canada and its own peculiar problems, customs and system of law and that while the Lord's Day Alliance of Canada may be able to deal with the problems which affect the Dominion as a whole, the problems of the Province of Quebec can be dealth [sic] with more effectively by the Quebec (Provincial) Lord's Day Alliance."[19]

He claimed that the Dominion Alliance was an English Protestant body acting as a foreign element in Quebec society and seeking to change Quebec with methods and an organization tested elsewhere. A "small group in Toronto who are practically responsible to noone [sic] but themselves," Mingie wrote, "consider themselves better fitted to know what the people of Quebec need than those who have spent their whole lives in Quebec."[20] When the Dominion Alliance insisted that Quebec be treated in the same way as the rest of the country, this could only mean ludicrous failure in Canada's only majority French and Catholic province. Toronto's isolation could be seen in the way the general secretaries of the Alliance, William Rochester and then Huestis, occasionally dropped in on Quebec and collected money from Montreal's rich, spiriting it away to pay Toronto's bills and then writing to Quebec's politicians over the heads of the Quebec Alliance in the name of Quebec's Protestants. Quebec's Alliance felt useless. Strengthened by hostility toward Toronto in the Quebec Protestant community, Mingie threatened the Alliance with a lawsuit and what might be called a smear campaign if it persisted in trying to oust him. When Huestis asked him what he did with donations, Mingie refused to answer.[21]

Mingie claimed also that the Dominion Alliance was participating in the new United Church's attempt to freeze all Presbyterians, such as Mingie, out of prominent positions. As for United Church dominance of the post-1925 Lord's Day Alliance of Canada, that was an undeniable fact. Since all Methodist and most Presbyterian clergy joined the United Church, most of the Alliance executive positions were suddenly filled with United Church adherents. In 1937, the Dominion Alliance was still staffed almost exclusively with United Churchmen. What with the Presbyterian Church's drastic reduction in size and importance, the disappearance of Methodist and Congregationalist organizations, problems within the Baptist communion over modernism, and continued Anglican coolness, the Alliance had clearly lost touch with many of its denominational constituents. Mingie's rival Quebec organization was successfully staffed with Quebec Anglicans, Baptists, and Presbyterians, in stark contrast to the Dominion Alliance.

Consequently, the Dominion Lord's Day Alliance was almost entirely cut off from both Catholic and Protestant Quebec. There were no French Canadians on executive committees, on staff, or in branches. Furthermore, it had some trouble convincing the Ligue du Dimanche that the familiar Mingie was no longer the Dominion Alliance representative.[22] Admittedly, it was hard for the Ligue to believe the Toronto-based Alliance represented Quebec's English Protestant population better than Mingie's organization, but Huestis continued to write from Toronto to the Ligue and to Father Archambault on behalf of the English Protestant minority in Quebec. Little by little, the two organizations, the Ligue du Dimanche and the Lord's Day Alliance of Canada, collaborated on small projects. For example, after a joint submission to Ottawa, both organizations obtained cancellation stamps with the engraving "Observe Sunday—Observez le Dimanche." Not surprisingly, the Ligue bought bilingual stamps and the Alliance English-only stamps—for lack of money, the Alliance claimed.[23] Later, Huestis wished the Ligue du Dimanche success in suppressing the Jewish exemption clause, and his kind remarks were gratefully acknowledged.[24]

When Huestis asked about Montreal's Sunday hockey games, however, the Ligue quickly responded that it was concentrating on business and the Jews, not on simple games.[25] The Ligue recognized that prosecuting hockey games would mean prosecuting French Canadians, who would not take kindly to the forceful hint that they were as criminal as non-Catholic "foreigners": Jews and English Protestants. While the Alliance tried to extend English Protestant Christian civilization (based on the Bible) to French Canada, French Catholics in Quebec extended their own definition of a Christian nation (based on the Catholic Church) to all of Quebec, including the English and Jews. Professional hockey had become a French-Canadian pastime and would not be prosecuted by French Canadians. Ironically, the prosecution of Jews became something of a joint Protestant and Catholic pastime.

The Ligue du Dimanche dared to use Duplessis against an aging Liberal government to legislate the morals of Quebec where Catholicism and the fourth commandment, the Ligue prayed, would form the constitution of the nation. After a lengthy battle, the Ligue succeeded at least in imposing sabbatarianism on many segments of Quebec: English and Jewish businesses.

The similarities between Quebec's experiences and those of the Alliance are striking. Catholic Action groups were rather like English Canada's Social Gospellers in using government power for religious ends. Ironically, too, the democratic creation of a Catholic day of rest, like the Protestant one, also meant the coercion of dissident Christians and Jews and the creation of a new class of criminals. The Ligue du Dimanche was a youthful, Quebec version of the Alliance. It was willing to do battle with all and sundry for Christian civilization. In the interests of uniformity within Quebec, the provincial Sunday law had been shorn of the Jewish exemption clause, which had distinguished Quebec from the rest of Canada. In the first half of the twentieth century, Quebec's Catholic Action mirrored Canada's Protestant Social Gospel. It fought to create a uniform, righteous, and sabbatarian nation, although its definitions of "nation" and its efforts were "largely unconnected"[26] with the English Protestant Sunday. Did anyone in the Ligue look at the moribund Quebec Alliance and wonder whether the future of Quebec's sabbatarianism could be seen there?

Duplessis had gained power with the help of the Ligue's critique of Taschereau's government over Sunday. The new Attorney General, Duplessis himself, continued to grant fiats to prosecute Jews. Somewhat satisfied by Duplessis' prosecution of Jews, members of the Ligue supported the Union Nationale. Although Sunday morning activities by Christians were prosecuted so that religious services were the only activities permitted, however, no prosecutions were allowed against afternoon activities. Theatres slowly reopened and the pulp-and-paper business went on its unimpeded way. In 1936, complaints against the mills doubled. In 1937, complaints doubled again to over one hundred and twenty cases. Factories successfully claimed industrial necessity. Price Brothers Paper Company ignored the law in 1937 and, in 1938, was fined fifty dollars under the Lord's Day Act.[27] Recognizing that the penalties needed to be increased, the Ligue turned to Ottawa. A member of Parliament and a Ligue supporter, Hector Brunelle introduced a private bill in 1937, 1938, and again in 1939 to increase fines and jail sentences, but the Senate merely amended his bill almost out of existence. Neither the federal nor the provincial government wanted to hamper companies that brought in needed capital and jobs during the 1930s. The Sunday inspectors' salaries went unpaid. Duplessis became unavailable for interviews. His assistant informed inspectors to ignore major companies and concentrate on closing small businesses in towns, such as pool halls, during mass.[28] Quebec's sabbatarians were forced to content themselves with prosecuting weak minorities such as Jews.

Prophetically, Chicoutimi's Bishop, Mgr Eugene Lapointe, castigated the Ligue for allowing itself to be deflected from its original mission against inhumane pulp-and-paper mills that employed thousands of Catholics. Why did the Ligue insist on wasting its time in pointless Jew-baiting? Jews were not the problem. "We are deluding ourselves when we say that we have won anything in this 20 year struggle against Sunday work. We have won nothing, or so little that it might as well be nothing. Events, the economic crisis, if you will, have caused a reduction of Sunday work. That's all!"[29] As the 1930s slipped by, fewer members attended meetings of the Ligue du Dimanche. People resigned to join other crusades such as the one against communism. Of the original members, only Archambault was left. And few fought "atheistic communism" and "anarcho-jewish socialism" with the same fervour as did Joseph-Papin Archambault and his retreatants. Quebec's national Sunday became much less important to them than the struggle against communism being waged and won in Franco's Spain, Mussolini's Italy, and Hitler's Germany.

All that remained to defend Quebec's hothouse sabbatarianism was a skeleton organization that met weekly, then monthly, then seasonally as its members aged. The Duplessis government had been elected with Ligue votes, and many Catholic leaders voted for the Union Nationale if they did not already belong to it. Yet the people of Quebec continued to work on Sundays, go to the hockey games, sometimes to the theatre, and occasionally stopped at the shop after Sunday mass to buy something needed for lunch or supper that day. The Ligue du Dimanche had gone into the political arena and, to defeat the Liberal government, had transferred its hopes, its moral authority, and its power to the Duplessis government. But the Duplessis government ignored the Ligue's demands in favour of other, more pressing secular ones. Ironically, the Ligue experienced the same reverses in the provincial political arena as the Lord's Day Alliance did elsewhere. Jews, almost exclusively, however, were still prosecuted for breaking the Roman Catholic Sabbath.

As in 1906, the transfer of religious authority to the political arena meant that institutional religious authority declined in favour of political and, ultimately, popular authority. By 1937, the businesses and people of Quebec went to work or play on Sunday, relatively unhampered by the question of a French-Canadian nationalism that had been shaped by Roman Catholicism.

You shall keep my sabbaths and reverence my sanctuary: I am the LORD. *If you walk in my statutes and observe my commandments and do them, then I will give you your rains in their season, and the land shall yield its increase, and the trees of the field shall yield their fruit.*—LEVITICUS 26:2–4

The main thing to be combatted now is Communism, and a disposition on the part of those who are unemployed to feel resentful toward established institutions. I think you will agree with me that this is a more important thing for Christianity than a more rigorous enforcement of the Lord's Day Act.
—W.H. PRICE, ATTORNEY GENERAL OF ONTARIO, 1931

CHAPTER SEVEN

SUNDAY DURING THE DEPRESSION

Politics, Provinces, and Pluralism, 1930–1938

IN 1938, THE PRESBYTERIAN CHURCH SURVEYED CANADA from east to west and declared: "In the Maritimes, the Sabbath appears to be still the Sabbath . . . As we go westward the Sabbath means less and less."[1] The Presbyterian Church had accurately described Canada's Sabbath. The Maritimes were bogged down in economic stagnation and could hardly produce more than the token Sabbath-breaking company. Quebec was in the powerful and only sometime sabbatarian hands of Maurice Duplessis and his fellow travellers in the Ligue du Dimanche. Premier Mitchell Hepburn's Liberal Ontario was locked in an industrial combat with the Depression and, incidentally, the federal Liberals; the federal Sunday law sometimes got in the way. Manitoba and Saskatchewan had thrown over the federal Lord's Day Act during the 1920s and were ignoring it as much as possible, even when it occasionally made an appearance in court. Alberta's Social Credit government, a religious movement in its own right and powerful competition for the mainstream churches, decided to ignore the federal law. In British Columbia, Christian fragmentation and the drive to make money steadily denied a hearing to the Alliance. In all, pluralism and provincial politics stripped the Alliance of secular power throughout the West. Canadians took advantage of the vacuum that this religious conflict created and introduced travel, tourism, music, radio, and sports on Sunday.

The secularization, or transfer of power over moral questions from religious authorities to the governments and people of Canada, was further advanced, because the Depression years were ones of general disorganization in the churches. Their creation, the Lord's Day Alliance of Canada, experienced a different form of secularization. Its leadership was reduced by age and financial want. With the Maritimes stuck in the Depression and Quebec promoting only an anti-Semitic sabbatarianism, the battles and training of young sabbatarians occurred in the West. Western sabbatarian leadership eventually infused the entire Alliance and allowed it to survive the Depression.

The financial crisis and drop in donations to the Alliance forced General Secretary Charles Huestis in 1933 to ask the churches for help. He was rebuffed by everyone except T. Albert Moore, former general secretary of the Alliance and now a doughty past moderator of the United Church of Canada. The United Church appointed this stout warhorse and the bespectacled and scholarly-looking George Pidgeon to head a committee of secretaries of the Board of Evangelism and Social Service to examine the Alliance finances and make recommendations. In 1936, the committee recommended retirements. Huestis remained the general secretary for one more year. His western successor, George G. Webber, a Methodist United Churchman, like Moore, remained in Alberta and British Columbia, and would succeed Huestis when he retired. W.N. Byers, also a Methodist United Churchman, was hired for the Maritimes and was expected to keep an eye on Quebec. The general secretary was to take care of Manitoba, Saskatchewan, Ontario, and Quebec with help from his retired ministers. Naturally, most of Canada fell between the cracks and little information about Saskatchewan or northern Ontario, for example, ever reappears in the Alliance records in spite of Lord's Day court cases from these places. William Rochester, another former general secretary of the Alliance, might not have been pleased to see that his old plan of a full-time field secretary in every province had been scuttled, but the same financial retrenchment was occurring in Canadian churches and in Sabbath-observance organizations around the world.[2]

There were no opportunities for expansion of Alliance activities during the financially pinched years of the Depression; even before the recommendation to cut staff, people were let go one by one—in 1931 alone, three field secretaries had been retired. Mingie had been fired earlier, of course, from Quebec and the Maritimes. These elderly ministers had often forfeited automatic church payments to their respective pension funds after joining the Alliance. Returning to their churches, they found that their diminished years of official church service and of pension payments left most of them with little to live on. Many ministers who had worked outside the Presbyterian, Methodist, or Congregationalist churches in non-denominational organizations found that their pensions had been cut. Older ministers, such as Lawson or Watson, lacking pensions, often took on the odd sermon for the Alliance. The small Alliance cheque for salary arrears and the occasional sermon helped them get by.

No longer was the image of the Alliance one of youth, dynamism, and power as it had been at the turn of the century. The face that the Alliance showed to the public became older and poorer every day. There were few incentives for young ministers to take difficult, often low paid, and insecure positions outside of a denomination. In spite of Huestis' and Webber's efforts, few ministers other than aging Presbyterian and United Church ministers came forward to fill Alliance field positions. Anglican bishops regularly refused to allow their young, Low Church ministers to work for non-denominational organizations such as the Lord's Day Alliance, or would allow it only if ministers waived their Anglican pension rights.[3] So, the average ages of the Alliance secretaries crept higher each year as the Alliance found it almost impossible to recruit younger people. The youngest were in their fifties. In 1937,

G.G. Webber, General Secretary, Lord's Day Alliance, 1937–1950, and a formerly Methodist minister who joined the United Church as had Huestis, his predecessor.

Huestis resigned and Webber stepped up from Alberta and British Columbia to take control of the Lord's Day Alliance of Canada. A sign of the greying of the Alliance, Webber had been active in Alliance circles since 1904! No one could be found to replace him in the West, so Byers was transferred from the Maritimes to British Columbia. Baxter J. Warr, another Methodist United Churchman who had studied with J.S. Woodsworth, succeeded him in Halifax.

In spite of the Alliance's visible decline, there had been no watering down of sabbatarian belief within Alliance circles throughout the Depression. The general secretary, Huestis, publicly tailored his newspaper articles and his book, *Sunday in the Home,* to the growing creed of secularism by emphasizing secular rest and recreation for body and mind. Within Alliance meetings, Huestis revealed that what he meant was that Sunday rest was "to bring us to God."[4] Rest was never, in his mind or in the minds of other sabbatarians, worthwhile in itself. Rest and recreation were to be used for the worship of God. Huestis himself found worship a form of recreation. When he advocated recreation, Huestis often meant prayer and religious services. His opinions and the opinions of his aging field secretaries had not changed since 1906.

Christian denominations had also kept their own opinions about Sunday since the turn of the century. Now numerically first among the Protestant denominations, the United Church of Canada, as a self-appointed national church, tried to "Christianize the Social Order."[5] This goal had been one reason for both church union and the Lord's Day Alliance of Canada. During the Depression, the United Church, desperate to save money, promoted Moore out of his secretary's chair to act as both moderator and secretary for an unusual cost-cutting term. The former Alliance general secretary preached as a moderator for "a virile Christianity permeating and dominating our life in its every relationship. . . . Our need is not more shibboleths, doctrines and formulas, but a keener realization of the inestimable values of and participation in prayer, Bible reading, Sabbath observance, assembling with His people, and responsibility in all the great enterprises of the Church."[6]

United Church presbyteries and United Church Evangelism and Social Service committees across the country discussed the Lord's Day Act during the 1930s. If there had been any wavering doubt about Sunday observance in the untried United Church, Moore encouraged a groundswell of efforts to protect the day of rest against "materialistic greed."[7] The United Church at least united and encouraged former Methodists and former Presbyterians in a strict sabbatarian position. All of Sunday was for absolute rest, so that all could worship God.

William Rochester, former general secretary of the Alliance and now respected editor of the Presbyterian *Record,* the official Presbyterian magazine, chaired the Presbyterians' Sabbath Observance Committee. Just prior to church union, the committee had been buried by successive reorganizations of the Board of Home Missions and Social Service, and had gradually dropped out of sight. Rochester's personal adherence to the Presbyterian Church helped keep Sunday observance in the forefront of Presbyterian concerns and saved the Alliance from condemnation as just another United Church organization surreptitiously sucking away Presbyterian members. Immediately after church union, Presbyterians blasted their omnibus boards as unwanted legacies of the uniting crowd and, in 1926, a committee dedicated only to Sabbath observance was re-established. With Rochester's support, in 1927 it set out a strict sabbatarian interpretation of Sunday. By 1929, Rochester was the acting convener, and he took complete control by 1930, writing lengthy reports on Sabbath observance in the *Acts and Proceedings of the Presbyterian Church in Canada.* These reports condemned all activities, all noise, and anything that was not related to the worship of God. Unfortunately for Presbyterians, Depression realities forced them to combine their Sabbath observance, temperance, and moral-reform committees into a new omnibus committee. At least, however, it was still chaired by Rochester. In 1936, the Sabbath committee was placed under Evangelism and Church Life and Work, but it received several pages in the annual *Acts and Proceedings* of the General Assembly. By 1937, Presbyterians had finally stabilized their membership and administration. Only then were they able to shift their attention from church life to church work, yet they were no longer a national church as they had been in 1906. By sheer force of numbers, the United Church had taken over Protestant leadership on the Sunday question.

Anglicans, as ever, were ambivalent about the Canadian Sunday. Their internal theological divisions kept them from speaking officially during the Depression on any matter dealing with society, to Huestis' annoyance.[8] Anglicans were perfectly content to allow leisure activities after religious services and were happy to commend the Alliance. But they never went further to pressure the government for stricter observance of the law and never freed one of their own ministers to help with Alliance work. Reflecting a middle- or an upper-class bias, Anglicans were still debating whether servants should be allowed Sunday off.[9] Although a small "unofficial" (and mainly Low Church) contingent of Anglicans excoriated the abuses of capitalism, demanded strict adherence to the Sunday laws, and participated in Alliance committees, no resolution was ever passed by its General Synod about the Depression. About Sunday and seven-day work weeks, too, nothing was said. A mild salute to the Lord's Day Alliance was all that was ever discussed at the highest levels. Moderation was ever the key word.

During the Depression years, however, Baptists gradually moved out of internecine theological strife and began to support interdenominational movements more readily. In 1931, Alliance field secretary and Baptist, George McLean, rammed through a resolution of support for the Alliance at a Baptist convention. The Baptists stated that their denomination had participated in the formation of the Alliance in 1899, and claimed that, in the financial crisis of 1931, the Alliance had been abandoned by all other churches. Since the Alliance "carefully refrains from invading the sphere of religion and conscience and is thus in harmony with the traditional principles of our churches," the United Baptists promised to raise some money. The entire premise of the resolution was inaccurate. The Alliance had been founded in 1888; other denominations, notably the Presbyterian and the United, had pledged financial support; and the Alliance had often invaded the sphere of religion (in a way entirely consonant with Baptist principles). But this resolution marked a new effort by Baptists in Canada to promote Sunday rest. Each year—1935, 1936, 1937, 1938, and 1939—saw resolutions of support for the Alliance in the *United Baptist Year Book.*

In the United, Presbyterian, Anglican, and Baptist churches, nothing had changed. Belief in the necessity for a Christian Sabbath remained. No secularism had affected the churches' beliefs on this. Lord's Day observance in Canada as a whole and especially in the West became the special concern of the United Church Board of Evangelism and Social Service under J.R. Mutchmor because of its great strength across the West, while the Presbyterians concerned themselves with Sabbath observance only among their own dwindling members and mainly in Ontario. The Alliance, as Mingie once claimed hysterically, became a peculiarly United Church organization. It now returned to the small structure it had known under Shearer and Moore, with one man in the West, one in the Maritimes, and one in Ontario. In spite of the fact that it still spoke only for sabbatarians, now primarily in the United Church of Canada and the Presbyterian Church, the Alliance continued to pretend as it had in 1906 that it represented all of Canada. The western imbalance in Alliance personnel had increased to such an extent that Ontario's deputy Attorney General claimed that it did not know Ontario conditions; Huestis came from the West, after all, and continually quoted western examples to Ontario.[10] Although the Alliance had as many paid workers in 1937 as it had had in 1907, they were now less representative, less active, and older. During the Depression, therefore, secularization of aging, not secularism of thought and theology, was the real challenge in Alliance ranks. With proportionately fewer secretaries for a growing Canadian population and those secretaries tiring, the organized sabbatarian message began to weaken across Canada.

TO COMBAT SUNDAY SECULARISM, the Alliance again turned to government authorities. Huestis first solicited letters of appreciation from federal parliamentarians: W.L. Mackenzie King, R.B. Bennett, H.H. Stevens, and other prominent political leaders on the occasion of the Alliance's anniversary in 1931. The politicians were glad to oblige. Huestis banked largely on the fact that he and Bennett were from Alberta and knew each other, and that Bennett, a former Methodist like Huestis, never worked on Sundays.[11] From these slim facts, Huestis and Webber, also from Alberta, wrote directly to Prime Minister Bennett about western problems: government post offices, military practices, and Sunday observance in the government work camps for the unemployed. In general, the Alliance approach to Bennett was sound, for Bennett ran a one-man government. Post offices were closed, recreational gun shoots were stopped, and work camps did no work on Sundays. Sabbatarians relied on government to enforce the Sabbath.

Although federal power over Sunday was re-established with sabbatarian blessing, Bennett refused to grant sabbatarians everything they wanted. He was more than willing to invade the sphere of religion, but as far as the economic world was concerned, he would not venture into new paths. Instead, he went in a more mystical direction and declared Sunday, 17 July 1932, to be a public "day of prayer and petition that Christ may sit in at the conference table and guide the deliberations" of the Imperial Economic Conference that he was hosting to solve problems created by the Depression. When the conference failed, Bennett frantically cast about for ideas to replace his bankrupt policies. "An Act to provide for a weekly day of rest in accordance with the Convention concerning the application of the Weekly Rest in Industrial Undertakings adopted by the General Conference of the International Labour Organization of the League of Nations, in accordance with the Labour Part of the Treaty of Versailles of 28th June, 1919" was passed with a myriad of other labour bills in the short session before the election of 1935.

Predictably, a storm of protest fell on the prime minister from the Canadian Manufacturers Association saying that these laws were unrealistic; members would not abide by them.[12] The CMA argument was interesting. On the one hand, it said, business was already moving to the proposed standards of 1919, so government really had no need to pass any laws. On the other hand, it claimed, these standards were economically impossible. In another paradox, international competition kept profits too low to afford better hours of work, but most Canadian businesses were too small to compete internationally and had too few workers to afford rest days. Seasonal work in agriculture demanded round-the-clock, seven-day work weeks, while factories required the same hours because of continuous production. Then, the CMA appealed to Bennett's baser sense by pointing out that they would be less able to pay taxes. They refused to conform, above all, unless other companies and even other countries did the same. The textile industries asked for permission to continue working women two shifts each day in the work week, the Railway Association asked for a blanket exemption, and the Employers Association of Manitoba asked for the right to seasonal overtime. From British Columbia lumber companies to Charlottetown sardine companies, complaints rolled in. This suggested that every business in the country would go under. Within the Conservative government itself, there was some stiff opposition. One cabinet member privately protested that the proposed laws would implicitly recognize the existence of employers' and workers' organizations, collective bargaining, and international unions! Obviously, cabinet had some catching up to do in labour history, because both employer and labour organizations were just then fiercely lobbying the government.[13]

To the Alliance's satisfaction, the successful law declared that "[t]his period of rest shall wherever possible be the Lord's Day" and also declared that the exemption for people working fewer than eight hours a day was repealed. The Conservatives of 1935 had basically adopted the 1906 law with minor changes. Shortly afterwards, the Liberals returned to power and had most of Bennett's programme thrown out. The Conservative Senate then turned back the Liberal Brunelle's Ligue du Dimanche-backed attempt to increase the 1906 fines to owners and employers. In spite of Bennett's good will, his feeble sabbatarian efforts were easily stopped by business and political opponents.

The Alliance appeared to be stuck. It could not touch businesses, and its campaigns against petty sports and sales, both activities of the masses, were gaining unfavourable publicity. In both cases, its sabbatarianism seemed an ineffectual middle-class phenomenon that was squeezed between those who had money and those who did not. Tom Moore, president of the Trades and Labour Congress of Canada, severely criticized the Alliance in 1931 for not defending the principle of one day of rest for all workers.[14] Huestis quickly wrote that the Alliance would be happy to collaborate and pressure the federal government into amending the Lord's Day Act to make employers give every employee one day off each week, no matter how essential the work or how few hours the employee worked in the rest of the week.[15] As always, the solution to sabbatarian weakness was sought in government strength. But although the governments of Canada accepted the endorsements and the authority to do what was necessary, they regularly refused to implement the sabbatarian programme.

The federal governments' refusal to implement the existing Lord's Day Act can be traced to its belief that responsibility for day-to-day administration of the Sunday law, as well as Depression relief, was in provincial hands.[16] The Alliance had to contend with individual provinces refusing to accept federal responsibilities delegated to them or thrust upon them by the federal government. Huestis' demand that the provinces institute prosecutions under the federal act fell upon deaf ears. The federal law was passed to impose unity on the nation, but provincial differences during the Depression, as always, created disunity. The Ontario Attorney General wrote to Huestis: "The main thing to be combatted now is Communism, and a disposition on the part of those who are unemployed to feel resentful toward established institutions. I think you will agree with me that this is a more important thing for Christianity than a more rigorous enforcement of the Lord's Day Act."[17] Ontario's Deputy Attorney General admitted that if a private citizen or the Alliance requested a fiat, it would be granted; but the police would not go out searching for offenses, because that would require an entire army of inspectors—and they had other things to do! Why, the Deputy asked, could the Alliance not institute proceedings on its own authority?[18] Obviously, there were even fewer Alliance secretaries and less money to do just that. As with all Alliance secretaries before him, Huestis' policy was to insist that the police prosecute Sunday offenders everywhere equally, because private individuals were often too shy to begin prosecutions of their neighbours, and the Alliance had too little money to pay for prosecutions. Once all offenders were prosecuted equally by vigilant governments, the Alliance itself could take a sabbatical. In this way, the Alliance offered to transfer its weakening authority to governments in the hope that political power would bolster sabbatarianism.

Unfortunately for the Alliance, provincial governments promoted the idea of giving the administration of the Sunday law to a third level of administration: municipalities. In 1930, Ontario led the way. The miniature-golf craze had swept across Canada and, by 1930, invaded Sunday. Walkerville, in Ontario's York Township, passed a bylaw closing miniature-golf courses from Saturday night to Monday morning. The key court case challenging the bylaw was *Rex v. Louis Epstein* (1931). Louis Epstein and his partner, a Mr. Altman, ran the Tom Thumb miniature-golf course on Sunday. This particular case gained the special attention of the Alliance, because, as the Toronto United Church secretary of Evangelism and Social Service noted, Tom Thumb was run by a "Jewish firm."[19] As far as the provincial government was concerned, miniature golf had to be closed on Sunday if public opinion so demanded. And public opinion demanded that Jewish businesses close on Sunday. Although the Deputy Attorney General could see no difference between a miniature and a regular golf course, he was instructed to close the former. After complying with the order and seeing his prosecution appealed, he then attended the appeal court to argue that the municipal Sunday bylaw was within municipal power, since it did not mention Sunday. Municipalities, he said, could pass their own bylaws to regulate hours of opening, including Sunday. In theory, municipalities were to exempt specific shops, sports, or other activities, and to inform the province of these exemptions so that the provincial Attorney General would refrain from granting fiats for prosecutions due to complaints. Thus, the provincial government would be able to avoid its federally imposed responsibility by passing it on to the municipalities. Newspapers across Canada eagerly watched as the City of Toronto opened wading pools on Sunday in 1938.

At the end of the summer of 1938, a new Attorney General, G.D. Conant, began a speaking tour against the enforcement of Sunday observance laws. He had vigorous approval from the *Globe and Mail.* Alliance officials complained that an old and very strict Ontario Sabbath law of 1845 was being confused with the 1906 Lord's Day Act. No fiats had been issued in almost twenty years, and the crazy legal tangle had been brought on by Ontario itself by bending to every pressure group claiming to represent public opinion asking for an exemption. The Alliance organized a huge delegation of United Church, Catholic, Anglican, Baptist, Presbyterian, Salvation Army, Toronto and National Labour Council, and Retail Merchant representatives. No matter, Attorney General Conant held firm. Premier Hepburn himself could not see anything wrong with Sunday sports and came to Conant's defence.[20] The pools stayed open, because the province refused to institute its own prosecutions.

Miniature golf hit British Columbia and Manitoba, too, in 1930. And both provinces brought cases to court. Although British Columbia had already thrown its responsibility to the municipalities in the 1920s, it now decided that miniature golf was similar to golf, which was legal under federal law as a quiet game. Saskatchewan allowed its municipalities to regulate Sunday hours. Manitoba, following its famous excursion precedent of 1925, decided that the province had a right to permit miniature golf or anything else forbidden under federal law. All provinces later asked their municipalities to decide what was legal or illegal on Sunday. By having different municipal Sunday laws in Quebec, Ontario, Manitoba, Saskatchewan, and British Columbia, Alliance secretaries believed that Canada had returned to the crazy quilt of conflicting, often illogical Sunday laws and exemptions that had been characteristic of the nineteenth century. The federal law would now be meaningless. Huestis demanded that each province appoint a provincial inspector to keep it in line with the federal Lord's Day Act of 1906.

The British Columbia Attorney General's department considered Sunday infractions to be mere misdemeanours, so prosecutions were discouraged.[21] As both minor and major businesses continued to make money on Sunday, Webber reminded British Columbia boards of trade that unemployment would be relieved if businesses refused to employ people on Sunday and employed more people during the rest of the week.[22] When that appeal failed, Huestis again turned to Bennett. But the federal government refused to act for fear that it would then logically be bound to take financial responsibility for social programmes during the Depression.[23]

For well-off British Columbians and Canadians in general, work was what other people did, gladly. While servants cleaned the dishes on Sunday night, richer British Columbians went out to the Vancouver Symphony. Many musicians were willing to overlook a Sunday law to earn money; the Symphony Society exploited this occasion to hear fine classical music and also to make some money.[24] Members of government and their wives, the mayor, and the lieutenant-governor placed their names on the patronage lists for this musical and "spiritual" endeavour.[25] Acting Premier R.H. Pooley then informed Webber that His Majesty's representatives were not to be "called upon for explanation of their actions by any of His Majesty's subjects . . . such as you."[26] The secretary of the Symphony Society put it more directly: "I have a very conscientious objection to being taken to a grimy police court to show cause why I should not be fined, especially when all we are doing is to benefit, intellectually, spiritually and educationally, those who attend our concerts"[27] and, one might add, those who could afford the ticket prices or were being paid. The chances of obtaining a fiat of prosecution were nil, the probability of ridicule certain. When the Attorney General told Webber to stop writing letters to people, because the Alliance could be charged with disturbing the peace, the Alliance was badly beaten.[28] Not so strangely, the Edmonton Symphony Society experienced the same success thanks to having the lieutenant-governor and the premier as patrons. Webber and his Vancouver Alliance colleagues pointed out that what was spiritually uplifting music was a matter of taste. What principle would stop Sunday theatrical shows, movies, vaudeville, dances, or keep the dreaded American jazz from the radio?[29]

While the monied upper classes indulged in expensive Sunday aestheticism, many British Columbians preferred cheap athleticism. Endurance contests, walkathons, skateathons, and danceathons swept the continent; in British Columbia the Alliance tried to stop yet another invasion of the Christian Sabbath. Webber used his experience in the miniature-golf cases to strike a deal with the Attorney General whereby any municipality could construct a municipal bylaw to prohibit sporting activities from Saturday night to Monday morning and prohibit Sunday sports—without actually saying Sunday. The unemployed who wanted to run dance halls and the employed who wanted to dance on Sundays pleaded with the Attorney General, but the bylaws remained.[30] I suspect that several more municipalities did not pass bylaws.

Given this administrative chaos, was there no standard? As the president of the Vancouver Alliance Branch said, "It is unnecessary to point out to you that the 'thin edge of the wedge' which has now been inserted, sets up a dangerous condition. It is rumoured that the Chinese are already thinking of opening [their shops on Sundays]."[31] That horror could never be allowed. On application from the police commissioners, the Attorney General authorized thousands of prosecutions against the Chinese. Urban British Columbians, Protestant and Catholic alike, especially in the Vancouver and Victoria areas, agreed that, if anyone, non-Christian Chinese Canadians should be prosecuted.[32] Again, the Christian churches pulled together to fight a perceived common foe. Xenophobia remained the lowest common denominator of Christian civilization in British Columbia for decades. Stopping Canadian aboriginal sporting events on Sundays ran a distant second. Otherwise, anything that helped white people make money during the Depression was allowed.

Events in Alberta followed a slightly different pattern from British Columbia, but the results were the same. Webber turned at first to the federal government to close tourist stands in Banff National Park. Since national parks were under federal jurisdiction, the federal government could not deny its responsibility. Yet the department of the interior refused to stop the Sunday sale of "essentials": tobacco, candy, gum, magazines, post-cards, refreshments, soft drinks, ice cream, camera films, or books. Only "souvenirs" were kept out of sight on Sunday.[33]

Beyond this, the federal authorities would not go and insisted that the administration of the Sunday federal law outside of national parks was a provincial responsibility. Webber then turned to the provincial government, headed by the United Farmers of Alberta. Although the Edmonton Symphony Society gave concerts, and the *Edmonton Journal* printed Sunday extras, the Depression stopped work (aside from the occasional Sunday farming) on the Lord's Day in Alberta. Webber and J.F. Lymburn, the Attorney General, conferred to clear up the legal problems.[34] Sunday newspaper extras were stopped. The United Grain Growers promised that their grain elevators would not operate on Sundays.[35] The only problem then plaguing Alberta was that black baseball teams were barnstorming across the border. The Attorney General suspected that The Texas Colored Giants, The Detroit Colored Giants, and others were the same team. It travelled so quickly across provincial boundaries to avoid prosecutions and worked under so many aliases that it was very difficult, if not impossible, to prosecute them under the Lord's Day Act.[36] Nonetheless, Alberta had found at least one group that all Albertans could agree to prosecute—if they could catch them.

Hoping that the scourge of locusts and bad harvests on the Prairies would be lifted, sabbatarians advised the state to obey God's commandments. But most politicians listened to the voices of Canadians and not the voice of a supposedly Sunday-Sabbath God. Business voices asked governments to keep their hands off business, or rather, to adopt business principles. Popular voices clamoured for more freedom to work if necessary and to play, if at all possible, on Sunday. Money was the key everywhere to popular approval during the Depression, not prosecutions under the Sunday laws.

In the interwar period, the rise of non-mainstream sects, especially in the West, chipped away at the Protestant cultural uniformity promoted by those larger denominations that went into the United Church of Canada. On the western frontier, where Christian civilization faced economic depression and cultural fragmentation, religious experiments flourished. Doukhobours, Christian Scientists, and Jehovah Witnesses farmed, lectured, sold pamphlets, and justified their Sunday activities as commanded by God. For them, all secular activities were blessed by God and, therefore, were religious. No division between the sacred and the secular existed among these sects. They were not interested in christianizing the world—if they were Christian at all, which was not the case for Mormons, Jehovah's Witnesses, and Buddhists. The greatest sectarian opposition to Canada's Sunday law came from Seventh-Day Adventists. They had always opposed federal, provincial, and municipal laws dealing with the Sunday-Sabbath.

In the Depression years, the growing number of Seventh-Day Adventists in Alberta and British Columbia fought the Sunday law both quietly and noisily. Quietly, several Adventists went on with their farming or other business on Sunday. Noisily, the Western Canadian Union Conference of Seventh-Day Adventists, the Adventists' British Columbia and Alberta conferences, the Religious Liberty Society, and individual Adventists wrote to Prime Minister Mackenzie King, to his ministers, to provincial premiers, to provincial Attorneys General, to newspapers, and to the Lord's Day Alliance. All of their letters denounced the Sunday-Sabbath as unscriptural and, therefore, iniquitous. All denounced the laws as fomenting religious persecution of a minority. Some called the Christian Sunday a pagan and papal creation and the Lord's Day Alliance the Pope's Day Alliance! In return, the Attorneys General sometimes did not prosecute Adventists.[37] Police in Alberta and British Columbia were more than once instructed to ignore the Adventists' Sunday activities. The Alliance vainly protested that the Lord's Day Act did not prescribe any religious duties; no one was forced to go to church. People were forced only not to work on "Canada's national day of rest." Adventists retorted that the Sabbath commandment stated: "Six days shalt thou work." This meant that they were commanded to work six days and rest only on the seventh, Saturday, not on both Saturday and Sunday.[38] It might seem amusing that when the League of Nations proposed a revised calendar with an intercalary day, creating one eight-day week each year, Adventists rushed to contact the Alliance to join them in opposing "this dynamite" against

Protestantism.[39] The debates among the sects appear similar to ones among siblings: eternally repetitive and quarrelsome but postponed when facing a common foe.

The importance of religious diversity in Alberta continued to make itself felt. General secretary Huestis had written to the leaders of each of the political parties in the election campaigns of 1935:

> and received from the leaders of the Conservative and Liberal parties assurances of their desire to keep Sundays free from political propaganda. The reply from the leader of the C.C.F. party indicated he regarded his program so close to the Christian standards he could not see any reason why Sunday should not be so used by them. . . . All efforts to get the leader of the Alberta Social Credit party to see that he was engaging in political propaganda on Sundays seemed useless, because of his obsession that his was not at all a political party but a religious movement.[40]

The radicalization of Depression politics in Canada had brought third parties to claim divine right of government. Whatever success sabbatarians experienced in Alberta was soon swept away by the election of Aberhart's Social Credit government in 1935.

William Aberhart (1878-1943) had travelled far from his Presbyterian boyhood in Perth County, Ontario. By 1935, he had gone through conversions to adult baptism, fundamentalism, and then to dispensationalism, a conservative anti-Social Gospel form of Christianity, finally leading his congregation and all of Alberta into Social Credit. On his Sunday radio programmes, broadcast to more than 350,000 people on the prairies and in the United States, Aberhart moved from dispensational to political oratory and advocated Social Credit, to the dismay of the United Farmers of Alberta government and the Lord's Day Alliance. As far back as 1927, the Alliance had rapped Aberhart's Calgary Prophetic Bible Institute for selling books on Sunday. Aberhart had bowed under pressure but protested that he did not see anything wrong.[41] Alliance letters to the Calgary radio station received scorching replies that Sunday advertisements, Sunday radio, and Sunday programming were none of its business; the radio station believed that it could broadcast anything anytime. When Aberhart announced a CPR railway excursion to a Sunday political rally for Social Credit, Webber and Huestis consulted lawyers but found that they could only shake their heads and lament that the sabbatarian former Prime Minister Bennett was no longer the legal advisor of the CPR.[42] Sunday political broadcasts and Sunday excursions became normal in Alberta.

The totalitarian nature of Social Credit's authority—divine, economic, and political—proved unstoppable. Older denominations, holding to the division of church and state, protested the "secularization" of the Lord's Day and probably lost supporters to Aberhart's Prophetic Bible Institute. There was a secularization of God's message in Social Credit. But if God could tell Aberhart how to rearrange the finances of Alberta so that every man, woman, and child would receive fifty dollars in dividends from the economy, then the secularization of God's message in a political movement seemed a mighty good thing. For the Alliance, however, Aberhart was just another political mudslinger, "even though he does mix up his mud with Scripture passages."[43] By the end of 1936, Webber and the Alliance gave up on Alberta and hoped that Aberhart would be torpedoed eventually by "his restless and impatient supporters" expecting "'dividends' yet to come."[44] The Alliance would wait a very long time, for Alberta's Social Credit government remained in power until 1971. The Attorney General's Lord's Day Act criminal-case files, now in the Alberta Archives, became thinner and thinner with each passing month. Warnings were sometimes sent out, but prosecutions rarely authorized. Excursions to the Rockies for skiing and sporting events boomed in Alberta.

Together, Alberta's Social Crediters and British Columbia's Adventists and other religious sects were able to convince their provincial governments that the majority of Canadians were, like them, opposed to the Sunday-Sabbath. The other provinces took note and frustrated the Lord's Day Alliance. By the end of the Depression, religious diversity hampered any united action on the Sunday question. The governments were free to do what they pleased about Sunday.

The federal government had fobbed Sunday onto the provinces. Ontario decided that sabbatarians did not represent the majority. The governments of western Canada agreed. All of these provinces took their cue from the federal government, delegated power to the municipalities, and thus shirked their responsibility to prosecute Lord's Day Act violators. The Alliance ran itself ragged trying to find the appropriate level of government to pressure into enforcing the Lord's Day Act. In their political sleights of hand, the various levels of government had performed a neat bit of secularization by taking authority for the Canadian Sabbath and hiding it among themselves. For most of the Depression, the Lord's Day Act, like other social legislation, was lost somewhere in the limbo between levels of government. The people of Canada were left free to do what they wished, because governments of the day could not give answers or leadership during the economic crisis.

In 1937, Huestis resigned as general secretary of the Alliance, muttering about the war to come. Webber stepped up from the Alberta-British Columbia Alliance organization to replace him as general secretary. Now facing Ontario's Attorney General Conant and Premier Hepburn was another United Churchman who had survived the municipal bylaw battles of the West. Recognizing that Ontario's sabbatarianism had always been the keystone to the Alliance throughout Canada, he organized vocal opposition to Conant, lobbied Hepburn, and kept the Alliance argument for the federal law in the newspapers. In 1938, Conant received a massive petition, organized by the Alliance, protesting the delegation of provincial power to the municipalities. When Conant and Hepburn ignored it, Webber grimly prepared to work even through the myriad municipal courts with the Ontario 1845 law, with the 1906 law, or with any municipal law that would close businesses on Sunday. He had a dance hall's Sunday frolic brought before a municipal court in Sydney Township, Ontario. The dance hall's owner argued that the municipality had no constitutional right to close the hall, because the provincial government had no right to delegate its power to a municipality. The Ontario government watched in horror as the court obliged the owner by striking down the municipal bylaw.[45] After that, the entire municipal debate fizzled out across Canada. The

Sunday law was back in provincial hands in spite of provincial attempts to hand the federal Lord's Day Act to municipalities. Although Ontario's Attorney General privately informed his deputy that the old arrangement of systematic neglect would prevail and the law be allowed to wither on the books, the Alliance had won a victory of a sort.[46] It need concern itself only with provincial authorities, not with thousands of municipalities across Canada.

The Depression had stripped an already aging Alliance of money and of men. By chance, its western organization survived because of the exceptional competence of two consecutive secretaries: Huestis and Webber, both United Churchmen. It was in the West, therefore, that the major battles were fought. These were provoked in part by the Alliance and abetted by the United Church of Canada which was struggling with new, vigorous sects and political movements. The Ontario government, eagerly watched by the western provinces, had tried to transfer authority from sabbatarians to municipalities. Little by little, in order to avoid sabbatarian pressures, governments avoided authority over Sunday activities and allowed people to make or spend money in business, sporting events, dance halls, tourism, sales, or contests. In response, to promote Protestant sabbatarian uniformity, the Alliance again attempted to transfer moral authority over Sunday to the federal government and continually tried to stop governments from fragmenting that authority or passing it back to the individual. When municipal bylaws of the 1930s were struck down in Ontario as unconstitutional, the 1906 federal law remained. A tattered remnant of the uniform national Canadian Christian vision had just barely survived the Depression.

Let us fight against every man who comes to attack us on the sabbath day; let us not all die as our brethren died in their hiding places.—1 MACCABEES 2:41

Sunday was a day to bring us to God.
We never needed it more than at the present time
when the world seemed on the brink of chaos.
—MINUTES OF THE MEETING OF THE LORD'S DAY ALLIANCE OF CANADA, 28 JANUARY 1937

CHAPTER EIGHT

THE WAR AGAINST SUNDAY

1938–1945

IN 1938, THE LORD'S DAY ALLIANCE CALLED A FIFTIETH anniversary celebration to commemorate the 1888 founding in Ottawa and to unite Protestant churches in a revived Alliance. Messages from the opposition leader, R.B. Bennett, from the Honourable Norman Rogers, Minister of Labour, and from the Anglican archbishop of Ottawa were read out to the assembled Alliance secretaries, church representatives, and sympathizers in Ottawa. An ex-moderator of the Presbyterian Church, Robert Johnson, presided over an almost faithful re-enactment of the original meeting. The alliance of Protestant denominations rededicated itself to a fifty-year-old sabbatarian crusade.

George Webber succeeded quickly in reorganizing its finances. Revenues, which had fallen to $21,000 in the depths of the Depression from an all time high of $57,000 in the boom days of 1920–21, crept up to over $25,000 in 1938. During the war, when the Canadian economy experienced a revival, Alliance revenues mounted even further to $30,000 and Webber was able to pay off all debts and salary arrears.

When war broke out, the Alliance was theoretically ready to face wartime problems. Tom Sinclair-Faulkner reports that "the Lord's Day Alliance issued a manifesto entitled 'Sunday in War-time' which pledged that the Alliance would redouble its efforts to ensure that Sunday remain a day of rest, and the manifesto was published in virtually every mainline Protestant newspaper in Canada."[1] Webber wrote in a revived Alliance newspaper, *The Bulletin,* that

> the future salvation of our nation, and the world, from tyranny and oppression, from selfishness and greed, from strife and bloodshed, demands the release of the spiritual dynamic revealed in our Lord and Master Jesus Christ. This is the day of challenge, and of opportunity for the Christian home and the Christian Church. And Sunday is the day of special opportunity for all Christian organizations in the task of building a Christian civilization and thus promote the interests of the Kingdom of God.[2]

To the editor of the *Calgary Albertan* on March 21, 1942, Webber more pithily stated, "At a time when we are facing a world war for freedom to develop a Christian democracy we can ill afford to allow our Sunday at home to be sabotaged." The Alliance had rebounded from the Depression and now reclaimed complete moral authority over Sunday, even in wartime. There was no creeping secularism in the claims, message, or theology of the Lord's Day Alliance.

Unfortunately for the Alliance, religious diversity continued to hamper a united sabbatarian stand. For example, when the Alliance protested the royal visit to Kingston on Sunday, 21 May 1939 and the other Sunday Royal visits across Canada, ministers told the Alliance that it had picked the wrong event to criticize.[3] The United Church of Canada had inherited both Methodist and Presbyterian attitudes. Although the Church eventually supported the Alliance, the government's disregard of Sunday regulations during the war forced many United Church ministers to reread St. Paul's letter enjoining respect for authority and to rethink Jesus' attitude to the Sabbath. Just as their Depression-era pacifism melted, so many now thought that Sunday war activities were permissible.[4] Ministers in the chaplaincy service believed that, in war time, the Lord's Day Act should not be strictly enforced.[5] One clergyman believed that Sunday sports would be just the thing to keep the soldiers occupied. It would be "Better Than Going to Bootleggers" as the *Toronto Telegram* trumpeted on 22 August 1942.

Catholics had additional concerns. The Roman Catholic Church in Quebec busily tried to secure Christmas, Good Friday, Easter Monday, Thanksgiving, Epiphany, All Saints Day, Immaculate Conception, Ascension, as well as Sunday, as legal holidays. And because of Catholic preponderance in Quebec, it was often successful with the provincial government. What one government gave, however, another took away. The federal Minister of Justice, Louis St. Laurent, declared that government business was mandatory during the war, even on holidays.[6] While the Ligue du Dimanche wrestled with governments, Catholic pastors installed bowling alleys in their church basements.[7] While one Jesuit, Archambault, promoted the Ligue du Dimanche, another promoted Sunday movies in the basement of Montreal's French Jesuit church, the founding place of the Ligue![8] Cardinal Villeneuve of Quebec granted Catholic women permission to knit socks on Sundays for the troops. This permission was to be only for the duration of the war; the work was to be unpaid; it was not to be done for more than four hours at a time; and socks were certainly not to be knitted during Sunday's traditional times for religious services.[9] Villeneuve was promoting a paternalistic, pre-industrial society, but many younger men and women were working seven days a week in war industries and making more money than many had ever seen at home; Villeneuve's outlook was irrelevant to the lives of working French Canadians. The English Catholic Church had no central apparatus or senior cardinal to shape social policy. Often it merely adopted American Catholic or, in the case of Toronto Catholics, English Protestant attitudes. So, Toronto Catholics were sometimes enjoined to be more respectful of Sunday quiet than, say, Windsor or a British Columbian Catholics.[10] Just a few hours from Toronto, in Windsor, the Basilian Fathers ran a Christian

Culture Sunday lecture series, at which prominent American Catholics spoke. The Basilians assured the Alliance that tickets were not being sold.[11]

In all of these denominations, whether Catholic or Protestant, differing sabbatarian beliefs made for disunity. The Alliance strove unsuccessfully to speak for all in one united, powerful voice during the war, but the churches splintered the sabbatarian cause. In their confusion and disunity, they again undermined the Alliance's ability to lobby the state. Religious differences within the Alliance allowed national secularization. For example, at the very summit of sabbatarian leadership, within the Lord's Day Alliance organization itself, former general secretary Charles Huestis publicly disagreed with his successor, George G. Webber, over the necessity for provincial Sunday laws. Why?

In 1938, Huestis wrote to newspapers calling for repeal of the Ontario pre-Confederation law.[12] The 1845 law made it illegal to sell anything, including liquor; to fight; to use profane language in the streets; to hold, convene or attend any public political meeting; to play skittles, ball, or football; to gamble, swim, run races of any kind; to fish, hunt, or shoot on Sunday. The older law had been useful to Ontario sabbatarians, because the Attorney General's consent had not been necessary for prosecutions. Since the language and provisions of the 1845 law had become quaint over the years, it suffered a great deal of abuse and ridicule from opponents. Huestis wanted legal uniformity across Canada, because ridicule of the Ontario law became a bad example everywhere else. By contrast to Huestis' position, Webber was still willing to use the 1845 law on the principle that an enforceable law on the books was worth far more than a 1906 federal law that a provincial Attorney General could ignore.

Just before the war, therefore, sabbatarians were torn between two leaders. The transfer of authority from Huestis to Webber had not been complete; Huestis insisted on his idea of a uniform sabbatarian Canada and weakened Webber's authority in Ontario. Going into the war, Webber's Lord's Day Alliance appeared strong, but in reality it had almost been destroyed in the Depression and had not re-established itself under a new, universally accepted leader and policy. In the fumble between Huestis and Webber, the Alliance effectively lost its credibility among the churches. Financial stability and more field secretaries could not offset the loss of authority that it had suffered. Henceforth, Sunday forces would be splintered as the badly divided and usually ineffectual churches took over from the Alliance. In 1939, the Alliance tried to be representative, but churches were now doing their own lobbying, and for other causes.

Webber's attempts to strengthen the Alliance's field staff failed. Wartime chaplaincy services were hiring younger ministers, and the two youngest field secretaries joined the war effort. As in the Depression, only older men were left behind. The same retired men continued the routine of chairing meetings of increasingly older ministers. In a difficult excursion case, Webber turned to Rochester for legal advice, but even this tapping of active older members had to end. Rochester fell on a Toronto street corner with a stroke and was confined to his bed, lingering until 1949. His place at the *Presbyterian Record* was quickly filled; the format he used in the *Record* and in the defunct *Lord's Day Advocate* was scrapped. T. Albert Moore died of a heart attack in 1940 at the age of seventy-nine. Sabbatarians everywhere were retiring, dying, or dead. An entire religious generation was passing away; fewer young clergymen in the rising generation were replacing the fallen. A declining organization had no attraction for younger religious leaders. The war held their attention.

The Alliance's organization in Quebec starkly illustrates the impact of the war on Alliance personnel. In Quebec, as always, personnel problems were compounded by the scarcity of English Protestant clergy, the presence of the Ligue du Dimanche, and the fact that the Alliance's head office in Toronto continued to bypass the Quebec office. In 1938, Webber tried to reorganize Quebec's Alliance by inundating presbytery, synod, bishop, and church offices with requests for delegates to an Alliance meeting. On 27 June 1939, in the board room of the Montreal Auxiliary of the British and Foreign Bible Societies, the representatives met; Webber chaired the meeting of Anglican, Baptist, Salvation Army, Presbyterian, and United Church representatives. Not one Catholic was invited, Webber stated, because the Ligue du Dimanche represented Catholics. The Quebec Provincial Lord's Day Alliance would provide a voice on Sunday problems "for the non-Roman Churches of the Province" and would cooperate with the Ligue du Dimanche.[13] Immediately, the Toronto office set its stamp on the organization. All costs were borne by Toronto; in return, Toronto named the Reverend Baxter J. Warr, another Methodist United Churchman, as field secretary for Quebec. He had been working for the Alliance in the Maritimes and his only previous connection with Quebec had been a term of study at Montreal Wesleyan College. All correspondence with the Ligue du Dimanche and with the Duplessis government was handled by Webber from Toronto.

The first Quebec meeting of 1940 saw several representatives missing. Some had died. The secretary, Warr, and others had become chaplains in the armed forces. The remainder listened to Webber read about his activities in the rest of Canada. A grandiose plan to start a branch in Sherbrooke, a major centre of English-speaking people, was quietly dropped for lack of personnel. Charles Racine, the secretary, heroically tried to continue alone. He called a 1941 meeting and conservatively hoped for thirty people, but only six people arrived, including Webber and himself. Webber dissuaded Racine from resigning and begged for at least one meeting a year to keep the organization going until the war was over. But the organization disappeared, because Racine was too old and too ill to continue.

The same personnel shortage that plagued Quebec spread across Canada. Warr was also the Maritime's field secretary, and the Maritimes lost him at the same time that Quebec did. Watson supposedly worked in Manitoba; in reality old age kept him in Winnipeg. A.R. Skinner, a retired Presbyterian minister, worked in eastern Ontario. Huestis lived in Alberta and wrote the occasional letter to the editor of a western newspaper. The rest had joined the armed forces. Only the older, less active members of the Alliance remained to report to Toronto on the Sunday activities of the nation.

The Ligue du Dimanche, too, experienced a greying of its organization. The same men had been in control since the early 1930s. The founder, Father Joseph-Papin Archambault, SJ, remained on the executive every year as chaplain; Alphonse de la Rochelle and J. Alfred Bernier shuffled the positions of president, vice president, secretary, and treasurer among themselves. Younger men came and soon left for other volunteer activities. In 1945, the minutes complain of low attendance. Only Archambault was active; only he kept the organization together. He was sixty-five years old in 1945; most of his colleagues were older and less active.

Although the Ligue was more tightly organized, because it was restricted to Quebec and avoided the problems of interdenominational cooperation by restricting its membership to Roman Catholics, close ties to the Catholic hierarchy hampered its effectiveness.[14] The French Catholic hierarchy was definitely not sabbatarian. When it decided that parish, not provincial centralization was needed, provincial committees such as the Ligue fell out of favour. Archambault obediently turned to organizing and promoting the parish-based Catholic Action committees. Younger people, given the choice between the limited interest group of the Ligue and the larger Catholic Action committees, naturally turned to Catholic Action. Catholic Action recruited the youth of French Canada; the Ligue du Dimanche remained an older man's preserve.

Secularization of the sabbatarians themselves, whether English Protestant or French Catholic, was the result of slow erosion by Father Time, of the incomplete transfer of religious authority from one generation to another, and of religious diversity sapping any united stand against government power. The governments of Canada were now willing to exercise that power for the war.

Even before war was declared, federal officials began to assert their control over new technologies and, consequently, Sunday activities. For example, C.D. Howe, Minister of Transport, was anxious that an aviation show be held and promised several squadrons of Royal Canadian Air Force planes to a show held in Goderich, Ontario, on a 1939 Sunday.[15] With the development of radio in the interwar period, the Canadian government passed the Canadian Radio Broadcasting Act (1932). Regulation of broadcasting during the week, including Sunday, became the new corporation's responsibility. The Alliance wrote many futile letters protesting to the CBC about advertising, sports, or other profane broadcasts over the national radio system. On the declaration of war against Germany by Great Britain, on Sunday, 3 September 1939, news bulletins were aired all day. Canada declared war seven days later, on Sunday, 10 September. The CBC and independent broadcasters filled the Sunday airwaves with international and national news. While radios blared every Sunday, the Alliance was silent and confused about this government-sponsored desecration until April 1942, when it rallied to call for commercial-free radio. At the same time, the CBC gradually reduced religiously inspired music and church services from its Sunday programming, claiming that they were not popular enough. In fact, the CBC officials believed that religious disunity was a threat to national unity during the war.[16]

Sunday military activities quickly expanded on government orders. Immediately after Parliament declared war on Germany, the Mackenzie King government moved to re-enact the War Measures Act, notorious from its use during the Great War. It again gave the federal government power not only to bypass Parliament and the judiciary but also to organize the war by order-in-council. In May of 1940, under the War Measures Act, the federal cabinet asked industries to speed production and labour to forego holidays and Sundays during the war emergency. For self-preservation, the state sacrificed Sunday just as it had done during the First World War.

The War Measures Act meant that the Canada Starch Company, Hinde and Dauch Paper Company, Heinz, Canadian Canners, Campbell Soups, Quaker Oats, Kellogg's, Proctor and Gamble, and all other packaging, paper, cardboard, canning, and prepackaged food companies went into expanded production. The Steel Company of Canada forced suppliers to work seven days every week. Railways hired more men and worked them overtime; in one case, a railway news company worked one man over eighty-nine hours each week. The company insisted he had enough time off during the week; it was not going to hire another man just for Sundays. As men enlisted, businesses suffered labour shortages and required Sunday work either to help the war effort or to offset what the war effort was doing to the labour pool.[17] Companies charged with a Sunday law infraction successfully argued wartime necessity. As the war dragged on, the Alliance requested, as in the First World War, that the principle of one rest day in seven be conceded for reasons of health and efficiency. The Minister of Labour responded by sending along a copy of Order-in-Council 2685 (19 June 1940) which declared that, for the war effort, "where increased output is desired it should be secured as far as practicable by the adoption of additional shifts throughout the week, experience during the last war having shown that an undue lengthening of working hours results in excessive fatigue and in a diminution of output."[18] There was no mention of Sunday.

The military took over Canada's Sunday life. Volunteer and mandatory reserve Sunday drill began in earnest on college and university campuses. After complaints, Sunday training in general was slowed in early 1941, but J.L. Ralston, minister of national defence, finally informed the Alliance's general secretary that Sunday training was inevitable given the world situation.[19] The military would train and fight on Sundays, as it had done during the First World War. Other priorities concerned the nation more than Sunday rest did.

The entertainment industry again took advantage of a plea of necessity to introduce entertainment for charity and soldiers. There had been the occasional Sunday film for charity prior to the war. For example, when Japan invaded China, a film toured Canada on Sunday to raise money for the Chinese Red Cross. During the war, an early scheme by the Motion Picture Film Distributors and backed by the Famous Players Motion Picture Corporation to sell government war stamps at patriotic Sunday shows was vigorously promoted as necessary to win the war. The Alliance wrote letters to the Attorneys General of each province explaining how the scheme was a way to evade the law. A timely explanation quashed the proposal.[20] Eighteen months later, as fears grew about the moral behaviour of uniformed troops during leisure hours, Famous Players privately approached the Imperial Order Daughters of the Empire (IODE) proposing that it sponsor Sunday films to keep young soldiers busy.[21] The Alliance informed it "that the Moving Picture people were using them as a blind to get the pictures going on Sunday."

When several ministerial associations, the Women's Christian Temperance Union, and theatre employees also protested, the IODE saw the point of the Alliance argument and scaled down its proposal.[22] Webber's victory led the Ontario government to ask him to serve as a Sunday film censor. All requests for patriotic Sunday shows in Ontario were handed to Webber. If he was satisfied that a show promoted the war effort or religion, and not the film industry, he and the province approved a Sunday showing.[23] By such steps, the state was able to co-opt even sabbatarians into its war crusade. Webber might not have realized that he was being used to condone Sunday films.

Although it was clear that film interests hid behind the patriotic skirts of the IODE, the result could be spectacularly different when these interests stopped bothering with small charitable organizations and approached the government directly. Famous Players convinced the department of munitions and supply that movies would be good for munition-worker morale. The munition workers were on shifts and had only Sundays off, so movies would be shown on Sunday, the film promoters proposed. Since there would be a choir and benediction by church representatives (Catholic, Jewish, and "Protestant"), the government asked, would the Lord's Day Alliance give its blessing to the shows? Webber declined.[24] Because it was a government-sponsored show, and because the federal government was above its own Sunday law, the show went on as planned, without the Alliance's blessing. This small success brought Famous Players to approach the Minister of National Defence. Famous Players' arguments convinced Ralston that the armed forces required "facilities" not provided by volunteer organizations. He accepted Famous Players' offer, and films opened in five cities in April 1943.[25] A Gallup poll, which claimed that a majority of Canadians would vote against Sunday movies, temporarily dampened official enthusiasm. But Ralston, on the more enthusiastic advice of his officers, authorized films in twenty more cities. Later still, Famous Players received the right to open two movie houses each Sunday in every city.[26] Movies remained free to uniformed Canadians. Civilians had to pay full weekday fares; many obviously did if two theatres were filled up every Sunday. The Alliance had fallen silent, because sabbatarians were disorganized. Some of them, mainly in the United Church, were half-convinced that all these government-sponsored activities might be necessary to safeguard the Christian nation from Hitler's pagan Germany.

Government secularization of the Sunday laws allowed individual Canadians to make choices about Sunday activities. Theatres, dance halls, Sunday radio, cabarets, and nickelodeons became popular. Governments turned a blind eye to any and all civilian entertainments in the interest of home-front morale. The police intervened in Sunday dancing only when uniformed soldiers took out their excess frustrations and energy on civilian bystanders. For example, a few sailors started a riot against some dancing zoot-suiters—ostensibly for being carefree dancing civilians during wartime—and wrecked Biggart's Milk Shake Stand at Sunnyside Amusement Park in Toronto. The sailor "heroes," obviously provoked by the music and the sight of expensive zoot suits in a time of war rationing, were ignored. The Wurlitzer, however, was impounded for being used on a Sunday.[27]

Another healthy activity that involved both young men and women was bowling. With more government-printed money, civilians and soldiers patronized bowling alleys during the war. Clubs sprang up everywhere to take advantage of gregarious spenders. Entertainments in a church were not against the Lord's Day Act, so bowling lanes again proliferated in church basements across Montreal, Ottawa, and Quebec City. From a legal point of view, unfortunately, businesses that rented space for bowling enthusiasts were guilty of breaking the Lord's Day Act. One famous case, *Rex v. Bol-O-Drome Ltd* (1944), dragged through the federal and Ontario superior courts for years until, finally, it was decided that the Bol-O-Drome Sunday bowling club was indeed just a dummy club set up by businessmen to get around the Sunday laws. Bowling fans were thereafter restricted to bowling in church basements, with which Ottawa was plentifully supplied, or in genuinely non-profit clubs, such as the Ottawa Civil Service Recreational Association. Until the case was settled, however, people, often civil servants, bowled on Sundays in churches or in thinly disguised money-making clubs.

Sunday vaudeville for charitable fundraising became the rage in every city: Vancouver, Victoria, Edmonton, Winnipeg, Montreal, and especially Windsor, where American vaudeville tours found a hearty welcome. American tourist dollars were even more welcome. Money, above all, was most welcome. In Windsor, sports and concerts became ways to raise money. The *Windsor Daily Star* of 13 October 1944, ran an advertisement that asked "Have You A Son Overseas?" How could the folks help? It promptly answered, "This Is The Way. A 2 1/2-Hour Vaudeville Show." Greyhound racing receipts went to war service clubs. Concert receipts went to Air Raid Victims. An Anglican congregation joined with the Windsor Symphony Orchestra to put on a Sunday evening concert for the Windsor Squadron Air Cadets. Another concert was for the Sea Cadets. War-business boosterism prevailed across the country. In British Columbia, the Red Cross wanted dances until dawn on Sunday. The Citizen's War Services Committee of Greater Victoria wanted skating rinks for the soldiers. Parks were opened in Vancouver to the public on Sunday "as a war-time policy."[28] In Sudbury, Ontario, as in Windsor, the Overseas Cigaret Fund was supported by the Royal Canadian Legion, the Lions, the Rotarians, the Knights of Columbus, the IODE, the Ukrainian Vets, the Finnish Democrats, the Catholic Women's League, and many other non-Protestant organizations. In response to growing war-boosterism, Quebec and Maritime cinemas and sporting events started up again. Even the YMCA put on Sunday entertainments wherever it had a branch. It was a sign that the Protestant youth of the nation was more caught up in the war than in Sunday righteousness.

Sometimes, the proceeds from all this charity never reached their destination. After the musicians, rent, projectionists, ushers, and managers were paid, there was little left over. These wartime benefits appeared a lot like weekly work to the Lord's Day Alliance. Only slim net proceeds ever went to charities; the larger, often very large gross proceeds went for salaries. One writer to the editor of the *Windsor Daily Star* summed up the entire film charity business as a "racket." He wrote: "I have recently quit my position with such racketeers . . . the midnight Sunday show business is just one of their ways to buck the Sunday laws."[29] This letter was later buried in a small avalanche of claims that workers needed Sunday entertainment. Wartime morale excused everything.

In Ontario, government sabotage of the Sunday laws had been slowly extended. In 1938, just before the war, the Liberal government under Hepburn, supported by Toronto councillors and the *Globe and Mail,* began an anti-blue-law crusade spearheaded by the Attorney General, Gordon Conant. Across the province and across Canada, newspapers breathlessly reported on Toronto the Good's revolutionary Sunday proposals. Sensing that the time was right during the war, when so much was already running on Sunday, Conant announced that Sunday ski trains could take American tourists back to their homes in the south after they spent the weekends in Ontario. He claimed that the war debt in Canada demanded American tourist dollars.[30] Church representatives threatened Conant with court action for bypassing the legislature and for not prosecuting railways when his duty clearly required it. The primate of the Church of England in Canada, the president of the Ontario Baptist Convention, the moderator of the Presbyterian Church in Canada, the commissioner of the Salvation Army, the moderator of the United Church of Canada, and the Roman Catholic archbishop of Toronto sent a resolution to the Legislative Assembly of Ontario.

> While our soldiers, our sailors, and our airmen offer their lives to stem this tide of tyrannous barbarism abroad, we realize the need also to safeguard the freedom of our Christian institutions in Canada. Legislation which seeks to commercialize the Lord's Day attacks our Christian civilization from within while its foes are attacking it from without. At a time when we are being urged to forego luxuries, and save our money to invest with the Government for the successful prosecution of this war, we fail to understand why encouragement should be given to the spending of additional money in expensive sporting activities.[31]

True patriotism, these church leaders claimed, did not mean Sunday ski trains. When the legislature met, it found that it could not rally enough followers to pass a proposed bill to legalize Conant's authorization. It is hard to say how many members were swayed by clerical pressure and how many refused to support Sunday sports from conscience's sake. It is significant that, although the Alliance participated in this letter campaign, its small victory belonged to the churches.

Conant next stated that provincial police were too busy to enforce any of the Sunday laws, which were, he wrongly claimed, a municipal responsibility. This created another furore among church leaders. When Hepburn resigned in October 1942, Conant became premier, causing even more consternation among religious leaders. His handling of the Ontario economy caused the *Globe and Mail* to run an article on 3 December 1942, entitled "Fun Era Dawns For Americans, Theatres Boom. Sunday Becomes Day of Merriment. Money Keeps Rolling Along." The churches charged Conant with fostering "moral laxity, marital infidelity, illegitimacy, juvenile delinquency, gambling, drunkenness and disregard for law and order."[32] Almost every newspaper in Ontario repeated these charges. Certainty of losing the approaching election convinced Conant to accept a position on the Ontario Supreme Court; until then, however, the holy day was a holiday. When the Liberals were finally defeated, partly by their handling of moral-reform issues, the Alliance breathed a deep sigh of relief.

The relief was immediately choked off by Dana Porter, the new Attorney General of Ontario. Porter became alarmed by so-called fanatics, who insisted on prosecuting some farmers under the 1845 law for working on Sundays in fields north of Toronto. These fanatics happened to be police officers of York Township, who were fulfilling their duties and enforcing the laws of Ontario. The *Globe and Mail* cried out that the wartime labour shortage required that farmers "work on Sunday to get their carrots and celery crops in before the ground froze," but "three York Township farmers and their 30 helpers will appear in court."[33] Newspapers across Canada took up the cry. Ontario's government reacted and asked the federal government to suspend the Ontario Lord's Day Act. The swift result was Order-in-

Council 8535, which declared that, during the war, all prosecutions by anyone in Canada under any Sunday law, regulation, or ordinance, would require the signed approval of a provincial Attorney General within sixty days after the infraction. The Attorney General of Ontario immediately sent out a memorandum informing all police that, henceforth, all prosecutions of Sunday offenses also required a written opinion on the case from the county Crown Attorney. For the duration of the war, the provincial law was safely buried under paperwork.

Ironically, farmers had always been exempt under the 1845 law, and the Alliance had nothing to do with the prosecution. Webber stated that the order-in-council threw more responsibility upon the Attorneys General, who were too busy to administer it. Webber suspected that someone set up the Alliance for the fall. He could not make up his mind whether it was someone in the provincial government, or the former general secretary of the Alliance, Huestis, who wanted provincial laws out of the way.[34] Webber tried to calm the fears of Alliance supporters in British Columbia and in Alberta, but the order-in-council applied to all of Canada. For once, Ontario's example made prairie farmers happy.[35] There were no more prosecutions of farmers for any Sunday activities across Canada, because, again, Ontario's example prevailed—although this time it was not in the direction of stricter Sunday observance.

The transfer of religious authority from Huestis to Webber had not been smooth. But the problem of transferring the mantle of Sunday leadership from Huestis to Webber became meaningless, since the Canadian governments of the day, federal and Ontario, decided that both the 1845 Ontario law and the 1906 federal law were under federal control; Ottawa could abrogate them at its own or the voters' pleasure. Huestis got his way when the federal government abrogated the 1845 law. But sabbatarians everywhere were defeated, because uniformity meant that there would be no Sunday prosecutions during the war.

More importantly, the transfer of sabbatarian moral authority from one generation to another was frustrated when service to the Canadian state became more important than service to the Canadian Sabbath. The Lord's Day Alliance and the Ligue du Dimanche both lost supporters to government recruitment, to government jobs, and to other religious organizations such as Catholic Action. As Canadian governments increased their authority during the Second World War, traditional religious authority declined.

This development left Canadians free from both sabbatarian and legal restrictions on Sunday activities. In fact, governments encouraged Sunday work along with Sunday morale-building entertainments and fundraising concerts, movies, and sports. Ontario governments played a leading role in muzzling sabbatarians. Since Ontario was also the sabbatarian fortress, every reverse in sabbatarian efforts there had an immediate effect on all of Canada. With the decline of traditional religious authority and the rise of government power, in the Second World War as in the First, some people tried to find "salvation in entertainment" and not in the Christian Sabbath.[36] More and more, authority to make decisions about daily life eventually found its way back into the hands of individuals. The consequence, during the Second World War, was that the Sabbath, the holy day, became simply Sunday, a holiday, if one so desired. At the end of the war in Europe, the government and the churches sponsored a Sunday set aside for prayer and thanksgiving. While the churches were at prayer, RCAF planes roared noisily overhead on their way to the Pacific theatre of war, disturbing Sunday's quiet. At the same time, the fly-past entertained those people who had decided not to go to church.

The Second World War, even more than the First, brought governments to assume an active and dominant role in Sunday secularization. Unlike the Depression years, these years gave the federal government the moral courage (or the excuse) to claim Sunday. Of course, the rise of organized state power further meant that Sunday choices, especially in leisure and entertainment, were further liberated from sabbatarian control. Anti-sabbatarianism, in regions such as British Columbia and the Windsor area, was allowed greater licence and contributed as powerful a secularizing influence on Sunday as it had during the Depression. During the war, both federal and provincial Sunday secularization were seen, especially in Ontario, whose example yet again determined Sunday observance, and the lack of it.

And you shall count seven weeks of years, seven times seven years, so that the time of the seven weeks of years shall be to you forty-nine years. . . . And you shall hallow the fiftieth year, and proclaim liberty throughout the land to all its inhabitants.
—LEVITICUS 25:8,10

Just because some old Scottish gentleman of past decades held that we couldn't smell on Sunday is that any reason why it should be made to apply today?—DAVID BALFOUR, TORONTO COMPTROLLER, *The Toronto Evening Telegram*, 24 SEPTEMBER 1947

CHAPTER NINE

TORONTO SUNDAY SPORTS

1946-1950

AT THE CLOSE OF THE SECOND WORLD WAR, THE Lord's Day Alliance naively expected that the War Measures Act would automatically lapse and that manufacturing would return to a prewar, Depression-induced sabbatarianism.[1] They were disillusioned. First, the government decided to extend the War Measures Act beyond the actual end of hostilities in order to face the problems of the Cold War world. Factories throughout Canada, abetted by government fear of a postwar recession, continued to crank out widgets and, in some cases, stepped up production as returned soldiers swelled both the labour and the consumer markets. After a small recession, the Canadian economy experienced a boom as wartime industries converted to peacetime production—usually with wartime Sunday work habits. Fear of Depression poverty overcame any residual Sunday-Sabbath scruples.

Retail businesses followed the lead of the manufacturers. Every small shop, drugstore, hardware, grocery, and five-and-dime store opened to take advantage of money in the pockets of passing people.

The greatest Sunday competition faced by retailers took place among gas stations. During the Second World War, as during the First, gas rationing had been imposed. Service stations closed Sundays and most evenings. When gas rationing ended, so did service-station regulations. Small businessmen found themselves in the middle of an expansion of competition with no end in sight except twenty-four-hour service seven days a week. Station attendants protested, but gas and oil companies promoted the expanded hours as being good for profits and for the consumers who would swell the profits. Station attendants tried to limit competition by agreeing to open on alternate Sundays or by agreeing to some form of Sunday rotation, but each rotation was upset by a new competitor who refused to be bound by a previous agreement. Soon, small businessmen turned to municipal bylaws to regulate competition. Support for the attendants' attempts to legislate control of their Sunday environment in the good old-fashioned, Social Gospel way were applauded by denominations across the country.[2]

The pull of profits and the unconstitutionality of any municipal prohibition of Sunday sales (still under federal jurisdiction) brought back longer hours for most gas attendants in Canada. The Industrial Standards Act was able to set hours in areas where most retailers were able to agree on hours. Many did not. It might have been less galling to service-station attendants if newspapers such as the *Globe and Mail* and the *Financial Post* had not righteously trumpeted the hard virtues of long hours of work, less government regulation, and survival of the fittest, and had not raised the spectre of veterans caught between hunger and an Industrial Standards Act forbidding them to work nights and Sundays.[3] The Retail Gasoline and Automotive Service Association expressed their feelings by having the Alliance general secretary, George G. Webber, give grace at the Association's 1946 luncheon. Unfortunately for this middle class luncheon, the large oil companies and their smaller, more desperate competitors were hungrier for money than for the convention's lunch. The same situation developed among all of the smaller retail businesses, such as drug stores, grocery stores in competition with wayside farmers markets, and trucks and buses in competition with the trains.

Postwar immigration worsened fears about unemployment and increased the drive to compete among small businesses as individuals and families of immigrants prepared to make their way in the Canadian economy. Farmers in Ontario, on the Prairies, and in British Columbia hired immigrant labourers. Other immigrants, and some that had started out on farms, set up grocery stores in small towns. Many immigrants went to cities, where industrial jobs were plentiful. The largest cities got the most immigrants. At the same time, across Canada, the number of Canadians of non-British ancestry had reached 50% in 1941 and rose in postwar Canada. Most new immigrants were from European countries without developed sabbatarian traditions. The common denominator among almost all immigrants was that they were desperately willing to work—even on Sunday.

On the other end of the economic scale, more prosperous classes had enough of work and wanted to be entertained after the war. New Canadians were able to provide Sunday labour. Although there were entertainments during the war, a feeling now spread that wartime tensions could be eased—though not completely, since the Cold War against communism replaced the war against Hitler. Canadians had, nevertheless, earned a rest. In spite of Sunday laws, dancing, roller skating, ice skating, curling, bowling, ball games, hockey practices, motorcycle races, boat races, and every other type of competitive game flourished in the postwar period. There were kennel shows, movies, excursions, carnivals, merry-go-rounds, games of skill and chance, symphonies, and vaudeville shows. Most of the games and the competitions were justified to the public as fundraising events for charity. A kennel show raised money to buy a seeing-eye dog. A symphony supposedly raised money for flood victims in Edmonton or in British Columbia and in general promoted "good" music as opposed to that of vaudeville. The latter raised money for the benefit of a non-profit club. An excursion benefitted veterans. Time and again, the Alliance inquired into some Sunday activity only to be rebuffed by good intentions and thin excuses. The clause in the Lord's Day Act that allowed "mercy and necessity" was stretched ever wider; businesses claimed necessity, and entertainments begged for mercy.

Much of this frenzied entertainment, not unexpectedly, took place along the Great Lakes and near the United States. Small towns such as Port Stanley and Crystal Beach and larger towns such as Windsor continued to woo American and Canadian tourists. Entertainments in shows and in beach-side amusement parks, small retail businesses such as hotdog or ice-cream stands, bowling alleys, and small stores opened on Sundays to cater to tourists. Port Dover's newspaper, *The Maple Leaf*, correctly sensed the mood in the region. It constantly poured ridicule on the Alliance and on its ministerial members in town.[4]

Sports were momentarily stopped by the Ontario Supreme Court case *Rex v. Icelandia Limited.* An indoor ice-skating rink was successfully prosecuted in 1947, at the Alliance's instigation, under provincial law. This Ontario Supreme Court case, reported in newspapers and law reviews across the country, declared that necessity was not a relative word; the concept of economic necessity did not allow a business to bypass the Sunday law. Necessity meant necessity relating to human life and death. The main Sunday users of the rink, incidentally, were members of a Catholic Youth Organization hockey team. The case roused newspapers and all entertainment and sports buffs to plead the innocence of Sunday skating.

In newspapers such as *The Maple Leaf*, a major argument for ridding Canada of Sunday restrictions was based on the fact that veterans were asked to fight on Sundays in Europe, which supposedly gave all veterans and their families the right to do what they pleased on Sundays. A second argument made much of the lack of enforcement in Quebec and the evident inconsistency in Sunday-law enforcement across Canada. A third stated that the law was basically unpopular and should be repealed by the law-abiding majority who wanted Sunday sports. So strong was the call to uniformity, majority rule, and veteran privileges that the underlying contradictions of the mutually exclusive arguments were hardly challenged except by the Alliance. If veterans were given privileges, then the law would be even more discriminatory and harder to enforce. The fact that Quebec (barring the Ligue du Dimanche) ignored the Sunday law did not necessarily mean that it was a bad law. If majority rule was the rule, then the rest of Canada should try to bring Quebec, veterans, and small newspapers such as *The Maple Leaf* into line with majority wishes expressed in 1906. Most importantly, each side in this argument realized that Canadian law rested on majority consent and consequently tried to claim that its side represented the majority. In a democracy, right ultimately does reside in popular might, no matter how illogical or transient popular desires are. The Alliance had risen to power by convincing the federal government in 1906 that sabbatarians represented the majority will of Canada; the Alliance's opponents would now use the same argument.

Allan Lamport (Lampy to his friends, Lumpy to his enemies), was born in 1903, long after sabbatarians began to build their successful organization. He represented the new, postwar generation. The contrast between the relatively youthful Lamport and the elderly sabbatarians can be seen in the differences between Lamport and his own father, W.A. Lamport. The latter was eighty-one years old in 1949. He had been a successful lawyer, an active Baptist layman, and had briefly served on the powerful Toronto Alliance executive before the First World War. As an infant in Toronto the Good, Allan Lamport attended Walmer Street Baptist Church and was sent to Upper Canada College, where he developed a fondness for sports. After graduation, though still claiming attendance at his father's family church, he regularly attended his wife's Anglican church.[5] During the war, he served concurrently in the provincial legislature and in the RCAF where, I suspect, he frequented the officers' club and bar. After the war, he was solidly upper-class, Anglican, and a sports fan with a taste for dry martinis. Upper Canada College education and Anglican connections reinforced his ready identification with the landowners of Toronto. His service record, drinking, and sports made him seem more of an average man, though, than his background promised. Voters in a broad middle class, aspiring to live comfortably off investments, were able to identify their hopes with him.

Significantly, he was more successful as a municipal politician than as a provincial one. Municipal elections were decided by property owners; those who did not own land, boarding-house inmates who supposedly wanted Sunday sports, were never given the chance to express their opinion of Lamport in his runs at the mayoralty.

Between 1941 and 1951, Ontario experienced a net migration increase of over 300,000 people, and most of them arrived after the end of the Second World War. Every other province, except British Columbia, experienced net migration decreases. Ontario and British Columbia then experienced major sabbatarian battles. Although Toronto's population increased very little (just over 1%) from 1941 to 1951, the number of immigrants pouring into Toronto was the highest in Canada, which meant that many older residents, many of them English and Protestant, were moving out. The face of Toronto changed drastically from 1946 to 1950. The predominantly English Protestant society in Toronto began to disintegrate. Although early attempts to place Sunday professional sports on the municipal ballot in 1947 and in 1948 were defeated, the dreaded "American" cocktail lounges were introduced in 1947.

The same coalition of forces that had advocated Sunday ski trains during the war came out strongly for sports in the postwar period. The *Globe and Mail,* the *Windsor Star,* some municipal councillors, and sporting organizations, such as the Maple Leaf Baseball and Hockey Clubs (owned in part by the publisher of the *Globe and Mail)* constantly asked for Sunday sports. Alderman Allan Lamport supported organized Sunday baseball for the enjoyment of roomers and renters. There was nothing intrinsically evil about paid sports. And, he added, they had been allowed during the war.[6] Frank Tumpane, Jim Coleman, and the other city and sports writers at the *Globe and Mail* played up Lamport's arguments in column after column. The proposal for a city plebiscite was beaten back in 1947 and in 1948, partly by Leslie Saunders, the "Orange" mayor of Toronto, and partly by the fact that Ontario's 1845 law allowed anyone to prosecute a person playing ball, let alone the person charging admission or receiving a salary for the game. Sunday laws were not yet in municipal hands.

In 1948, after years of prodding by the former Alliance general secretary, Charles Huestis, and after growing calls from individuals and groups, the Ontario government decided to ask the federal government to repeal its pre-Confederation Sunday laws permanently. Ostensibly, the Ontario government wanted to do away with conflicting laws. Federal law allowed the Attorney General to decide among cases at his discretion; provincial law left prosecutions up to individuals. During the Second World War, as noted previously, a police officer had tried to prosecute farmers under the provincial law in spite of the provincial government's policy of not prosecuting farmers under the federal law. So, the provincial government decided that one of the two laws had to be repealed. Since it could easily ask the federal government to repeal provincial laws, that was the route Ontario followed. The federal government quickly obliged and, henceforth, there was to be only one law for all of Canada. Because prosecutions under the federal Lord's Day Act were placed firmly in the hands of Attorneys General, prosecutions were taken out of the hands of the individual, sometime sabbatarian citizens of Ontario.[7]

The Alliance's general secretary, George Webber, publicly rejoiced that never again would Alliance opponents be able to ridicule Ontario's strict law or point to Ontario's refusal to enforce the federal law because of a provincial law on the books.[8] Privately, however, he lamented the repeal of Ontario's stricter law. He knew that a stricter, more personal standard of sabbatarianism had been abandoned.[9] Sunday gambling in a poker game among neighbours or friends, for example, illegal under Ontario law, was legal under the 1906 Act. The simple ball game that a boy would play on the streets of Ontario had been illegal on Sundays prior to 1948. After 1948, no more young children would be told by Toronto policemen to stop playing whatever game they were playing. In 1949, under pressure from small tourist towns, the Attorney General further exempted the following: all grocery stores and butcher shops at summer resorts; souvenir stands; ice-cream booths; hotdog and refreshment stands, cigarette, cigar and tobacco sales; rental of boats, canoes, horses, bicycles; rides in aeroplanes and all Sunday excursions.[10]

Encouraged by the Ontario government's attitude, opposition to Sunday restrictions grew tremendously. The Alliance had used rhymes, tunes, and poems during the first rush of organization and published them in the *Lord's Day Advocate.* Opponents had also used the same means to capture public attention. But between 1946 and 1950, ridicule of Sunday laws and customs flooded the airwaves and newspapers. Lister Sinclair caught the rebellious, satirical mood in a play called *Nobody Likes Toronto* which was first performed on CBC radio in 1946 and replayed in 1947. The narrator in the story grandly announced that the young hero, Charlie,

> came at last to Toronto, the great teeming city of eastern Canada; the swarming, seething tumultuous sky-scraper-ridden heart of Ontario! Toronto: the wealthiest city in the Dominion, its sidewalks paved with gold and obscured by an endless throng of eager, excited, happy, bustling people!
> Only he happened to arrive on a Sunday.
>
> *(There is a vast silence)*
>
> *Charlie: (His voice echoing in the emptiness)* Hello-o-o-o! Hello-o-o-o-o-o-o-o!! Is there anybody about?
>
> *Narrator: (Bitterly)* In Toronto on a Sunday? What a question![11]

Webber objected to the play on behalf of sabbatarians everywhere, but the play had already been broadcast. The CBC general supervisor insisted that it was only "good-natured fun."[12] Sinclair later published the skit in a popular book of radio plays in 1948 and went on to a long career in CBC broadcasting.

Bandleader Ozzie Williams and writer Lige McKelvy wrote a satirical song in 1948, which they entitled "Sunday in Toronto." This song, among the many ditties, poems, jokes, and newspaper filler that characterized the Sunday debate, ingeniously combined many familiar themes: alcohol, Quebec, the United States, entertainment, and dancing. Williams and his fans sang:

We can't have no fun on SUNDAY IN TORONTO,
And we're off when once we see dawn's early light.
We just jump into our car or we catch the C.P.R.
And we won't be home till late on Sunday night!

(Chorus) Oh, Toronto, oh, Toronto is O.K.
in ev'ry way—
Ev'ry way and ev'ry day—
Except Sunday.

They don't have no movies SUNDAY IN TORONTO,
Ev'ry place you wanna go is closed up tight.
So when Sunday rolls around, That's when I'll be leavin' town,
And I won't be home till late on Sunday night!

Oh nobody's happy SUNDAY IN TORONTO,
They have set that day aside for doin' right.
So we wink and off we go, spend the day in Buffalo,
And we won't be home till late on Sunday night!

They don't have no sidewalks SUNDAY IN TORONTO,
They just roll 'em up and put them out of sight.
But before they roll 'em in, I'll be leavin' town again,
And I won't be home till late on Sunday night!

They don't have no bar-rooms SUNDAY IN TORONTO,
All the beer and gin and rye is out of sight.
I don't want no ice cream sodas, I want alcoholic odours,
And I won't be home till late on Sunday night!

They don't have no fun on SUNDAY IN TORONTO,
There's no dancing when the moon is shining bright.
So when Sunday comes, by heck, You will find me in Quebec,
And I won't be home till late on Sunday night!

> They don't have no sunlight SUNDAY IN TORONTO,
> They don't have no moon ashining big and bright.
> All the homes are dark and bare, 'cause there ain't nobody there,
> And they won't be home till late on Sunday night!
>
> So don't ever get caught SUNDAY IN TORONTO,
> There will never be a living soul in sight.
> For it's very very true, they have made our Sunday blue,
> And we won't be home till late on Sunday night!

Of course, the *Globe and Mail* reported that Lamport approved of the song.[13] Anti-sabbatarians everywhere took heart; they had laughter on their side.

Believing that the people, too, were on their side, anti-sabbatarians now shifted their attack from Ontario's laws to the federal law. A verbal battle raged over who were in the real majority—sabbatarians or sports fans—and whether the City of Toronto could actually hold a plebiscite to decide. The *Kingston Whig-Standard* on 4 July 1947, declared that "Sports and Movies on Sunday Favored by Majority Polled." Only six people were polled. Arguing that the question was one of majority rule

A 1950 Toronto billboard

and that if the Alliance had the majority, then they had nothing to fear, Lamport succeeded in bringing sports to a municipal vote to be held at the 1950 municipal elections.

Lamport asked: "Are you in favour of the City Council of Toronto requesting the Provincial Government to enact such legislation as may be necessary to permit the playing of organized baseball and other sports on Sunday, and the holding of concerts, cultural and educational performances and meetings at which an admission charge may be made, provided the same does not interfere with regular church services."[14]

The Ontario Attorney General's office asked one of its lawyers to find out what the issues were. He reported that the proposed question was so vague as to be meaningless, and he could never find an explicit policy statement by Lamport. He decided that Lamport was in favour of a totally open Sunday, but Lamport would never say so in order not to frighten those voters who were willing to support baseball in the afternoon but nothing else.[15] Popular support had to be cultivated very carefully. In chorus, small towns in northern Ontario and towns along the American border sent in resolutions of support for the proposed Toronto municipal question.

Windsor quickly followed Toronto's liberal example. After the city proposed its own plebiscite, the *Windsor Daily Star* editorially thumbed its nose at the Alliance in the sports columns and announced an illegal Sunday baseball game between the African Zulu Colored Giants (the same of Depression Prairie fame) and the Windsor United Auto Workers.[16] The Alliance protested the vague wording of the plebiscites and demanded a shorter question: "Are you in favour of seeking legislation to make professional and other forms of commercial sport and entertainment legal on Sundays?" Such a clear question, the Alliance believed, could be defeated.[17] Toronto accepted the challenge of the revised question; Windsor decided to ask its citizens a still vaguer question, which emphasized local option (as in the temperance plebiscites of recent memory).

Webber organized the Toronto sabbatarians. A Baptist minister, Alvin S. McGrath, rejoined the Alliance, became field secretary for western Ontario, and organized Windsor. Both secretaries decided to avoid the standard ridicule thrown at the Alliance and played down the Alliance's participation. They set up citizens' committees, independent of the Alliance, in both cities. These committees were heavily made up of clergymen, especially United and Presbyterian, who would normally have been Alliance members. The debates, meetings, and newspaper editorial columns filled with speakers both for and against. On 6 December 1949, over twenty-four thousand people, (40% of the eligible voters) turned out in Windsor and voted 54% to 46% in favour of local option. The Alliance shrugged off this defeat in what they considered an americanized, Catholic, and alcoholic city and turned its attention to Toronto.

In Toronto, the executives of every sympathetic Christian denomination collaborated in buying advertisements to fight the plebiscite. Although ex-Mayor Leslie Saunders chose to see the plebiscite as a Catholic plot to undermine the Protestant nature of Ontario, even Catholic Cardinal Archbishop McGuigan cautiously supported the Citizens' Committee.[18] The Toronto vote attracted a surprisingly large turnout: over 170,000 people, or 45% of the eligible municipal electors who voted 51.56% for Sunday sports. Lamport, the *Globe and Mail,* and other sports enthusiasts claimed total victory—politically adding that if everyone had been allowed to vote, not just the supposedly conservative ratepayers, the majority would have crushed the sabbatarians.[19] Newspapers exaggerated the thumping and claimed two to one majorities. Historians can never know how Toronto would have voted if everyone had been allowed to vote.

The Alliance saw this vote differently. It believed "that the heavy vote for commercialized Sunday sports came from the sections of this city where the non-Anglo Saxons are most numerous, and the Communists drew their greatest voting strength. It is also significant that the largest proportion of liquor outlets are to be found in the same areas." Webber could not hide his disappointment, however, over "the fact that the Christian people in other parts of the city did not give us the substantial majorities against commercialized Sunday Sports that were expected and needed."[20]

In fact, many stay-at-home Christian voters might have been Cardinal McGuigan's followers. Although McGuigan responded to the

Alliance's careful, long-term wooing and came out at the last moment against Sunday sports, Toronto's Catholics splintered into approval, indifference, denunciation and, in one case, schism.[21] Catholics such as Henry Somerville, the socially minded editor of the officially Catholic *Canadian Register,* were willing to follow McGuigan into a pan-Toronto, omnibus, social Christianity. Toronto's Catholic hierarchy had long had a tradition of cooperation with the Protestant majority, especially in matters of practical, social Christianity. Most Catholics, however, preferred to keep clear of Toronto's Protestants, led by such as the ex-mayor and Orangeman, Leslie Saunders.

The provincial government took Toronto's will to be that of Ontario, if not of God, and drafted a local option law. Webber tried to convince the legislators that it could not pass a law, since all Sunday legislation was in federal hands. When Ontario pointed at the enabling legislation once passed in Manitoba to allow excursions, the Alliance retreated to the position that an older English law of 1677 forbade sports, and it had never been repealed. The government ignored this last, desperate argument and proceeded with the bill.

"The Lord's Day (Ontario) Act 1950" stated that when a majority of voters favoured commercialized sport on Sundays, the municipal council could enact a bylaw to permit sports (horseracing excepted) between the hours of 1:30 p.m. and 6 p.m. Windsor and Toronto quickly permitted baseball. Symbolically, the first Toronto professional Sunday ball game started late, as the teams dithered, so that Councillor Hamilton tossed the ball to Councillor Lamport at bat for the amusement of 17,388 bored spectators.[22] Other municipalities across Ontario held plebiscites. Tourist centres near the United States such as Port Dover, Crystal Beach, Port Stanley, and Port Dalhousie naturally voted for sports. Hamilton, birthplace of the Alliance, did not.

The Alliance totted up the numbers in the plebiscites and came up with a majority of municipalities that had voted for Sunday sports but also with a majority of people voting against them.[23] The Alliance did not know what to make of the numbers. Looking at the figures closely, one can now see that most sabbatarians were found in large municipalities such as Hamilton, Kitchener, Oakville, Guelph, Chatham, and

Waterloo. Stated in another way, parts of Ontario that contained a majority of English Protestants voted against Sunday sports. Most of the municipalities that voted for Sunday activities were very small and dependent on tourism. In fact, a majority of Ontario voters would probably have rejected Sunday sports if given the chance to speak. CBC radio had conducted an informal poll in a 25 March 1949 national radio programme and received over 16,000 calls from all over Canada to oppose an open Sunday and only 693 calls to support Sunday activities. Then again, people in favour of an active Sunday might not have been listening quietly to CBC radio. Either way, it was very likely that a good argument could have been presented to the government of Ontario that a majority of Canadians favoured Sunday laws. The Lord's Day Alliance had failed miserably in organizing its own people.

Sporting events of questionable value, such as carnival games of skill or, rather, chance, came into the open. Billiard, snooker, or just plain "pool parlours" opened in some municipalities. Races were authorized in others. Alcohol and gambling crept in. There was no more uniformity, so confusion reigned across Ontario. With swift communications, municipalities in the rest of Canada, especially in British Columbia, caught the same restlessness and liberalized Sunday activities—to the growing alarm of the Christian denominations. Toronto had once led the way in Sabbath righteousness. Now it led the way in Sunday liberty.

WHY DID THE ALLIANCE ORGANIZATION FAIL in the sports plebiscites? Its organization after the Second World War seemed strong. The old field secretaries had returned to Canada from their chaplaincy positions in the armed forces, and new ones were hired as well. Webber started a new Alliance newspaper, the *Bulletin,* out of the increased donations that began to fill Alliance coffers. The 1948 sixtieth anniversary celebrations were large and well attended. As Newfoundland moved to join Confederation, the Alliance planned to set up a branch in St. John's and to give islanders the benefit of Canada's national Sunday. Almost all Christian denominations supported the Alliance. In Quebec, Joseph-Papin Archambault still headed the Ligue du

Dimanche, now as president as well as founder and chaplain. His vision of a French Catholic nation seemed more assured than ever. For his work in French Canada, in Social Catholicism, and in the Ecole Sociale Populaire, he received an honorary doctorate from the University of Montreal in 1945 during a glittering ceremony filled with Quebec's notables. The Ligue du Dimanche launched a campaign for "the return of the pre-war Sunday." In numerous short talks, Pope Pius XII emphasized Sunday's importance for the family, for rest, and for worship. Even the independent Quebec Provincial Lord's Day Alliance revived briefly. Sunday promised to be Quebec's, Canada's, and God's Sabbath day.

Ballooning postwar hopes for the Canadian Sunday were quietly deflated by sheer lack of unified leadership. Returning chaplains, like veterans, found other things to do and resigned from the Alliance shortly after arriving in Canada. For example, the Reverend Major Baxter J. Warr returned to Quebec and the Maritimes only to find the organizations in such pitiful condition that he immediately sent in his letter of resignation. Warr left to work as a chaplain of the Camp Hill Hospital, housing wounded veterans in Halifax. Almost every member of the Quebec Alliance had moved west, either to Ontario or further. The newspaper that Webber launched seemed to spend an inordinate amount of space announcing the deaths and resignations of "esteemed veteran workers." W.N. Byers of Alberta and British Columbia resigned in 1949 just before the crucial plebiscites of 1950. R.L. Taylor of Manitoba and Saskatchewan resigned to return to the Anglican pastorate. Rochester died in 1949; his old enemy, George Mingie of the splinter Quebec Provincial Lord's Day Alliance, died in 1950. Huestis died at the age of eighty-eight in 1951. His colleague for Manitoba and Saskatchewan, J.S. Watson, died at the age of eighty-three in 1953. Even the office secretary, Miss Davidson, who had typed almost every letter, every newspaper article, every report since 1926, retired in 1951 after a quarter century of service.[24] Webber concentrated on getting retired ministers to take over, at a low salary, but the generation of men who knew about the Alliance's glorious past was thin. One old Presbyterian layman volunteered to do some door-to-door fundraising. After the defeat of the Toronto plebiscite, Webber resigned. The Toronto

A.S. McGrath, General Secretary, Lord's Day Alliance, 1950–1972, and a Baptist minister.

campaign had seriously harmed the organization's finances. Hardly anyone was left in the office even to pay the bills. By the 1950s, the generation of sabbatarian leaders that had organized the successful 1906 lobby had passed away. Because other and more popular causes beckoned, few younger religious leaders stepped forward for the cause of sabbatarianism. During most of the crucial votes in Ontario and municipalities elsewhere in Canada, there were few trained sabbatarian religious leaders to organize against Sunday commercialization. No one went to Newfoundland. Donations dropped off, because people said, "what's the good of donating, the L.D.A. simply doesn't do anything."[25]

The Ligue du Dimanche was restricted mainly to the activities of one man: Archambault. Catholic Action became an umbrella organization whose efficiency decreased as its mandate broadened. All Catholic Action activities were becoming increasingly marginal to Canadian Catholic life, because postwar comforts and government service beckoned to French-Canadian youth. In 1949, the Asbestos Strike brought out a new generation of workers and intellectuals, including Pierre Trudeau, in a broad coalition against the Duplessis government. Although the church was prominent in the 1949 battle against Duplessis, most writers saw it, including the Ligue du Dimanche, as part of the Duplessis regime. In 1950, Catholic Action Young Catholic Workers barred chaplains and church dignitaries from their deliberations. The idea of separating church and state, popular under Taschereau's Liberal government, again came to the fore. Ironically, the church and the Ligue never received much satisfaction from Duplessis during the years that the popular mind associated Archambault and the

Roman Catholic Church with Duplessis. Also ironically, the Catholic Church in the postwar period had actively promoted sporting events, weekend camps, and other healthy outdoor activities centred around the parish club. The Ligue du Dimanche, like most of the elderly in North America, had become peripheral to Quebec society.

Every major church loudly denounced the commercial secularization of the Lord's Day, but most did not realize that their efforts were bound to fail without dedicated, fulltime workers and without money to fuel the campaigns. One denomination did realize this and began to do more than print sympathetic editorials. The new general secretary of the Alliance was Alvin Starr McGrath. Born in 1897, he was a Baptist minister recruited from southwestern Ontario in 1946. This appointment by the executive directors (who usually consisted of one or two clergyman from each province and from twenty to thirty members, or more, from Ontario) reflected the shift of organized sabbatarianism from traditional sabbatarian churches, Presbyterian and United, to other churches.

The shift to minority churches could be seen also in the financial records of the Alliance. Donations had been shifting subtly since the Depression. Ontario still predominated in giving over 50% of all donations, with the Prairies and British Columbia just ahead of the impoverished Maritimes for the remainder, but donations were no longer coming as readily from the major Protestant denominations. Donations in 1940 were almost $13,000. In 1950, they were just over $21,000. In 1940, United Church members and congregations gave over $7000, or over 50% of all donations while they held almost 20% of the Canadian population. Presbyterians gave almost $2000, or roughly 15% when they were just over 7% of the population. In 1950, these percentages changed significantly. From 1940 to 1950, Baptist donations almost tripled to over $2000, forming 10% of the donations while the Baptists themselves declined from 4.2% to 3.7% of the Canadian population. United Church members gave just over $10,000 in 1950—under 50% of the donations—while their percentage of the population increased to over 20%. Presbyterians marginally increased their donations from around $2000 to $2500 and fell in the total percentage of donations and of the Canadian population. Anglicans gave just over $1000 in 1940 and almost the same amount in 1950. Naturally, their percentage of the total donations fell drastically. Anglicans, however, were over 15% of the population in 1951. In real terms, these numbers show that smaller churches such as the Baptists, traditionally labelled evangelical, and congregational churches such as the Mennonites were giving proportionately more than their population among Protestants in Canada would suggest. In fact, they were giving as much as Presbyterians, the original sabbatarians.

For comparison, it is useful to look at donations from Jews and Roman Catholics. The records show that all the Jews of Canada together gave under $35 in 1940 and a little over $50 in 1950. Perhaps this minuscule amount could be termed a rock-bottom nuisance fee paid out by some Jewish shopkeepers to keep the Christian community and Alliance ministers quiet. In contrast, donations from Catholics to the Alliance fell from just under $90 in 1940 to around $60 in 1950. These figures represent official Catholic donations from all of Canada, over 40% of the population. Perhaps the argument could be made that the lion's share of Roman Catholic money went to the Ligue du Dimanche in Quebec, but this would not be true. Ligue records show that all of the annual expenses from 1940 to 1950 put together were under $100 for postage. Two gala congresses in 1946 were played up in newspaper and radio. The total bill to the Ligue came to $7.93. The tab was generously taken up by the Jesuits, Archambault's order. There were few if any donations to the Ligue. In these few financial records, one can see how truly popular Catholic sabbatarianism was. Catholics sided with the Jews in opposing the national and Protestant day of rest.

More Baptists appeared on the executive board of the Alliance, and the *Baptist Year Book* increasingly reported Alliance activities. It made sense to appoint a Baptist as the general secretary of a sabbatarian organization. Of course, naming a younger Baptist minister, who was relatively new to the Alliance, alienated some of the older mainstream members, who then withdrew their support of the Alliance.[26] As a sign of things to come, General Secretary McGrath attracted another Baptist, Dr. Elbert Paul, to become the Alberta and British Columbia Alliance field secretary.

The Alliance, in consequence, became more and more visible in churches of a minority of Canadians and less and less visible in those of the majority. In general, it seemed as if sabbatarianism was disappearing; Canada's Sunday would necessarily suffer some form of secularization, however defined. In reality, 1950 was the year when one generation of sabbatarian leaders handed over control to a new leader and a different Christian denomination, with a different vision of Christianity. The results required time and exposure to assume national prominence.

The slightly differing versions of Christian nationalism among Methodists and Presbyterians really did not hamper the transfer of authority to any great extent. There had been few problems when Shearer, a Presbyterian, handed over the Alliance to Moore, a Methodist. One reason for creating the United Church of Canada was just this unity: a national English Protestant vision. The transfer to Baptists, however, meant a greater adjustment. Baptists had strong traditions of separating church from state and the role of lay Christians. The first tradition meant that Baptists were not often close to the centre of political power and would not be expected to play many political games with provincial or federal governments. The second tradition meant that lay people would certainly be expected to play a greater part in the councils of the Alliance and act as liaisons with government and church. The Alliance was already beginning to hand over some of its organized authority and power to lay people under Webber. Webber received the support of retired lay people to canvass for donations door-to-door. The Alliance realized that if the people wanted a Sunday set apart from the rest of the week, they themselves would have to make the effort by joining citizen committees and voting to pressure the government. With the rise of Baptists in the organization, there came a distinct transfer of sabbatarian authority to lay people. The history of the Sunday movement in the twentieth century is also the decline of traditional, hierarchical religious authority and the rise of individual lay people, as church-goers and voters.

SABBATARIANS EVERYWHERE were shocked at Toronto's fall from Sabbath righteousness. For fifty years, sabbatarians had written to the Lord's Day Alliance head office in Toronto, had sent delegates to Toronto "the Good" where not one but two laws on Sabbath observance had regulated conduct. Hamilton had been the birthplace of the sabbatarian battles, but Toronto had been the centre from which sabbatarians had travelled to Ottawa and to the rest of Canada to lobby for laws and spread the benefits of Sabbath rest for worship. Every time Ontario deemed it necessary to loosen the Sunday observance laws, newspapers elsewhere took note and provinces soon followed its example. Toronto itself now allowed commercial sports on Sundays. The rest of Ontario was soon embroiled in plebiscite battles, and all of Canada followed. The centre of sabbatarian organization had disintegrated. Sabbatarians everywhere were disorganized and ineffective in opposing liberty leagues set up to promote everything from alcohol to zoos on Sundays and on every other day of the week.

In 1950, as in 1925, Canadian diversity fragmented religious and national authority over Sunday; Sunday laws were given to the provinces and then to the municipalities. Eventually, public decisions about Sunday behaviour were made by individuals in their own consciences. The "national Sabbath" was no longer either national or a Sabbath. In some cases, it was not even a day of rest. The sabbatarian desire for a united and uniform nation was defeated by the splintered nature of Canadian religious, political, and popular culture. The death of the older generation of sabbatarians, the role of government power under federalism, and the rise of a new generation of lay people claiming Sunday as their own, not belonging solely to the church or to the government, meant the disintegration of Canada's Sunday.

Children of the postwar generation were allowed and even encouraged to play ball in the streets and parks. God, the people believed, if he or she existed, would not be offended and would probably approve. Strangely, it seemed that the children of this postwar generation were also being encouraged to pay for the privilege of watching other, older people play those same games or even sing songs. Naturally, the children could pay for it all by working Sundays and making some pocket money. Of course, children were supposed to be living with their parents and did not need to be paid very much for their Sunday work behind counters, delivering papers, mowing lawns, selling or painting. Work was supposed to teach them the value of what little money they received. For the children of a wealthy family, who did not need money or time to study during the summer, perhaps the work did teach them something; work might even have been as much fun as a baseball game on a Sunday afternoon. But for most younger and poorer people, this was unlikely.

Opposition to sabbatarianism triumphed in the Toronto 1950 municipal referendum on Sunday sports, and that victory was hailed as the people's victory. In an age of popular democracy, the results of the municipal votes were enshrined by the Ontario government in a 1950 law, which allowed Toronto's wishes to become the norm for all of Ontario and an example for all of Canada. In 1950, the men of 1900 were no longer in charge of the nation's righteousness; their children had come through the Depression and the Second World War to decree that nationalism, especially the fascist kind, was no substitute religion and that the nation could not enforce a uniform religious law upon the diversity found in Canada. A righteous and united nation no longer meant a religiously uniform nation. The business of professional sporting entertainments was the people's fancy, or so governments believed, and professional sports were what the people were going to get. The Lord's Day Alliance was busy with its internal staffing problems and lost control of the situation. Sunday was given to the people of Canada. The national day of worshipful rest became a day for work and, perhaps, recreation.

The sabbath was made for man,
not man for the sabbath; so the Son of man
is lord even of the sabbath.—MARK 3:27–28

EPILOGUE

THE SUNDAY-SABBATH
after 1950

ALTHOUGH THE LORD'S DAY ALLIANCE APPEARED IN sabbatarian battles across the country after 1950, it fought mainly Ontario battles. Ontario still had the bulk of the Canadian population; it was still the headquarters for most Protestant denominations; and, increasingly, Toronto held the headquarters of most of the businesses and the banks of the nation. As always, therefore, sabbatarian battles in Ontario set the pace for the entire country.

From 1950 to 1970, Sunday secularization continued to spread. Unfortunately, since Sunday prosecutions are part of criminal records, government files are closed to researchers, and information must be found through painstaking newspaper research. Movies in Alberta, retail stores in Ontario, pulp-and-paper mills in Quebec and New Brunswick, and automatic vending and washing machines everywhere inspired new court cases and government commissions. In the 1950s, Henry Birks and Sons fought against Catholic holiday closing laws in Montreal, British Columbia fought for sports, and Alberta fought for laundromats. New

Telegram *22 September 1956.*

Brunswick legalized Sunday bowling in 1961. The Supreme Court bowling case, *Walter Robertson and Fred Rosetani v. the Queen,* 18 October 1963, decided that the Lord's Day Act did not infringe any religious freedom and that its effect was purely secular. Recognizing that any religious legislation will have a purely secular effect, the famed legalist Bora Laskin then concluded that John Diefenbaker's Bill of Rights guaranteeing religious freedom meant little in Canadian life. Only a later Supreme Court, one that had felt Laskin's personal presence for several years and worked with the 1982 *Charter of Rights and Freedoms* enshrined in the Constitution, would attack the Lord's Day Act directly. In the meantime, Canada's sabbatarians tried to make their version of Christianity part of the civil religion of Canadian life. But the Lord's Day became increasingly hard to see among the growing secular demands of contemporary Canadian society.

In 1970, the Ontario department of justice's Law Reform Commission produced a comprehensive *Report on Sunday Observance Legislation* which studied all aspects of the Sunday laws. It concluded by recommending an almost unworkable intermediate policy of stopping businesses on Sunday and allowing time for leisure—ignoring the fact that leisure had become big business. The commission advised strongly against exceptions for any religious group, such as Seventh-Day Adventists or Jews. The result of political compromise satisfied no one.

The Alliance began to distance itself from churches. Individual instead of institutional donors had become more important to it. By 1970, only one-third of the Alliance budget came from churches; the rest came from individual donations and from investments made in earlier, more prosperous years. By 1986, church contributions fell to one-sixth of the entire budget. Another third came from unions and retail businesses concerned about Sunday rest. In 1971, 1976, and 1979, the papers of the Alliance were given away—not to any religious archive but to the University of Toronto, in order to avoid identifying itself with any religious organization. Fifty years after McGrath first joined the Alliance, he handed over the organization in 1972 to another Baptist pastor, Gordon Walker, who continued to transform the Alliance into a more lay-oriented organization. In 1982, after years of agonizing debate, the Alliance changed its name to the People for Sunday Association of Canada. After Walker stepped down from the position of general secretary, the first lay general secretary was chosen; this secretary was a woman. The traditional male and clerical Alliance, apparently, disappeared.

The Alliance had always recognized that power lay in majority rule. Otherwise, why had it bothered to lobby governments for majority-based laws? So the modern Alliance moved to a broader-based, apparently secular name that would attract retailers, labour unions and other non-religious organizations. Later still, the People for Sunday Association helped form the Coalition Against Open Sunday Shopping and similar lobby groups. No matter what the name, the aim was the same. Secularization of the Alliance could be used for religious ends.

The Ligue du Dimanche suffered a less ambiguous and less lengthy demise. After the Alleyn Commission reported in 1966, the Liberal Lesage government openly legalized Sunday pulp-and-paper work.

Economic necessity and unemployment were bigger problems than the lack of Sunday rest. When Archambault died in 1966, the few remaining, aging Ligue du Dimanche members wrote a collective request to the bishops of Quebec for some leadership. The bishops, busy coping with the chaos of Vatican II renewal, advised the Ligue to dissolve, which it obediently did.[1] Without Archambault, there was no desire to continue the half-hearted Sunday sabbatarianism that Catholicism sponsored. Only Cardinal Léger, the archbishop of Montreal, the most highly industrialized city of Canada, continued to warn his diocesan clergy and lay people against giving in to the financial or leisure gods of the moment.[2] When Léger retired, French-Canadian Catholics, both lay and clerical, returned to their original, secular attitude towards Sunday. In a 1984 publication, *The Meaning of Sunday in a Pluralistic Society,* the Catholic bishops wrote that Sunday was a customary day of rest and said very little else. The People for Sunday Association were upset at how little sabbatarianism informed the Canadian Conference of Catholic Bishops' statement. The Association incorrectly believed that secularism had seized modern Quebec, but Catholics had never believed it to be a fundamental principle within Christianity. Catholic bishops realized that the Sunday-Sabbath had little meaning in a fragmented society. Only later, when biblical studies and the new social sciences began to make their influence felt, did a greater emphasis on Sunday rest for worship creep back into Catholicism. By that time, though, it was too late for the sabbatarian movement in Canada.

On 1 April 1985, the Supreme Court of Canada decided that the 1906 Lord's Day Act, "to the extent that it binds all to a sectarian Christian ideal, works a form of coercion inimical to the spirit of the *Charter.*" The Lord's Day Act was indeed based on a restricted set of Christian religious principles to promote a religious concept. It discriminated against both non-Christians and non-Sunday sabbatarians. It was neither labour legislation nor business legislation, both of which would have been, in general, beyond federal jurisdiction. After 1985, Sunday legislation was back in the hands of the provinces, a century after Sir John A. Macdonald stated that Sunday was a matter of custom and,

Advertising that appeared in newspapers, magazines and handbills in 1971.

therefore, a provincial matter. The provinces warily passed Sunday or weekend regulations, shops closing acts, day of rest acts, urban municipality acts, and business and retail holiday acts. These carefully avoided mentioning the "Lord's Day," that dreaded phrase which would have created yet another religious and unconstitutional law. Many provinces merely handed on the bothersome business to municipalities. Paul

Magder of Toronto ran a fur shop in Chinatown and immediately began to violate the Ontario Retail Business Holidays Act, as did other Jews in Toronto. His case reached the Supreme Court in 1987.[3] Other provinces soon faced the same question. By 2003, Nova Scotia was the only province in Canada that had not yet struck down its Sunday-shopping ban. Not surprisingly, it has a high number of Presbyterians.

Secularization of Canada's Sunday after 1985 meant, as it always had, that governments co-opted moral authority and divided it among government agencies. Moral authority over Sunday was then carefully fragmented into its lowest common political denominator in the hope that it would disappear. It usually did.

Finally, public opinion meant a great deal to the People for Sunday Association and to the governments of Canada, because power, both religious and political, is a reflection of collective choices. To the people of Canada, sports, movies, summer jobs, part-time jobs, tourist jobs, and just plain ordinary jobs were sometimes more important than Sunday rest. People wanted to shop or watch baseball games on Sunday, but they still did not want to work the cash register or clean up the mess after the game was over. This confused and collective opinion about what Sunday was for—rest as well as for restless leisure—continues to make Sunday different from the rest of the week. Sabbatarians, to some extent, succeeded in their education of the masses about Sunday rest and surprisingly kept Sunday free for many who wanted to go to church. As long as the majority of Canadians remain attached to one day of the week that is different from all others, democratic governments of Canada must act accordingly and propose compromise solutions about what exactly may be done on that day. When the majority desires Sunday activities, governments will obviously allow it. Stated in another way: Canadians believe that Sunday was created for them and not they for Sunday. Canadians, therefore, are in charge of what they do on Sunday. For sabbatarian Christians, God is in charge of Sunday. For other Christians and, therefore, most Canadians, the liberty to choose what to do on Sunday is a gift from God. This uneasy coexistence explains why Canadians still feel the need to post possibly guilty signs proclaiming an "Open Sunday."

But it is easier for heaven and earth to pass away, than for one dot of the law to become void.—LUKE 16:17

CONCLUSION

THE MEANING OF SUNDAY SECULARISM

THE MOST POWERFUL EXPLANATION FOR THE decline of Sunday observance in Canada can be found in Canada's religious and ethnic diversity. Jews, Americans, blacks, Seventh-Day Adventists, Catholics, French-Canadians, Indians, Chinese, and Japanese found themselves pitted against a supposed English Protestant uniformity. Jews and Protestants in Quebec found themselves at odds with the same attempt at a French Catholic uniformity. How many opposed Sunday sabbatarianism will never be known, but we do know that the Alliance was a careful balance of Protestant and lay groups. Thus constituted, supposedly of most Canadians, it was able to launch a crusade throughout Canada to convince Parliament that the Christian Sunday-Sabbath needed uniform legal protection. The people of Canada were to be made moral by force of law and the coercive power of the state.

The Protestant crusade excluded Catholics, however, because of regional and linguistic differences between Protestants, most of whom spoke English, and Catholics, most of whom spoke French and lived mainly in Quebec. Quebec developed a French and Roman Catholic Ligue du Dimanche, which worked only in Quebec and with Catholics. All French-speaking Catholics outside of Quebec, all English-speaking Catholics, and all other minorities were always excluded and became a constant source of friction to English-speaking Protestant sabbatarians for their supposed lack of respect for Sunday rest.

The Sunday crusades, Protestant or Catholic, by self-definition, did not include Jews, Seventh-Day Adventists, or any other seventh-day sabbatarians. Jews, therefore, were prosecuted all across Canada and often launched court appeals that eventually whittled away the federal Lord's Day Act.

Lastly, many religious groups that supposedly belonged to the Protestant crusade for a Christian Canada were not entirely convinced of the crusade's necessity and, therefore, were not entirely part of the Alliance. Before 1950, Anglicans were more preoccupied with missions than with sabbatarian civilization. After 1950, along with members of the United Church, most of them had moved into the liberal Protestant camp and were not interested in evangelical or transcendent Christian concerns. Baptists were often busy with modernism, orthodoxy, and the organizational disruptions arising from these questions. When Baptists and other evangelical denominations stabilized, and centralized administrations were able to control their congregations, they began to participate more and more in the coercive efforts of the Alliance. The Sabbath crusade faltered only because of religious fragmentation and disorganization, not loss of belief in the sabbatarian ideal. Religious diversity or fragmentation and disorganization brought on crisis after crisis which severely weakened the sabbatarians and qualified the success of 1906.

The second most important explanation for the Sunday-Sabbath's decline in Canada is time itself. Simply, many of the organizers had died. Other causes (peace, disarmament, anti-communism, urbanism, etc.) occupied the time of the younger leaders. Sabbatarianism became a national issue only when a well-trained, dedicated, and organized sabbatarian elite took the time to force a Sunday debate on the national level. These were the years of the Lord's Day Act of 1906 and of the Privy Council decision striking down the Quebec Lord's Day Act as unconstitutional. As their leaders drifted away, grew old, and died, so did their creations: the Lord's Day Alliance and the Ligue du Dimanche.

There were problems of transferring power from one generation to another. The transfer would often be incomplete, because the authority one person had accumulated could not be passed entirely to untried successors—some of whom, belonging to different denominations, did not necessarily believe in the same kind of Sabbath. William Rochester often helped his successors, but Charles Huestis rarely did. In one important case, Huestis severely hampered his successor, although both belonged to the United Church. When Sabbath organizations, especially the Ligue du Dimanche, did not find any acceptable, trained, and ordained leaders to replace the former generation, it turned to lay leaders. These, many of them old and working only part time or as volunteers, could not keep elaborate national structures together. Their organizations fell apart. The Ligue du Dimanche disbanded in 1966. At first, the Alliance became more closely affiliated with smaller Christian denominations, such as the Baptists. Then it changed its name to the People for Sunday Association, an amorphous group of organizations and individuals, many of them lay, working mainly in Ontario.

The inner meaning of secularization is one intimately related to time, secular and eternal. With time, the sabbatarian elite gradually went to their eternal reward. And, with time, sabbatarian leadership was handed on to less experienced people.

The third reason for the decline of the Sunday-Sabbath is the political secularization of traditional religious authority. Christian denominations in Canada, beset by fragmentation, could not agree on whether Sunday was necessary, or if necessary, what kind of Sabbath Canada should have. So, they foisted the final decision onto governments, Attorneys General, and provincial leaders. The transfer ultimately meant loss of power among sabbatarians, because secular power was not given to them in return. Nor did many sabbatarians want it. No one wanted—or stated that they wanted—a union of church and state.[1] So, for many years, the Alliance refused to institute prosecutions, claiming that police functions were the duty of the police. Jean-Pierre Sironneau noticed the same phenomenon in Europe and commented: "Until modern times, the political used to depend on the religious: politics used to seek its ultimate legitimacy in religion . . . Then, in a typical reversal, politics has tended to replace religion as the last authority and main activity which must subordinate all the other ones, the first and last foundation of social life, and the guarantee of truth as well."[2]

The sabbatarians approached the governments of Canada in the belief that governments would obey their wishes, appoint inspectors, prosecute non-sabbatarians, jail dissenters, and fine companies. In Europe, religious property has been often seized. But in Canada, especially during the world wars, national conscription of people's time became more acceptable to Canadian religious leaders than the conscription of wealth. "Time is money." Sometimes, it is more valuable.

The Canadian nation was given power over the days of the week, yet it had never wanted to dabble in religious debates, fearful that they would explode in religious strife and destroy the nation or, at least, the government of the day. Governments suspected that religious disunity, eroding the Lord's Day Alliance behind the scenes, could also undermine any nation wielding religious arguments for the sake of uniformity. The Lord's Day Alliance and the Ligue du Dimanche both lobbied openly for changes in laws and prosecutions, but neither wished to take responsibility for the consequences: anger and disunity should the laws be strictly enforced. Sabbatarians often seemed to have the attitude that the Sabbath had to be enforced even if the nation perish, since a righteous nation might arise from the ruins. The government shuffled this issue into a limbo of the provinces, the municipalities, and then the masses. Popular culture took hold of Sunday. The holy day became a holiday.

Nonetheless, a distinct Sunday is still with us and might even stage a revival. Many people who laughed at the satires and read the newspaper jokes, are now working at more than one job. Their spouses and even their children are working to make ends meet as our economic culture "restructures" for more efficiency and higher profits. Those who have survived restructuring and kept their salaried position find themselves putting in unpaid overtime, equivalent to second jobs, as a matter of course. Both immigrants and Canadians drive the machines on Sunday, sell tickets, sweep, stack chairs, clean, and cook perhaps seven days every week, working hard for those with the time and money to enjoy restaurants, cinemas, clubs and golf courses on Sunday. This is all done in an age when leisure time was supposed to increase. Each new generation of workers, wage-earning lower class or salaried middle class, looks longingly at Sunday. Religious goals suddenly appear reasonable and the battles begin again. Sunday sabbatarianism might be a middle-class achievement from which those with more leisure and money excuse themselves and for which those with less leisure and money merely aspire. Sunday's decline (and the rise of secularism) could be part of the decline of that amorphous, hard-to-define Canadian middle class.

Nevertheless, Christianity still underlies the laws of Canada. National sabbatarianism, as part of Canada's civil religion—in bylaws, in regulations, and in provincial and federal laws—continues to surface and confront Canadians. Christianity has gone underground and is no longer in the antechambers of power, much less in the seats of power. But Christians have the amazing knack of working in the catacombs, in the corridors of legislatures, as organized and powerful lobby groups trying to shape a Christian Canada. Christians underground use secular weapons and hide themselves behind secular names, while religious authorities or clergy stand behind lay people. It is only natural that the fruits of secular organization and its result, power, should reappear. The struggle for and against the nation's Sunday has merely been passed on to another generation of Canadians. The spread of biblical literacy and literalism within Catholic circles, strongly encouraged by a Pope also interested in christianizing culture, may join with the steadily growing evangelical denominations of Canada to create a new Sunday crusade. The political "right-wing" has dominated debates throughout North America and has surprised many with its ability to gain votes. It is not surprising to those who pay attention to religion.

In summary, after a surprising, unusual, and powerful groundswell of sabbatarian organization united to Christian nationalism, Canada became legally sabbatarian in the early twentieth century. Religious fragmentation, the growth of government as the final authority among religious groups, and the death of key sabbatarians eroded the Sunday-Sabbath. The whittling away of Sabbath laws does not mean secularism, or the decline of religion, as many authors have thought, but it does mean secularization: the decline of traditional sabbatarian authority and its transfer to new forms of organization, whether lay or governmental. Secularization does not mean the end of religion but its transfer to the secular realm. Secularization eventually succeeded in destroying the power of the sabbatarian lobby, but sabbatarianism still exists in the minds of Canadians. How many Canadians we do not quite know, but we do know that the sabbatarian belief in a transcendent God and similar beliefs affecting other moral issues, are still alive, organizing, and waiting in the antechambers of power in Canada.

APPENDIX

AN ACT RESPECTING THE LORD'S DAY

(Revised Statutes of Canada 1906, chapter 153)
(Formerly 6 E. VII., c.27)

SHORT TITLE.

1. This Act may be cited as the Lord's Day Act.

INTERPRETATION.

2. In this Act, unless the context otherwise requires,
   (a) "Lord's Day" means the period of time which begins at twelve o'clock on Saturday afternoon and ends at twelve o'clock on the following afternoon;
   (b) "person" has the meaning which it has in the Criminal Code;
   (c) "vessel" includes any kind of vessel or boat used for conveying passengers or freight by water;
   (d) "railway" includes steam railway, electric railway, street railway and tramway;
   (e) "performance" includes any game, match, sport, contest, exhibition or entertainment;
   (f) "employer" includes every person to whose orders or directions any other person is by his employment bound to conform;
   (g) "provincial Act" means the charter of any municipality, or any public Act of any province, whether passed before or since Confederation.

3. Nothing herein shall prevent the operation on the Lord's Day for passenger traffic by any railway company incorporated by or subject to the legislative authority of the Parliament of Canada of its railway where such operation is not otherwise prohibited.

   2. Nothing herein shall prevent the operation on the Lord's Day for passenger traffic of any railway subject to the legislative authority of any province, unless such railway is prohibited by provincial authority from so operating.

COMMENCEMENT.

4. This Act shall come into force on the first day of March, one thousand nine hundred and seven.

PROHIBITIONS.

5. It shall not be lawful for any person on the Lord's Day, except as provided herein, or in any provincial Act or law now or hereafter in force, to sell or offer for sale or purchase any goods, chattels, or other personal property, or any real estate, or to carry on or transact any business of his ordinary calling, or in connection with such calling, or for gain to do, or employ any other person to do, on that day, any work, business, or labour.

6. Except in cases of emergency, it shall not be lawful for any person to require any employee

engaged in any work of receiving, transmitting or delivering telegraph or telephone messages, or in the work of any industrial process, or in connection with transportation, to do on the Lord's Day the usual work of his ordinary calling, unless such employee is allowed during the next six days of such week, twenty-four consecutive hours without labour.

2. This section shall not apply to any employee engaged in the work of any industrial process in which the regular day's labour of such employee is not of more than eight hours' duration.

7. It shall not be lawful for any person, on the Lord's Day, except as provided in any provincial Act or law now or hereafter in force, to engage in any public game or contest for gain, or for any prize or reward, or to be present at any performance or public meeting, elsewhere than in a church, at which any fee is charged, directly or indirectly, either for admission to such performance or meeting, or to any place within which the same is provided, or for any service or privilege thereat.

2. When any performance at which an admission fee or any other fee is so charged is provided in any building or place to which persons are conveyed for hire by the proprietors or managers of such performance or by any one acting as their agent or under their control, the charge for such conveyance shall be deemed an indirect payment of such fee within the meaning of this section.

8. It shall not be lawful for any person on the Lord's Day, except as provided by any provincial Act or law now or hereafter in force, to run, conduct, or convey by any mode of conveyance any excursion on which passengers are conveyed for hire, and having for its principal or only object the carriage on that day of such passengers for amusement or pleasure, and passengers so conveyed shall not be deemed to be travellers within the meaning of this Act.

9. It shall not be lawful for any person to advertise in any manner whatsoever any performance or other thing prohibited by this Act.

2. It shall not be lawful for any person to advertise in Canada in any manner whatsoever any performance or other thing which if given or done in Canada would be a violation of this Act.

10. It shall not be lawful for any person on the Lord's Day to shoot with or use any gun, rifle or other similar engine, either for gain, or in such a manner or in such places as to disturb other persons in attendance at public worship on in the observance of that day.

11. It shall not be lawful for any person to bring into Canada for sale or distribution, or to sell or distribute within Canada, on the Lord's Day, any foreign newspaper or publication classified as a newspaper.

WORKS OF NECESSITY AND MERCY EXCEPTED

12. Notwithstanding anything herein contained, any person may on the Lord's Day do any work of necessity or mercy, and for greater certainty, but not so as to restrict the ordinary meaning of the expression "work of necessity or mercy," it is hereby declared that it shall be deemed to include the following classes of work:

(a) Any necessary or customary work in connection with divine worship;
(b) Work for the relief of sickness and suffering, including the sale of drugs, medicines and surgical appliances by retail;
(c) Receiving, transmitting, or delivering telegraph or telephone messages;
(d) Starting or maintaining fires, making repairs to furnaces and repairs in cases of emergency, and doing any other work, when such fires, repairs or work are essential to any industry or industrial process of such a continuous nature that it cannot be stopped without serious injury to such industry, or its product, or to the plant or property used in such process;
(e) Starting or maintaining fires, and ventilating, pumping out and inspecting mines, when any such work is essential to the protection of property, life or health;
(f) Any work without the doing of which on the Lord's Day, electric current, light, heat,

cold air, water or gas cannot be continuously supplied for lawful purposes;
(g) The conveying of travellers and work incidental thereto;
(h) The continuance to their destination of trains and vessels in transit when the Lord's Day begins, and work incidental thereto;
(i) Loading and unloading merchandise, at intermediate points, on or from passenger boats or passenger trains;
(j) Keeping railway tracks clear of snow or ice, making repairs in cases of emergency or doing any other work of a like incidental character necessary to keep the lines and tracks open on the Lord's Day;
(k) Work before six o'clock in the forenoon and after eight o'clock in the afternoon of yard crews in handling cars in railway yards;
(l) Loading, unloading and operating any ocean-going vessel which otherwise would be unduly delayed after her scheduled time of sailing, or any vessel which otherwise would be in imminent danger of being stopped by the closing of navigation; or loading or unloading before seven o'clock in the morning or after eight o'clock in the afternoon any grain, coal or ore carrying vessel after the fifteenth of September;
(m) The caring for milk, cheese, and live animals, and the unloading of and caring for perishable products and live animals, arriving at any point during the Lord's Day;
(n) The operation of any toll or drawbridge, or any ferry or boat authorized by competent authority to carry passengers on the Lord's Day;
(o) The hiring of horses and carriages or small boats for the personal use of the hirer or his family for any purpose not prohibited by this Act;
(p) Any unavoidable work after six o'clock in the afternoon of the Lord's Day, in the preparation of the regular Monday morning edition of a daily newspaper;
(q) The conveying His Majesty's mails and work incidental thereto;
(r) The delivery of milk for domestic use, and the work of domestic servants and watchmen;
(s) The operation by any Canadian electric street railway company, whose line is interprovincial or international, of its cars, for passenger traffic, on the Lord's Day, on any line or branch which is, on the day of the coming into force of this Act, regularly so operated;
(t) Work done by any person in the public service of His Majesty while acting therein under any regulation or direction of any department of the Government;
(u) Any unavoidable work by fishermen after six o'clock in the afternoon of the Lord's Day, in the taking of fish;
(v) All operations connected with the making of maple sugar and maple syrup in the maple grove;
(w) Any unavoidable work on the Lord's Day to save property in cases of emergency, or where such property is in imminent danger of destruction or serious injury;
(x) Any work which the Board of Railway Commissioners for Canada, having regard to the object of this Act, and with the object of preventing undue delay, deems necessary to permit in connection with the freight traffic of any railway.

OFFENCES AND PENALTIES.

13. Any person who violates any of the provisions of this Act shall for each offence be liable, on summary conviction, to a fine, not less than one dollar and not exceeding forty dollars, together with the cost of prosecution.
14. Every employer who authorizes or directs anything to be done in violation of any provision of this Act, shall for each offence be liable, on summary conviction, to a fine not exceeding one hundred dollars and not less than twenty dollars, in addition to any other penalty prescribed by law for the same offence.
15. Every corporation which authorizes, directs or permits its employees to carry on any part of the business of such corporation in violation of any of the provisions of this Act, shall be liable, on

summary conviction before two justices of the peace, for the first offence, to a penalty not exceeding two hundred and fifty dollars and not less than fifty dollars, and, for each subsequent offence, to a penalty not exceeding five hundred dollars and not less than one hundred dollars, in addition to any other penalty prescribed by law for the same offence.

PROCEDURE

16. Nothing herein shall be construed to repeal or in any way affect any provisions of any Act or law relating in any way to the observance of the Lord's Day in force in any province of Canada when this Act comes into force; and where any person violates any of the provisions of this Act, and such offence is also a violation of any other Act or law, the offender may be proceeded against either under the provisions of this Act or under the provisions of any other Act or law applicable to the offence charged.
17. No action or prosecution for a violation of this Act shall be commenced without the leave of the Attorney General for the province in which the offence is alleged to have been committed, nor after the expiration of sixty days from the time of the commission of the alleged offence.

Note On Archival Sources

The essential source for all studies in Sunday observance, laws, or attitudes in Canada are the papers of the Lord's Day Alliance of Canada deposited in the Thomas Fisher Rare Book Collection of the University of Toronto. The Lord's Day Alliance collection now consists of over two hundred boxes and items. Before 1986, most of the collection was restricted, but it is now fully accessible.

The Alliance materials comprise a large collection of newspaper clippings from across the country, from the smallest town to the largest city, from east to west, and from Canada, the United States, and overseas. The collection also contains newspaper clippings, letters, and pamphlets of organizations that opposed sabbatarianism. Opposition to the Alliance's aims often crystallized in ad hoc and ephemeral organizations that left few traces except in newspapers and in Alliance papers. Judging by the quantity of newspaper materials in these papers, one can assume that almost everything pertinent to both sides of any Sunday question was kept by the Alliance.

The only other major source of Alliance material is held at the United Church British Columbia Conference Archives. This source contains mainly British Columbia and Alberta post-1950s materials. Also useful in the same archives are the Hugh Dobson Papers.

Although the archives of the Salvation Army and the Canadian Baptist churches, the Presbyterian Church in Canada, the General Synod of the Anglican Church, and the United Church of Canada were examined, these denominations considered Sunday observance legislation the Alliance's responsibility. Published annual minutes and journals were the only available valuable source on Protestant denominational attitudes to Sunday, Lord's Day legislation, or to sabbatarian concerns. Other Protestant denominations, such as the Seventh-Day Adventist and Lutheran churches, have only just established archives and hold few pertinent resources. Because of the number and geographic dispersal of Anglican diocesan archives, research in Canadian Anglicanism, in general, was restricted to the General Synod's Archives.

The second most important archival collection for a study of Canadian Sunday attitudes is the archive of the French-Canadian province of the Society of Jesus, now in St. Jerome, Quebec. The restricted papers of the founder and only chaplain of the Ligue du Dimanche, Father Joseph-Papin Archambault, SJ, contain the private and public documents of the organization as well as many French-language newspaper clippings not available in the Alliance collection. The Ligue du Dimanche papers, dealing with the observance of Sunday and Sunday laws in Quebec between 1906 and 1966, are organized in twelve archival boxes. These materials, as well as Archambault's papers as a whole, are essential to any future comparative work of French and English, Catholic and Protestant attitudes to Christian social action in Canada.

Most English Catholic archdiocesan archives contain nothing of value or are closed to the public. One exception is the archives of the Archdiocese of Toronto which contain an excellent collection of Cardinal Archbishop McGuigan's papers for the period 1935 to 1960. These papers of the largest English-speaking Catholic diocese can be considered representative of the hierarchy of the English-Canadian Catholic church until new evidence from other, currently restricted archives is found.

In French Canada, many Catholic archives are closed to researchers. Montreal's archdiocesan archives were opened for this study. Aside from the 1906 debates, however, the materials were mainly copies of documents in the Jesuit archives in St. Jerome. Pastoral letters and diocesan newspapers for Quebec's and Manitoba's French-speaking dioceses were consulted in Montreal's archdiocesan archives.

The third most important source for sabbatarian and anti-sabbatarian attitudes can be found in provincial criminal files. Access to criminal files deposited in provincial archives was made possible by a series of legal agreements negotiated with provincial governments. Because of restrictions placed on the use of the Attorneys General's materials, and to avoid the possibility of censorship or prosecution by the Attorneys General's departments, citations to the Attorneys Generals' papers of all provinces have been used only when no duplicate reference—for example, to the now public Alliance papers—could be found and used in its stead.

The value of provincial archives varied. Prince Edward Island and Newfoundland wrote that they held nothing remotely concerned with Sunday. Manitoba claimed to have no files on Sunday, Sabbath, or Lord's Day when consulted in 1985. Later correspondence about their Attorney General files produced nothing further. The Yukon and Northwest Territories papers are in Ottawa and held nothing relevant. Upon examination, New Brunswick and Nova Scotia held very little of value, since much of the Attorney Generals' files were missing, entirely restricted or destroyed and an examination of other ministries proved unrewarding. The Lord's Day Alliance holds more papers, more legal digests, and more information about the provinces than the respective provincial archives. Provincial law reports and statute books were more valuable than the often incomplete debates of provincial legislatures.

The public archives of British Columbia and Alberta hold extensive files on the criminal prosecution of Sunday observance and Lord's Day Act violations. Unfortunately, a fire in 1939 destroyed almost all of the British Columbia Attorney General's letterbooks for 1872–1917. Other files were destroyed by flooding. The surviving files of the ministry of the Attorney General for the post-1917 period are fascinating treasures of xenophobic and religious prosecutions. But because the files were often generated by active Alliance field secretaries who were in British Columbia and Alberta, much of the information is duplicated in Alliance files. Ontario, where the head office of the Alliance and usually two field secretaries were stationed, holds quantitatively more material than other provinces. The records are extensive, but all criminal files and materials after 1938 were restricted under the Freedom of Information Act. Quebec had its Ligue du Dimanche, so the files in the Attorney

General's ministry are voluminous but often repeat the Ligue's files. Criminal and civil files between 1938 and 1976, at which time the Parti Québécois replaced the Liberals, were destroyed by the out-going Liberal government, but the restricted criminal materials prior to 1938 were opened for this study.

The Department of Justice's papers in the National Archives of Canada, Record Group 13, include files on legislation for 1867 to 1934 and 1948–1960. In the swamp of missing, destroyed, and collated criminal and civil files, some valuable material is available in the Central Registry Series. The Political and Public Affairs branch of the National Archives hold the personal papers of the ministers of justice from 1900 to 1950, but there is little of interest there. Record Group 27, the ministry of labour, proved void of material. There is occasional tangential correspondence scattered throughout other collections in the National Archives, but it is not worth the time involved in searching. The debates of the House of Commons and of the Senate and the journals of the select committees, all published sources, were better sources of government activities and attitudes than manuscript files, especially for the passage of the federal Lord's Day Act in 1906.

Because most of the materials used in this book are rare, unpublished or manuscript sources, the following conventions have been used for the endnotes. Many available clippings did not list the newspaper title, date of publication or page number, so I cite only clippings that were identified at least by publication title, article title, and by date, although masses of incomplete clippings were also available. The citation of legal cases used by *The Canadian Abridgment* (Toronto: 2d ed., 1974) has been followed and the reader is referred to that authority and to its successors. Original submissions, arguments, decisions, and appeals were often conserved in the Alliance collection, but are cited from *The Canadian Abridgment,* when possible, for greater ease of access. Although Protestants used the King James Version during the period discussed in this book, Catholics used translations of the Vulgate, so quotations and references to the Bible are taken from the Revised Standard Version.

Many references to archival sources have been combined and references to generally available published works have been shortened to the author's name and the pages on which the citation is found. All are listed in the bibliography of works cited. For more detailed references to primary sources, I refer readers to my doctoral dissertation in the Department of History at the University of Toronto.

In summary, government and religious archives, if they survived fire, flood, and administrative clear-cutting, hold valuable materials. But they are often restricted, hold copies or originals of the Alliance materials, or are too dispersed in vast collections with varying purposes. Moreover, while the quotation or identification of writers has been forbidden by the public and private archives consulted, the papers of the Lord's Day Alliance have no restrictions and usually contain the originals or copies of correspondence in other archives. The Alliance played a public role and urged all of its writers to go public and thus give more weight to the sabbatarian lobby. Since Alliance officials considered themselves public representatives, it is not a disservice to persons connected with the Alliance to publish their names and opinions. Newspaper reports and opinions across Canada can be found in Alliance and in Ligue records. As historians become aware of the Lord's Day Alliance collection and the value of its papers dealing with sports, transportation, the retail trade, labour, alcohol, legal issues, libraries, real estate, entertainment and, in fact, most aspects of Canadian life, more and more historians will make use of its papers.

Abbreviations

ADV *The Lord's Day Advocate*. New Series. Newspaper published by the Lord's Day Alliance of Canada, Toronto, Ontario, 1903–1926. Thomas Fisher Rare Book Library and Archives of the United Church of Canada.

HC Debates of the House of Commons.

JPA Papers of the Ligue du Dimanche in the Joseph-Papin Archambault Collection (R3) of the French-Canadian Provincial Archives of the Society of Jesus, Saint-Jerome, Quebec.

LDA Lord's Day Alliance of Canada, Manuscript Collection 129, housed in the Thomas Fisher Rare Book Library of the University of Toronto.

NAC National Archives of Canada

Endnotes

INTRODUCTION

1. Vahanian, 138.
2. Eliade, 13. Also, Cox, *The Secular City,* 2.
3 Cox, *The Religious and the Secular,* 6.
4. Chadwick, 156.
5 I borrow this concept from the late Roland Chagnon, who pithily summarizes the sociological literature dealing with "Religion, sécularisation et déplacements du sacré," pp.21–51 in Desrosiers.
6. Eliade, 34, 70–71, 110–11.
7. Rordorf, 34, 162–6.

CHAPTER ONE

1. Meen, "Battle for the Sabbath," 70.
2. LDA 71, minutes of 21 March 1889.
3. Sermons xiii, xiv, and xv in Jonathan Edwards, *Twenty Sermons on Various Subjects* (Edinburgh 1804).
4. Hopkins, 318.
5. LDA 115, 23 Sept 1886, "Second General Conference of the Methodist Church 1886. Report of the Committee on Sabbath Observance." Jews would never denounce social visiting and worldly pleasure on the Sabbath, because the real focus of the day is not public worship but family and home. See Heschel.
6. Jable, 109.
7. LDA 71, minutes of 22 March 1889 and 20 March 1890; "Travail du dimanche dans les beurreries et les fromageries" (27 décembre 1898), *Mandements. Lettres Pastorales et Circulaires des Evêques de Montréal,* vol.13, p.117.
8. LDA 5, 18 December 1905, Shearer to the Reverend P.L. Richardson.
9. NAC, Senator Eugene Forsey Papers, "Labour and Sunday Observance 1883–1902" (typescript, n.d.), pp. 2–3; Bryan Palmer, "'Give us the road and we will run it': The Social and Cultural Matrix of an Emerging Labour Movement," 106–24 in Kealey and Warrian, 109 refers to the post-1888 period.
10. LDA 71, minutes of 8 August 1899; Armstrong and Nelles acknowledge that the bicycle took no revenge. Methodists and Presbyterians were

worried by Sunday bicycling, a solitary sin, but Sunday streetcar traveling involved forced, public Sunday labour for transportation workers as well as sin for travelers.

11. Allen, *The Social Passion,* 17.
12. LDA 71, p.111, 25 June 1901.
13. LDA 2, 16 January 1901, Shearer to J.S. Woodsworth. In LDA 71, pp.50, 52–3, 59, James Woodsworth's name appears as a member from 1896 to 1898.
14. LDA 2, 1 May 1901, Shearer to the Bryant Press, Toronto. *Christian Guardian,* 16 January 1901, p.10, 22 May 1901, p.7, November 1900, p.5.
15. Howell, 275.
16. LDA 3, 23 July 1903, Moore to Rev. A.I. Snyder, Freelton, Ontario. LDA 5, 7 May 1906, Shearer to Rev. Dr. F. Crafts. ADV II:10 (July 1905) "Sunday Excursions in the Name of Religion."
17. LDA 2, 3 July 1901, Shearer to Rev. W.R. Johnston. LDA 5, 17 November 1905, Moore to Rev. A.K. Sharp. LDA 2, 17 June 1901, Shearer to W.R. Johnston. ADV I:2 (October 1903) "The Bishops of the Anglican Communion and the Lord's Day."
18. LDA 4, 24 August 1904, [Shearer] to Rev. S.C. Murray.
19. LDA 72, Minute Book Special Committees 1902-5, Moore to Caven, 10 December 1902.
20. ADV II:2 (November 1904).
21. ADV II:5 (February 1905).
22. Public Archives of Ontario, Record Group (RG) 4-32, file 1902-1227, 20 September 1902, Herbert D. Smith, County Crown Attorney, to Acting Deputy Attorney General Allan M. Dymond.
23. LDA 4, 11 March 1905, Moore to Rev. H.A. Cook.
24. ADV I.2, (October 1903).
25. Archives of the Roman Catholic Archdiocese of Montreal, file 782.046, "Lord's Day Alliance," 5 November 1903, Vicar General Alexander MacDonald of Antigonish County to Bruchési; for Roman Catholic-Protestant relations in Nova Scotia before 1900, see Waite.
26. ADV I:12 (October 1903) and II:2 (November 1904).
27. Archives of the Roman Catholic Archdiocese of Montreal, file 782.046, "Lord's Day Alliance," 14 January 1904, Bruchési to Shearer; 730.113, "Gouvernement Federale & Provinciale 1903–04," 22 February 1904, Bishop of Sherbrooke to Bruchési, 10 March 1904, vicar general of Québec to Bruchési.
28. Archives of the Roman Catholic Archdiocese of Montreal, file 730.003, "Gouvernement Federale & Provincial 1903–04," 25 March 1904.
29. LDA 2, 31 July 1900, Shearer to Hon. J.R. Stratton.

30. ADV II:3 (December 1904).
31. LDA 4, 11 March 1905, Moore to Rev. H.A. Cook.

CHAPTER TWO

1. Joint Anglican pastoral in ADV III:2 (December 1905), "The Anglican Bishops and the Lord's Day"; for correspondence about Anglican participation, LDA 5, 25 September 1905, 15 and 23 February 1906, Shearer to the Bishop of Saskatchewan; 14 December 1905, 19 February 1906, Shearer to Archdeacon Lloyd; 18 December 1905, Shearer to Richardson, and 8 August 1905, Shearer to Chegwin.
2. ADV III:4 (February 1906) "Views on Sunday Observance of the Roman Catholic Bishops of Canada."
3. LDA 5, 12 January 1906, Moore to the Rev. J.L. George of Montreal, 15 July 1905, Shearer to the Rev. W.S. McLaren of Huntingdon, Quebec, 7 February 1906, Moore to George, etc.
4. LDA 5, 10 November 1905, Shearer to Father McAdam of Antigonish; 18 and 28 December 1905, Shearer to Archbishop O'Brien, 7 December 1905, Shearer to D.D. Mackenzie, M.P., North Sydney. ADV III:6 "Orangemen of Nova Scotia and the Lord's Day Bill."
5. LDA 5, 20 July 1905, Shearer to I.B. Colwell of Freeport, Nova Scotia.
6. Waterman, 114; LDA 5, 4 July 1905, where Shearer writes, "It is a disgrace to Pictou County if a sheet of that kind can carry on such a campaign with impunity, and nothing will be so effective as a vigorous kick, accompanied by boycotting features ... of course, this would have to be done privately." Others of like type are LDA 5, 10 May 1906, Shearer to Editor of the *Sunday School Times,* Philadelphia, and to the *Homiletic Review,* New York, and 8 June 1906, Shearer to Messrs Funk & Wagnalls.
7. ADV III:3 (January 1906) "Quebec Provincial Annual Meeting."
8. LDA 6, Correspondence 1902-13, File 1906; Sales and Labour, 1 February 1906, Moore to J.J. Foy, Attorney General, Toronto.
9. *The Book of Mormon* states that the sabbath must be observed (p.161, verse 16) and that it was observed by the Mormon ancestors, the people of Nephi (p.128, verse 5, and p.169, verse 23). See also LDA 5, 7 August 1905, Shearer to Moore, and 24 July 1905, Shearer to the Rt. Reverend (Mormon) Bishop of Raymond, Alberta.
10. This list included McMullen, Macdonald, Stewart, Guthrie, Thomas Greenway, Thomas Martin, A.H. Scott, opposition leader Borden, Telford, etc., as seen in LDA 41, Minutes of the executive Board 1901–18, 9 November 1905 and LDA 5, 16 November 1905 and 5 July 1905, Shearer to Ralph Smith.
11. LDA 5, 8 June 1906, Shearer wrote to Messrs Funk & Wagnalls, of the *Homiletic Review,* New York, to claim that over 30,000 people read the

Advocate and that if the *Review* continued its advertisements for the Seventh-Day Adventists, then 30,000 people would be informed of it. Later, Shearer claimed 36,000 people received the *Advocate,* 9 October 1906, Shearer to A.S. Busby, Canadian Newspaper and Magazine Subscription Agency.

12. LDA 5, 12 January 1905, Shearer to Laurier, (actually 1906, since it is filed in sequence and refers to the December 1905 *Advocate*).
13. NAC, RG13 A2, vol.139, file 1208, 20 November 1905. "The Draft Dominion Lord's Day Act."
14. Archives of the Roman Catholic Archdiocese of Montreal, file 730-004, "1906–1907 Gouvernement federale," 13 April 1906 Bruchési to Fitzpatrick; LDA 68, p.187 and ADV III:8 (June 1906) "His Grace Archbishop Bruchesi Again Speaks Out On The Lord's Day Question."
15. Letter, 16 June 1906, Laurier to Bruchési.
16. HC (1906) 1014.
17. LDA 5, 7 May 1906, Shearer to Wilbur F. Crafts, Washington, D.C.
18. HC *Appendix* 1906, Committees of Representative Jews on pp.15–7, letter by Goldstein on p.13, full text of amendment on p.146.
19. ADV III:8 (June 1906) "The Battle At Ottawa."
20. HC (1906) 5630.
21. HC (1906) 5638.
22. HC (1906) 5636.
23. HC (1906) 6363.
24. Aylesworth, HC (1906) 6295-6. Miller, HC (1906) 6305.
25. HC (1906) 6291–92.
26. HC (1906) 6347, spoken by John W. Daniel, a Conservative and a Methodist.
27. British subjects, HC (1906) 6308, by Emmanuel Devlin, a Roman Catholic; on Christianity, HC (1906) 6296, Lavergne.
28. HC (1906) 6303 by J.G. Horace Bergeron, a Roman Catholic and HC (1906) 6316 by William S. Fielding, a Baptist.
29. HC (1906) 6356.
30. HC (1906) 5779.
31. HC (1906) 6563, Aylesworth.
32. HC (1906) 7210.
33. HC (1906) 7308–9.
34. LDA 5, 2 October 1906, Moore to H.A. Thorne of Butternut Ridge, New Brunswick.
35. Waterman, 116.
36. Tucker, 733.

CHAPTER THREE

1. LDA 5, 14 July 1906, Shearer to J.B. Mitchell.
2. LDA 72, file "International Federation of Sunday Rest Associations of America. Executive Committee 1904–10"; Pettibone, 34, and, for example, the Federal Council of Churches 1908; LDA 5, 24 August 1906, Shearer to Rev. Dr. W. Crafts, Washington, D.C. ADV III:10 (August–September 1906); "World-wide Revival in Lord's Day Observance"; LDA 5, 16 October 1906, Shearer to Rev. Elie Deluz, Geneva, Switzerland; ADV II:11 (October 1906) "The Japanese and the Lord's Day," "China Declares for the Sabbath"; VI:3 (December 1908) "Our European Letter"; VII:8, (June 1910) "China and the Lord's Day."
3. ADV IV:8 (August-September 1907) "The New General Secretary"; ADV VI:3 (December 1908) "Provincial Annual Meetings."
4. LDA 5, 24 November 1906, Shearer to Laurier, 3 October 1906, Moore to Hill, etc.; LDA 5, 27 August 1906, Moore to Rev. C.S. Deeprose, Sherbrooke, Quebec.
5. LDA 144, *Montreal Witness,* 15 July 1909.
6. LDA 142, *Eleventh Annual Report of the Quebec (Provincial) Lord's Day Alliance 1910–1911,* p.5; for Louis St. Laurent: National Archives of Quebec, E17-267, file 4024, 4 October 1909; for controversies, E17-1461, "Index 1910" and E17-271, file 828, 15 February 1910, Moore to the Attorney General.
7. National Archives of Quebec, E17-273, file 1995, 6 May 1910, Moore to Gouin. ADV VII:7 (May 1910) "Another Battle in Montreal."
8. LDA 6, 29 July 1909, E.E. Boyce to Moore; LDA 6, 10 August 1909, J.R. Booth to Moore; Public Archives of Ontario, RG4-32, file 1910-1278; LDA 6, 8 January 1908, T.P. Phelan, president of the Canadian Railway News Company to Moore, and 3 August 1909, Phelan to W.G. Hanna.
9 LDA 6, 7 September 1910, C.G. Dunlop to Moore and 9 September, Moore to Dunlop.
10. LDA 6, 7 June 1911, W.R. Mackay to the Alliance; quotation in LDA 6, 12 June 1911, John Shirreffs to W.M. Mackay; LDA 6, 19 June 1911, Hudon to W.G. Hanna.
11. LDA 6, 23 June 1911, J. Maxwell to the Rev. W.J. Hanna.
12. LDA 6, 26 June 1912, J.R. Turnbull to the Alliance.
13. Public Archives of Ontario, RG4-32, files 1909-1703 and 1910-789; ADV VII:7 (May 1910) "Effort to Evade Sunday Laws," and LDA 146, *London Free Press,* 9 February 1910, "Dominion Charter Settles the Matter"; NAC, RG13 A2, volume 1923, file 1390, 8 October 1912, Rochester to the Hon. C.H. Doherty; 21 October 1912, memo Rochester to Doherty; 28 October 1912, E.S. Hunt to Prime Minister Borden re Petition from London and Lake Erie Traction Co.

14. LDA 144, *Canadian Rational Sunday League* [Toronto, June 1907] Broadsheet; Alliance's response: ADV VI:10 (July–August 1909) "Rational(?) Sunday League."
15. ADV IV:6 (June 1907) "The Irrational Sunday League's First Effort Proves Abortive."
16. LDA 144, "Action of 'Rational Sunday League' at the Annual Meeting, in Toronto, October, 1907. Rev. V.J. Gilpin, London, Chairman," Typescript, 1p.
17. LDA 144, 24 October 1907. "Call for Meeting On Sunday Cars. Rational League Promises Hot Fight—Getting Desperate Now"; *Toronto Star,* 24 October 1907, "Rational Sunday League is Short"; *Free Press,* 26 October 1907, "League Not Broke. Can Get Money"; 12 November 1907, "Letters to the Editor"; *Advertiser,* 8 November 1907, "Rational Sunday League Answered."
18. LDA 2, 14 November 1900, Shearer to W.H. Hayes, Windsor.
19. ADV I:8 (April 1904) "The Windsor Standard"; LDA 3, 9 June 1904, [Shearer] to James Duncan.
20. LDA 6, 1 February 1906, Moore to J.J. Foy.
21. LDA 6, 22 May and 8 June 1908, Edward Bayly, Attorney General solicitor, to Moore.
22. LDA 6, 16 November 1909, T.A. Moore to W.G. Hanna, 15 January 1910, J.J. Foy to Moore.
23. LDA 6, 1 April 1910, A.J. Cadman to Hanna.
24. LDA 6, 12 March 1909, the Alliance to the ministers and Alliance officers of Latchford, Haileybury, New Liskeard, etc.; Public Archives of Ontario, RG4-32, file 1906-1946, 17 August 1906, Moore to Attorney General, J.J. Foy, LDA 6, 27 October 1913, J.J. Sparling to Rochester for construction and films in a Catholic church and 9 July 1909, the Reverend P.T. Pilkey to the Alliance; Public Archives of Ontario, RG4-32, files 1907-1595, 1909-330, 1909-1172, 1910-1042, 1910-1058, 1910-1349, and 1912-900.
25. LDA 8, 10 June 1914, Rev. F.O. Nichol to the Alliance.
26. LDA 145, *Mail and Empire,* 1 February 1912, "Female Preacher Disturbs Meeting . . . Riot Threatened Until Mrs. Baker, Female Evangelist, is Firmly Ejected."
27. LDA 5, 22 June 1906, Shearer to the Reverend W.J. Hinchey, Nanton, Alberta; also ADV III:7 (May 1906) "The Battle at Ottawa."
28. ADV II:1 (October 1904) "British Columbia—Notes By The Way."
29. LDA 5, 9 December 1905, Shearer to J.R. Seymour *et al;* 18 December 1906, Shearer to James Ramsay, Vancouver.
30. LDA 5, 17 February 1906, Shearer to the Rev. H.S. Akehurst.

31. ADV III:4 (February 1906) "Well Done Vancouver!"; LDA 144, *Vancouver Daily Province,* 18 February 1907, "Record Number of 'Drunks' Arrested, for Many persons obtained Liquor in Resorts of Nearby Towns"; *Vancouver World,* 26 April 1907, "Sunday Drinking"; *Montreal Witness,* 22 October 1907, "Will Watch Sunday Sellers. Good Templars"; 5 November 1907, "Of Course There Is Sunday Drinking"; LDA 145, *Victoria Colonist,* 19 May 1908, "Pass Gleason Bylaw in Amended Form. Measure to Enforce Sunday Closing Finally Gets the Council's Assent"; LDA 144, *Vancouver Daily Province,* 5 September 1908, "For a Strict Sunday and a Real Dry Province," and ADV VII:7 (May 1910) "No Liquor With Sunday Meals"; Provincial Archives of British Columbia, GR429, box 14, file 1-554, 5 March 1907.
32. Re Turner and Laity (1913), *(sub nom. R. v. Laity);* also *Rex v. Walden;* ADV VII:6 (April 1910) "Police Up to Date"; LDA 149, *Manitoba Free Press,* 9 May 1913, "May Not Apply to Vancouver Island"; ADV IX:10 (October 1913) "Vancouver Island and the Lord's Day Act."
33. LDA 142, "Annual Report of the General Executive, 1910-11" in *Ontario Lord's Day Alliance Annual Reports,* p.5.
34. LDA 8, 23 July 1914, Rochester to W.G. Jackson.
35. Howell, 271.

CHAPTER FOUR

1. LDA 149, 4 September 1914.
2. LDA 9, 2 March 1915, Rochester to H. Bamwell re the National Car Co., Hamilton.
3. For Prairies, LDA 9, 20 October 1915, Robin Hood Mills to Rochester; for government announcement, ADV XIV:3 (April–May 1918) "Sunday Work on Farm and Garden," LDA 150, *Regina Leader,* 12 March 1918, "Sunday Work on the Farm," *Toronto Telegram,* 30 April 1918, "Stop the Waste of Food," *Montreal Gazette,* 4 July 1918, "Permit Gardeners to Work on Sunday. Outremont City Council Direct Police"; *Regina Leader,* 1 October 1918, "Lord's Day Act To Be Strictly Enforced Now."
4. LDA 10, 11 May 1916, telegram, Rev. H.A. Goodwin, Buctouche, N.B., to Rochester; 15 May 1916, Goodwin, Central Methodist Church, Moncton, to Rochester re Buctouche, and 17 May 1916, Rochester to Goodwin.
5. LDA 10, 18 August 1916, Rochester to the editor of the *Ottawa Citizen;* see also 22 August 1916, Rochester to editor.
6. LDA 8, *c.*13 June 1915, D. Ellison, Fort William, Ontario, to Shearer.
7. LDA 143, *Toronto Globe,* 25 September 1915, "Lord's Day Alliance Gets After Sportsmen. Organization Wants to Know the Nature of S.P.A.'s Sunday Concerts. On the heels of the objection raised by the Methodist Social Reform Association regarding the showing in this city of the

Johnson–Willard fight pictures"; LDA 8, 11 November 1915, Rev. James H. Boyd, London, to Rochester; LDA 10, 29 March 1916, Rev. D.W. Snider to Rev. J.D. Fitzpatrick, Hamilton.

8. ADV XIV:3 (April-May 1918) "Various Matters."
9. LDA 10, 23 June 1916, 12 July 1916, Barber to Rochester; LDA 10, 14 July 1916, Rochester to Mr. James Butters, Niagara Falls; 31 July 1916, Mrs. D.J. Nichols, Welland Co. Pres. WCTU, Niagara Falls, to Snider.
10. LDA 7, 26 March [1914], 28 April 1914, 30 October 1914, Rev. James Barber, Methodist, Niagara Falls, to Rochester.
11. LDA 7, 17 October 1914, Rev. John H. MacVicar, St. [*sic*] John, N.B., to Rochester; 27 October 1914, Rochester to MacVicar; 28 November 1914, Rochester to the Mayor of Saint John; 1 December 1914, the Mayor of Saint John to Rochester; 3 December 1914, A.A. Wilson, Saint John, to Rochester.
12. LDA 8, 20 April 1915, Rev. Hugh S. Dougall, St. Thomas, Ontario, to Moore; also 20 April 1915, Rev. D. Rogers, St. Thomas, to Moore (an Anglican minister presided); 22 April 1915, Rev. W.A. Bremner, St. Thomas, to Rev. D.W. Snider.
13. LDA 8, 12 November 1915, Rev. D.W. Snider to Rev. James H. Boyd, London, Ontario.
14. For end of New Brunswick concerts, LDA 7, 14 December 1914, Rev. Herbert E. Thomas to Rochester; LDA 8, 5 May 1915, Rochester to Rev. W.A. Stellarton, Nova Scotia; for Saskatchewan, LDA 7, 1 December 1914, James A. Hallan, Sask. Pres. LDA, to Rochester.
15. ADV I:3 (November 1903) "Emperor and Empress of Germany and the Lord's Day"; an ominous indication that all was not well with the German emperor came when the *London Free Press* in 1914 reported that the emperor had bought sausages on a Sunday: LDA 149, 25 May 1914, "German Emperor Must Buy Sausage Saturday Night. Courts Decide He Has No Special Standing in Trade and Must Obey Laws."
16. LDA 10, 9 February 1916, The Record Publishing Co., Niagara Falls, Ont., to Rochester re their loss of advertising; also ADV XIII:10 (November 1916) "Sunday Papers, Windsor, Ont.," and LDA 11, 25 May 1916, Rochester to J.A. Auld, Mayor of Amherstburg, Ontario.
17. Public Archives of Ontario, RG4-32, file 1915-1074, newspaper clippings; LDA 11, 25 November 1916, Snider to H.L. Chilver, Snider to W.E. Prescott [actually for Pescott]; also ADV XV:2 (February 1919) "With whom we have to do"; LDA 10, 3 January 1916, E.H. Macklin, president and general manager of the *Manitoba Free Press* to Rochester; LDA 11, 3 December 1916, Pescott to Snider. I am grateful to Mr. Lawlor Rochester for allowing me to consult the records compiled by his uncle, Lloyd B. Rochester, in *The John Rochester Family in Canada,* listed in the bibliog-

raphy. Lloyd Rochester was Dr. Rochester's nephew. See also LDA 10, 3 January 1916, Rochester to E.H. Macklin, president of the *Manitoba Free Press.*

18. LDA 9, 9 April 1915, Canadian Explosives Ltd, Nobel, Ontario, to the Rev. D.W. Snyder.
19. LDA 9, 15 November 1915, Hawthorn Mills to Snider.
20. ADV XI:3 (March 1915) "Fourteenth International Lord's Day Congress."
21. LDA 79, "Ontario Lord's Day Annual Report. 1915," p.2; ADV XI:1 (January 1915) p.8, and ADV XIII:3 (March 1916) "Extract from the Address of the Right Rev. The Lord Bishop of Toronto, at the Annual Meeting of the Ontario Lord's Day Alliance." He claimed the war was God's punishment for neglecting Sunday observance.
22. LDA 9, 23 March 1915, Walter E. Sieber to the Lord's Day Alliance re the Canadian Explosive Company, Nobel, Ontario.
23. LDA 10, 17 July 1916, H. Lamont to Rev. D.W. Snider.
24. LDA 10, 13 October 1916, Rochester to Lt.-Gen. Sir Sam Hughes.
25. LDA 7, 2 June 1914, Mrs. R. Boville, Blind River, Ont., V.P. of WCTU to Rochester; 9 July 1914, Mr. A.S. Evans of Upper Gagetown, N.B. to Rochester.
26. ADV X:8 (July-August 1914) "Word and Work.... Never before ..."; LDA 11, 18 March 1919, Rochester to Mingie.
27. LDA 9, 14 December 1915, Hon. I.B. Lucas to Snider.
28. Provincial Archives of British Columbia, GR1323, reel B2146, file 1153-1-1918, 2 August 1918, Chairman to J.W. DeB. Farris, Attorney General.
29. ADV X:11 (November 1914) "The Personal Liberty League"; LDA 148, *Toronto Globe,* 6 September 1919, "Liberty League Humbug"; LDA 148, 1919, "Border Cities Liberty League. Organized to Oppose All Legislation." (n.p., n.d.); Hallowell, 70, 86; Fort William officials allowed the Sunday opening of refreshment booths to sell ice cream, soda water, and other things on Sunday supposedly to give the population an alternative to alcohol: LDA 8, 29 July 1914, Mayor of Fort William, Ontario, to Rochester.
30. LDA 9, 8 September 1915, Rev. George A. McLean, Whitby, to Rochester.
31. LDA 10, 20 March 1916, Fred Ross to the Alliance re Debden; LDA 11, 13 March 1916, Rev. T.H. Lockhart, Union Church, Henribourg, Saskatchewan, to Rochester; LDA 8, Rev. Robert Eadie about Ottawa entertainments to Rochester, 2 July 1915.
32. LDA 11, 6 April 1916, Rev. Fred Brasier, Rector Grand Falls, N.B., to Rochester.
33. ADV XIII:11 (December-January 1916–1917) "Give Church a Chance."
34. Public Archives of Ontario, RG4-32, file 1915-1793, "Re Sale of Newspapers on Sunday at Cobalt," 24 June 1918, A.W. Hone, Methodist missionary, to the Attorney General.

35. LDA 149, *La Presse,* 3 December 1915, "Tout Travail Le Dimanche Cessera"; ADV XIII:1 (January 1916) "Some Recent Events." *R. v. Donnacona Paper Co.* (1917).
36. LDA 9, Mrs. John Gillis, Montreal, to Rochester, 17 May 1915.
37. LDA 9, 14 July 1915, Rochester to Mr. C.E. Dyer, Presbyterian Student Missionary.
38. LDA 8, 24 August 1914, Moore to Rochester; 1 September 1914, R.Y. Tindale to Rochester; LDA 9, 19 September 1914, Rochester to Tindale; LDA 8, 22 October 1914, RNWMP Commissioner's Office, Regina, to Rochester re Luseland and Derrick, Saskatchewan, etc.
39. LDA 142, *Annual Report of the Alberta and British Columbia Lord's Day Alliance* 1914–15, p.11.
40. Provincial Archives of British Columbia, GR1323, file 38-1-18, 20 June 1918, Attorney General to Mayor Todd of Victoria, criticizing his refusal to accept delegated authority. See also L-256-3, 20 June 1918, L-256-1 and 2, 14 November 1919, J.W. deB. Farris, Attorney General, to Rev. C.H. Huestis.
41. LDA 150, 21 July 1916, *Victoria Daily Times,* 21 July 1916, "Sunday Closing By-Law Is Declared Illegal"; Provincial Archives of British Columbia, GR1323, file l-256, 7 February 1918, Peter Gardult, Clerk to the Board of Police Commissioners, Victoria, to the Attorney General, "it is not desirable to prosecute everyone who may be technically guilty . . . "; File 38-1-18, 18 August 1918, Police chief of Victoria sends 70 cases to the Attorney General in one day and then 50–70 cases each week.
42. Public Archives of Nova Scotia, RG10-A-18, (Letterbook 1908) 25 June 1908–18 December 1908, Correspondence between Moore and the Attorney General of Nova Scotia; LDA 6, 1 April 1913, "Extract from Debates of the House of Assembly of Nova Scotia, p. 499" typescript; 10 September 1913, "Extract from Minutes of Meeting of Board of Control of City of Halifax held 4 September 1913" typescript; ADV IX:11 (November 1913) "The Attorney General and The Lord's Day Act."
43. ADV XIII:6 (June 1916) "Outsporting the Sports."
44. For leaflets, LDA 8, 3 September 1914, Rev. J. Edwards, London, Ont., to Rochester; ADV X:9 (September 1914) "The Sunday Press" and "Sunday War Extras"; quotation, 21 September 1914, Rev. H.L. Chilver, Walkerville, Ont., to Rochester.
45. LDA 11, 21 November 1916, Snider, citing the *Catholic Citizen,* to the Hon. I.B. Lucas, Attorney General.
46. Public Archives of Ontario, RG4-32, file 1915-740, 13 May 1915, Rochester to the Hon. I.B. Lucas, Attorney General; *R. v. World Newspaper Co.* (1915); ADV XI:6 (June 1915) "Making Money Out of Public Anxiety"; LDA 9, 10 July 1915, Rochester to Rev. H.L. Chilver, Walkerville, Ont.

47. LDA 9, 3 August 1915, D.C. Bawtinheimer, Walkerville, to Rochester; Public Archives of Ontario, RG4-32, file 1915-1074, 29 January 1916, *Detroit Free Press* to Edward Bayly, Solicitor to the Attorney General; 21 February 1916 and 14 March 1916, Bayly to the Attorney General.
48. LDA 9, 19 September 1915, Rev. E. Pescott *et al.* to Rochester; 10 September 1915, Rev. A.J. Love, Port Lambton, to Rochester.
49. LDA 11, 3 May 1916, Rev. A.J. Love to the Alliance.
50. Public Archives of Ontario, RG4-32, file 1915-1074, 10 February 1916, Windsor Board of Trade to the Attorney General; [November 20, 1916] Municipal Council of Windsor to the Attorney General; November 27, 1916, A.W. Jackson, Mayor of Windsor to the Hon. I.B. Lucas, Attorney General, asking for local option.
51. LDA 143, *Toronto Globe,* 22 January 1918, "Wilson Commands Forces to Observe Sabbath."
52. LDA 11, 15 November 1916, Rochester to the editor of the Windsor *Evening Record;* LDA 10, 6 January 1916, Hugh MacKay, manager *Evening Province and Standard* (Regina) to Rochester; LDA 11, January 1916, M.C. McCullough, Prince Albert, Sask., to Rochester, re Seattle and British Columbian newspapers.
53. Provincial Archives of Alberta, 83.192, file 400, 8 September 1919, Charles H. Huestis to A.G. Browning, deputy Attorney General.
54. LDA 150, *Sarnia Observer,* 16 September 1918, "Gasoline Kicker Was Advised to Wear White Flag"; *Moncton Times,* 13 September 1918, "Gasoline-Less Sunday in Montreal Has Been Failure. French Section of the City Paid Little or No Heed to the Appeal to Save Gasoline, but the English-Speaking Section, Generally Speaking, Observed the Day"; *Quebec Chronicle,* 20 September 1918, "Gasless Sunday Well Observed"; *Regina Post,* 23 September 1918, "Montreal Fails In Observance of 'Gasless' Sunday"; *Ottawa Citizen,* 25 September 1918, "No Respect for the 'Gas' Slacker"; *Montreal Star,* 17 October 1918, "Can Now Motor on Sundays. Washington Lifts the Ban and Canada Will Follow Suit."
55. LDA 148, *Presbyterian Witness,* 30 August 1919, "Correspondence. What is the Matter with Canada?"

CHAPTER FIVE

1. LDA 142, *Report of World Commission On The Christian Sabbath. Read at the Third World's Christian Citizenship Conference. Pittsburgh, PA., U.S.A. By Dr. Wm. M. Rochester, Chairman. Published by the National Reform Association* (Pittsburgh n.d.), p.6.
2. Provincial Archives of British Columbia, RG1323, file L256-2, 8 November 1919, L.D.A. secretary for Alberta and British Columbia, Charles H. Huestis to the Hon. J.W. Farris, Attorney General; 31 October 1919, Huestis to all Christian ministers in British Columbia and Alberta.

3. ADV XV:4 (April 1919) "The Returned Soldier"; For workers dying, ADV XVII:2 (February 1921) "Annual Report. The Lord's Day Alliance-Quebec and Maritime Provinces"; Also LDA 13, 27 July 1925, Rev. T.E. Richards to the Rev. A.I. Terryberry re the Grimsby waterworks; Provincial Archives of British Columbia, RG1323, file L256-27, 25 August 1922, F. Watson to the Attorney General; HC (1926–1927) 1060; LDA 14, 25 October 1927, the Rev. George G. Webber to Charles Stewart, minister of the interior; LDA 14, 4 February 1929, the Rev. Charles Huestis to Mr. W.H. Bischoff, general Superintendent, Dominion Iron and Steel Co., Sydney, N.S.; Provincial Archives of British Columbia, file L256-27, 19 May 1925, Consolidated Mining and Smelting Co. of Canada to the Attorney General; LDA 13, 14 November 1925, Chaudiere Local no. 34, International Brotherhood of Paper Makers, to Rochester.
4. ADV XV:6 (June 1919) "A Place in the Sun"; LDA 142, Royal Commission on Industrial Relations, *Report of Commission appointed under Order-in-Council (P.C. 670) to enquire into Industrial Relations in Canada together with a Minority Report and Supplementary Report* (printed as a supplement to the LABOUR GAZETTE, July 1919) p.10; NAC, RG13 A2 vol.396, file 152, "Lord's Day Act. Sundry questions. Consolidated fyle" 22 January 1925, James Murdoch, Minister of Labour, to Ernest Lapointe, Minister of Justice; Privy Council Order 1537, 7 September 1925, re the International Labour Conference of the League of Nations.
5. LDA 157, 12 January 1924, "The Church Union Controversy."
6. LDA 13, 9 May 1925, Mingie to Rochester; LDA 12, 1 May 1924, LDA 13, 5 May 1925, and LDA 13, 5 June 1925.
7. LDA 13, 23 December 1925, Mingie to Rochester.
8. ADV XXI:7 (July 1925) "Quite New."
9. ADV XXII:9 (September 1926) "Mistaken"; ADV XXI:10 (October 1925) "Modern Scribes and Pharisees. Ontario Sunday Called Bigotry."
10. Allen, "The Social Gospel as the Religion of the Agrarian Revolt," 174-86 in Berger and Cook, 181.
11. NAC, RG13 A2, vol.369, file 152, 26 January 1920, C.K. Bourne, secretary of the Grain Growers Association of Nipawin, Saskatchewan, to the Minister of Justice.
12. Vol.271, file 1669, 15 September 1922, E.L. Newcombe, Deputy Minister of Justice, re complaint by Chas. Harrington, St. Giles Rectory, Estevan.
13. ADV XVI:10 (October 1920) "Liberty League Protests"; LDA 153, *Vancouver Province,* 13 April 1922, "Anti-Blue Sunday League Gets Busy"; *Victoria Times,* 19 April 1922, "Establish League to Oppose Drastic Sunday Law Enforcement Here"; *Victoria Colonist,* 25 April 1922, "Blue Sundays"; Provincial Archives of British Columbia, RG1323, file L256-1,

8 May 1922, Dunlop and Foot, attorneys for the Anti-Blue Sunday League, to the Attorney General.

14. Provincial Archives of British Columbia, RG1323, file L256-1, 25 October 1922, Office of the Board of Police Commissioners to the Attorney General; 2 December 1922, J.G. Shearer to the Attorney General, and ADV XVIII:12 (December 1922) "Victoria."
15. LDA 153, *Victoria Colonist,* 16 May 1922, "The Lord's Day Act"; the *Victoria Colonist,* 25 April, editorials 11, 12, and 13 May.
16. LDA 152, *Victoria Colonist,* 15 June 1922, "An Echo of Blue Sunday Campaign. Dr. Rochester and Mr. Herbert Kent Discusses Circumstances of Recent Plebiscite."
17. See Provincial Archives of British Columbia, RG1323, files L289-1, L220-4, L256-1, L256-3, L256-4, L256-11, L256-21, and L256-27, which contain thousands of letters and fiats for the prosecutions from 1919 to 1929 of Chinese and Japanese inhabitants of British Columbia.
18. LDA 154, *Winnipeg Tribune,* 19 October 1922, "Sunday Observance"; ADV XVIII:11 (November 1922) "A Fresh Start"; LDA 155, *Winnipeg Tribune,* 8 February 1923, "Rochester Says Act Ultra Vires of Legislature. Lord's Day Alliance and Seventh Day Adventists Take Opposite Sides"; 15 March 1923, "Dominion Will Not Obstruct Sunday Trains"; LDA 156, *Winnipeg Free Press,* 23 May 1923, "Sunday Trains Held Legal By Appeal Judge"; 29 May 1923, "The Sunday Trains Appeal"; *Winnipeg Tribune,* 19 June 1923, "Manitoba Free of 'Blue' Laws, Court Decides. Theatres, Amusements, Games, Business, etc., Held Legal on Sabbath"; *Winnipeg Free Press,* 20 June 1923, "Craig Declares Lord's Day Act Needs Revision. Amendments to the B.N.A. Act or Appeal to the Privy Council Recommended. Movie Men Meet"; quoted in several B.C. papers. See also LDA 159, *Victoria Colonist,* 14 January 1925, "Note and Comment By R.B.D."; *Calgary Albertan,* 8 December 1924, "City Now Breaks The Principle of Lord's Day Act."
19. *Re Jorgenson* 1923; *Demchenko v. Fricke* 1926; ADV XX:4 (April 1924) "Saskatchewan Concerned."
20. NAC, RG13 A2, vol.396, file 152, 16 January 1926 "Memo re. expense of the appeal by the Lord's Day Alliance to the Privy Council"; 25 April 1927, R.W. Craig, Attorney General of Manitoba, C.H. Huestis, Lord's Day Alliance of Canada, and H.A. Bergman, solicitor, Alliance, to the Hon. Ernest Lapointe, Minister of Justice; 29 November 1927, "Memo re. The Lord's Day Act. by W. Stuart Edward, Deputy Minister of Justice to John Allen, Deputy Attorney General of Manitoba"; copies in LDA 14.
21. LDA 13, 14 May 1925, K.M. Millar, Fort Erie, to the Rev. A.I. Terryberry.
22. ADV XV:6 (June 1919) "A Correspondent to the Toronto Star."

23. ADV XVI:6 (June 1920) "Windsor, Ont."; ADV XVI:9 (September 1920) "Sunday Advertising"; ADV XVII:8 (August 1921) "More Illegal Advertising" LDA 161, 1926, "Cadillac Burlesque"; ADV XXI:10 (October 1925) "Advertising Sunday"; Public Archives of Ontario, RG56 A1, box 5, file 8, "Theatre Branch Early Correspondence. Sunday Shows 1917–1932."
24. Public Archives of Ontario, RG56 A1, box 1, "Censorship Files" 23 June 1921, Social Service Council of Canada to the Attorney General; LDA 143, *Victoria Times,* 20 May 1921, "Methodists Warned of Sunday Motion Picture Campaign. Way Being Paved For People to Resent Blue Laws, Says Rev. Dr. Huestis; Conference Wants Censorship More Efficient and Enlightened or Abolished."
25. LDA 154, 29 October [1922] "Annual Meeting of the Grenfell Branch of the Lord's Day Alliance."
26. LDA 14, 5 July 1928, the Rev. R.G. Howell to Webber: "That such things can be done at all is a commentary upon the spiritual attitude of the men who are given command of our younger men, who don the uniform of soldiers of the King, sworn to maintain the laws and freedom of the State, and yet urged to desecrate the Sabbath day by Field Sports in the afternoon, and a free for all Beach party with bonfires, common and coarse songs, and ribald jests in the evening hours"; Liberty League: ADV XVI:3 (March 1920) "Revived"; Public Archives of Ontario, RG4-32, file 1925-2416, Edward Bayly memorandum for the Premier; file 1925-2963, 28 November 1925, F.W. White, M.P.P., Windsor, to Bayly.
27. LDA 13, 11 May 1925, A.I. Terryberry, Ontario Lord's Day Alliance, to the Rev. Ivan E. Kennedy, Hornepayne, Ontario; LDA 161, *Hamilton Spectator,* 9 April 1926, "Sunday Baseball Taboo, But Golf Can Be Played. Boys Wonder Why Distinction Drawn"; LDA 156, *Toronto Star,* 7 May 1923, "Golf On Sunday Tends To Empty Pews-Rochester."
28. LDA 13, 3 August 1925, Mrs. Hammersley, Hespeler, Ontario, to the Lord's Day Alliance.
29. Also found in ADV XVI:1 (January 1920) "The Sabbath and the State."
30. LDA 156, (Nova Scotia) *Sydney Record,* 22 October 1923, "K.K.K. Branch Forming Here Pastor Hears. When Law Officers Fail, Drastic Steps Follow."
31. Provincial Archives of British Columbia, RG1323, file L256-3, 9 January 1924.

CHAPTER SIX

1. JPA, Box 39, file 2, item 59 (abbreviated as JPA, 39-2,59), "Prière à Saint Joseph pour la sanctification du dimanche." 300 days of indulgence granted by Pius X, 1905.

2. French-Canadian sabbatarianism outside Quebec can be seen in JPA, 35-1,59, 15 November 1930, S.S.J.B., Saint Boniface, Manitoba, to Alphonse de la Rochelle, secretary of the Ligue du Dimanche and in 35-1,64 12 June 1931, de la Rochelle to Papin Archambault about the Association Canadienne-française d'Education d'Ontario, Association Canadienne-française de l'Alberta, Association Catholique Franco-canadienne de la Saskatchewan and, from New Brunswick, *L'Evangeline,* Ltd.; *Les Cloches de St Boniface* (Winnipeg) 1902–32.
3. Joseph-Papin Archambault, SJ, "Les trois phases de l'École Sociale Populaire" p. 42–50 in *Les vingt-cinq ans de l'École Sociale Populaire. 1911–1936. Une oeuvre de doctrine et de salut* by the E.S.P.:269-70 (juin-juillet 1936) 62p.; also JPA, 38-5,1-32, in which Archambault's sermon plans about Sunday observance were published in the *Bulletin de la Ligue du Sacré Coeur* (1914), 180, and in other religious newspapers.
4. JPA, 34-5,27, 22 November 1923, E. Moreau to Martineau, secretary of the Ligue du Dimanche. Also JPA, 34-5,28-30 and National Archives of Quebec, E17-410, files 4288, 4289, 4290, and 4306; E17 Indexes show that from 1919 to 1931, the pulp-and-paper mills caused the most complaints.
5. National Archives of Quebec, E17-1469, file 1C26-1414A, Index for 1918, and files 363, 365, 366, etc.; ADV XV:6 (July 1919) "It was a Famous Victory."
6. JPA, 34-5,81, "Le Travail Du Dimanche," broadsheet originally published in *Le Bien Public,* 25 January 1927.
7. National Archives of Quebec, E26-35, file 223-1.
8. JPA. 34-5,88, "Lettre Pastorale de Nos Seigneurs les Archevêques et Evêques de la Province civile de Québec, sur la Sanctification du Dimanche" 21 November 1927, p.65; partial translation available in LDA 14, *Montreal Gazette,* 26 November 1927, "Pastoral Reminds of Sunday Duties."
9. JPA, 35-2,45, 9 March 1932.
10. "Le travail du dimanche. Autour d'une fausse manoeuvre," *La Semaine religieuse de Montréal,* vol.89, no.40, 2 October 1930.
11. JPA, 44-4,1, 7 October 1930; 44-4,1, 4 and 36, de la Rochelle to Bray; 44-4,9, Bray to de la Rochelle.
12. National Archives of Quebec, E17-793, file 475, 20 December 1933, memo.
13. JPA, 44-4,68, 3 March 1933, Archambault to de la Rochelle.
14. Rome, *The Jewish Congress Archival Record of 1936;* Arcand: pp. 5A, 12A, 13A, 22A; Laurendeau: p.17A.
15. NAC, RG13 A2, vol.400, file 406, 12 March 1934, the Attorney General of Quebec to the Minister of Justice. 20 June 1934, "Note concernant la demande d'abrogation de l'article de la Loi du dimanche (S.R.Q., 1925, c.199)."

16. Letter, 12 July 1934, "Memo . . . for Mr. Edwards."
17. ADV XIX;11 (November 1923) "Pressing Forward"; also ADV XVIII:11 (November 1922) "Again Active" for other comments.
18. LDA 14, 10 April 1928, Huestis to the Reverend James Fee, Montreal.
19. LDA 15, 22 June 1929, Mingie to Huestis.
20. LDA 15, 10 December 1929, Mingie to Huestis; 13 December 1929, Huestis to Mingie.
21. LDA 15, 16 March 1932, Huestis to Mingie; LDA 16, 3 March 1930, Mingie to Huestis.
22. JPA, 35-2,55, 8 April 1932, Huestis to Alphonse de la Rochelle, secretary of the Ligue du Dimanche.
23. JPA, 42-3,13, 1 March 1932, Alphonse de la Rochelle, secretary of the Ligue, to Arthur Sauvé, Minister of Post; JPA, 42-3,16, 9 March 1932, 42-3,83, 19 March 1937, 42-3,89, 24 March 1938, Webber to de la Rochelle; LDA 15, 20 March 1929, E. Fabre Surveyer, president of the Ligue, to Huestis.
24. JPA, 35-2,193, 23 May 1933, Huestis to de la Rochelle.
25. LDA 18, 17 January 1934, Huestis to J.C. McRuer, re sports in Montreal; JPA, 35-2,206, 23 October 1933, de la Rochelle to Huestis.
26. Allen, *Social Passion,* xxiii, noted some similarities between the two movements: "The social gospel, properly speaking, was a Protestant phenomenon, but an analogous social Catholic movement covered approximately the same years. While it would be tempting to try to weave the Social Gospel and social Catholic movements in Canada into one account, the winds of ecumenism had not yet, in 1914, begun to blow Canadian Catholics and Protestants together, and despite certain similarities in development, the two movements ran on parallel, but largely unconnected, lines."
27. For indexes, National Archives of Quebec, E17-1487 "Index 1936" and E17-1489 "Index 1937"; Price Bros.: E17-1286, file 3515, 8 Avril 1938.
28. JPA, 35-4,77, 29 October 1936, Arthur LaRue to de la Rochelle; National Archives of Quebec, E17-1241, file 515, 6 September 1938, assistant Procurer General reply to the Report of the Inspector for Trois-Rivières.
29. JPA, 35-3,89, 10 October 1934, Lapointe to de la Rochelle: my translation.

CHAPTER SEVEN

1. *Acts and Proceedings of the General Assembly of the Presbyterian Church in Canada,* 1938, "Committee on Evangelism and Church Life and Work," p.106.
2. LDA 15, 2 May 1929, Huestis to H.H. Martin, general secretary, Society for Promoting the Due Observance of the Lord's Day, London, England; 27 June 1929, George McAlpine, secretary of the Church of Scotland Committee on Christian Life and Work, Edinburgh, Scotland, to Huestis.

3. LDA 19, 10 May 1937, G.G. Webber to A.C. Newcomb, L.D.A. Alberta president. p.2.
4. For a typical newspaper article, see LDA 199, *Christian Century,* 9 November 1932, "Sunday Manners. By Charles Herbert Huestis." LDA 80, p.175, 28 January 1937, Minutes of the Meeting of the Lord's Day Alliance of Canada; for misunderstanding of his public statements by another sabbatarian: LDA 14, *Globe,* 28 June 1928, "Was Isaiah Wrong?"
5. *Christianizing the Social Order. A Statement Prepared by a Commission Appointed by the Board of Evangelism and Social Service* (Toronto: The United Church of Canada, 1934).
6. United Church Archives, Personal Papers of T.A. Moore, box 1, file 7, address "The Moderator's Message" 2p. [1932?] Fifth General Council of The United Church of Canada.
7. E.g. Minutes of the British Columbia Conference of the United Church of Canada, Minutes 1934, (Reel 130A in the Provincial Archives of British Columbia) p.264., 1935, p.401, etc.; Board of Evangelism and Social Service of the United Church of Canada, *Annual Report* 1935; *Minutes of Conferences,* 1932ff.
8. LDA 15, 2 September 1929, Huestis to J. Woodford Causer, general secretary of the Imperial Alliance for the Defense of Sunday–Sunday Lay Movement, Westminster, England. LDA 18, 10 December 1935, Huestis to Rev. Dr. D.N. McLachlan, Toronto. See also Pulker, 97.
9. *Journal of Proceedings of General Synod,* 1931, p.129; Anglican Church General Synod Archives, Toronto, MM54.1.R58, *Sunday Observance, a Message From the Archbishop* [Ottawa 1939] 8p.; LDA 199, *Montreal Herald,* 17 December 1938, "Sunday Observance."
10. Public Archives of Ontario, RG4-32, file 1930-3293, 3 November 1930, memo from the Deputy Attorney General to the Attorney General; file 1933-1707, 29 June 1933, Huestis to the Deputy Attorney General.
11. LDA 17, 17 March 1931, Huestis to W.H. Price; NAC, Papers of Prime Minister R.B. Bennett, p.46946, 24 May 1929, Bennett to the Rev. D.A. Armstrong. "My long experience has taught me that it is highly desirable to observe one day in seven as a day of rest and I have not worked on Sunday, neither do I intend to do so—neither do I ask others to work on Sunday for me."
12. NAC, Bennett Papers, p.266770-2, 21 February 1935.
13. P.266895-6, 5 March 1935, R.B. Hanson, Trade and Commerce minister to R.K. Finlayson, private secretary to the prime minister.
14. LDA 17, 26 January 1931, Tom Moore to Huestis. LDA 18, 6 December 1934, Tom Moore to Huestis.
15. International Labor Office, *Report of the governing body of the International Labor Office upon the working of the convention concerning the application of the weekly rest in industrial undertakings* (Geneva 1933); NAC, Bennett Papers, p.266649, 31 January 1935, Huestis to Bennett.

16. NAC, Bennett Papers, p.381432, 17 February 1932, Bennett to M.B. Wilson.
17. LDA 17, 11 December 1931, W.H. Price, Attorney General of Ontario, to Huestis.
18. Public Archives of Ontario, RG4-32, file 1930-3293, 3 November 1930, Deputy Attorney General in a memo to the Attorney General; also file 1931-931, 12 November 1930, memo by I.A. Humphries, Solicitor to the Attorney General.
19. File 1930-1705, 2 July 1930, the Rev. D.N. McLachlan to the Attorney General, Huestis to the Attorney General; also file 1930-32 and LDA 16, 25 September 1930, chief constable of Walkerville to Huestis.
20. LDA 20, *Windsor Star*, 30 December 1938, "'Blue Laws' Irk Hepburn. Premier Backs Conant's Suggestion That They Be Relaxed. Games on Sunday."
21. Provincial Archives of British Columbia, GR1323, file L289-1, 23 June 1930, deputy Attorney General in memo to the Attorney General; 18 July 1930, Attorney General to C. Fairbank.
22. LDA 16, 30 December 1930, Webber to Board of Trade, Dawson Creek, B.C.
23. LDA 18, 15 February 1934, Adam Bell, Deputy Minister of Labour to Webber; 23 May 1935, Bennett to Webber.
24. LDA 16, 24 September 1930, Anonymous to Webber re Vancouver Symphony Society; 20 October 1930, Webber to the Vancouver Alliance; Provincial Archives of British Columbia, GR1323, file L289-1, 18 November 1932, Musicians Union to the Attorney General requesting stay of prosecution against them or the Vancouver Symphony Society which supports them in "grave economic times."
25. LDA 16, 8 September 1930, L.C. Thomas, honorary secretary of the Vancouver Symphony Society, to Webber.
26. LDA 16, 17 September 1930, Pooley to Webber.
27. LDA 199, c.7 October 1930. "An Open Letter to Rev. Geo. G. Webber."
28. Provincial Archives of British Columbia, GR1323, file L289-1, 24 April 1930.
29. LDA 17, 29 July 1933, Webber to Hector Charlesworth, Canadian Radio Commission, Ottawa.
30. Provincial Archives of British Columbia, GR1323, file L289-1, 17 June 1932, 22 July 1932, 18 March 1933, 26 June 1933, etc.; LDA 17, *[Nanaimo] Daily Herald*, 21 January 1933, "An Important Local Case."
31. LDA 17, 19 November 1932, the Venerable Archdeacon Heathcote to R.H. Pooley, Attorney General; also in Provincial Archives of British Columbia, GR1323, file 289-1.

32. LDA 18, September 1934, copy, Lord's Day Alliance of British Columbia to the Hon. Gordon Sloan, Attorney General; Archives of the Roman Catholic Archdiocese of Vancouver, "Pastoral Letter" no.14 by Archbishop Timothy Casey, 11 February 1931, p.38.
33. LDA 17, 10 August 1931, "Outline of Agreement on the Operation of the Lord's Day Act in Banff Alberta, as Approved by the Department of the Interior."
34. LDA 24, August 1932, Webber to J.F. Lymburn, Attorney General of Alberta, re grain elevators; Provincial Archives of Alberta, 79.289, box 24, Attorney General Civil Law, uncatalogued, file 17A-100, Lord's Day Act, Section 2, 15 March 1933, Medicine Hat Ministerial Association to the Attorney General about concerts; 83.192, file 400, 29 February 1934, Deputy Attorney General to the chief constable of Calgary; LDA 18, 22 May 1934, Webber to Lymburn, 20 June 1934, Lymburn to Webber, and 15 August 1934, Webber to Lymburn, etc.
35. LDA 18, 8 August 1934, United Grain Growers, Eastern Division (Manitoba) Superintendent to Webber.
36. Provincial Archives of Alberta, 79.289, Attorney General Civil Law, uncatalogued, box 24, file 17A-100. LDA 17, 14 November 1931, deputy Attorney General of Saskatchewan, A. Blackwood to Webber; LDA 17, 23 June 1933, Webber to J.F. Lymburn, Attorney General, Alberta.
37. Provincial Archives of Alberta, 83.192, file 400; also 75.126, file 3508, 8 September 1926, Deputy Attorney General to the M.L.A. for Gleichen, Alberta; Public Archives of Ontario, RG4-32, file 1928-1364, Deputy Attorney General of Alberta to the deputy Attorney General of Ontario; for attempt by federal government to give Seventh-Day Adventists a legal exemption: NAC, RG13 A2, vol.396, file 152, "Lord's Day Act. Sundry questions. Consolidated fyle," 17 January 1930, "Memorandum for Mr. Chisholm" [from W. Stuart Edwards], and later correspondence.
38. NAC, RG13 A2, vol.369, file 152, "Lord's Day Act. Sundry Questions. Consolidated fyle" 27 April 1923, private secretary, Minister of Justice, to private secretary, minister of justice.
39. LDA 19, 27 August 1937, E.A. Beavon, B.C. Conference of Seventh-Day Adventists to the Lord's Day Alliance.
40. LDA 18, 21 February 1936, Webber to Hugh Farthing, K.C., Calgary.
41. LDA 161, *Calgary Albertan,* 15 November 1927, "Facing Problem of Right to Sell Books on Sunday. Lord's Day Alliance Official Objects to Sale of Religious Work."
42. LDA 18, 28 November 1936, C.F.C.N. to Webber; LDA 18, 12 August 1935, Webber to Huestis.
43. LDA 18, 12 June 1936, Huestis to Webber.
44. LDA 18, 18 September 1936, Webber to Huestis.

45. LDA 20, file "Amusements" 1938-1939, 29 June 1939, the Rev. James E. Beckel to Webber.
46. Public Archives of Ontario, RG4-32, file 1939-242, 21 April 1939, Deputy Attorney General memo to the Attorney General and 3 May 1939, Conant to Deputy Attorney General.

CHAPTER EIGHT

1. Sinclair-Faulkner, 77; also LDA 199 for clippings.
2. *Lord's Day Bulletin,* No.3. (c. 1940), "The Lord's Day"; also LDA 97, "Annual Report for 1940" by Webber.
3. LDA 21, *Vancouver Daily Province,* 28 February 1939, "Viceroy visit plans issued," 6 May 1939, Webber to the C.P.R. and subsequent correspondence.
4. Provincial Archives of British Columbia, RG1323, file L220-3, 28 April 1942, Rev. J.H. Davies, United Church, to the Attorney General; similar ideas in Socknat, *Witness Against War.*
5. Letter, 14 August 1942, Canadian Chaplain Service, District 11, to Col. Lighbody.
6. JPA, 40-7,25, 19 April 1944.
7. LDA 25, 29 April 1943, Walter F. Schroeder, K.C., Ottawa, to Webber; 14 October 1943, Rev. A. Ross Skinner, Eastern Ontario secretary, to Webber.
8. JPA, 36-2,109, 7 October 1941, Ligue du Dimanche to the Auxiliary Bishop of Montreal, Whelan.
9. LDA 169, *Montreal Star,* 5 June 1941, "Quebec Women To Aid Troops."
10. Beck, "Henry Somerville and the Development of Catholic Social Thought in Canada." (Ph.D. 1977), 290; but for a more complete analysis of Toronto Catholic adaptation to English Protestant Toronto, see McGowan, *The Waning of the Green;* contrast the Provincial Archives of British Columbia, RG1323, file L220-3, 28 February 1940, Bishop John C. Cody of Victoria to the Attorney General, asking if the Eucharistic Congress can have a Sunday expedition train and 6 March 1943, asking for permission to show a Sunday film, with the material in the Archives of the Roman Catholic Archdiocese of Toronto, MGPO05 (Political Papers of James C. Cardinal McGuigan—Sunday Laws).
11. LDA 23, 22 November 1941, Webber to the Rev. T.A. MacDonald, C.S.B., Superior of Assumption College.
12. LDA 20, *Globe and Mail,* 1 December 1938, "End The Legalized Sham" editorial; letter to the editor by Webber on 1 December and by Huestis on 2 December.
13. LDA 97, 27 June 1939 minutes, p.2; list of officers, elections, and correspondence in LDA 97.

14. JPA, 38-4,22, and Clément, 68, 90.
15. LDA 21, *London Evening Free Press,* 5 July 1939, "Old Dobbin Runs Poor Second When Racing"; *Goderich Signal-Star,* 13 July 1939, "Canada's Largest International Air Pageant."
16. Zolf and Taylor for a brief and partial view of the relations between churches and the federal government in broadcasting.
17. LDA 21, 28 September 1939, 11 November 1939, Webber to war industries; November 18, 1939, Alliance to the Steel Company of Canada; LDA 22, 17 July 1940, Canadian Railway News to the Alliance; LDA 23, 5 August 1941, Niagara Peninsula Canners to the Alliance; JPA, 40-3,14, January 22, 1940, Report of the inspector for 1939.
18. LDA 22, 27 December 1940, Webber to the Hon. Norman McLarty, minister of labour, Ottawa; 30 December 1940, McLarty to Webber, sending "P.C. 2685. Copy of a Minute of a Meeting of the Committee of the Privy Council, approved by His Excellency the Administrator on the 19th June, 1940" Section 3.
19. LDA 23, *Ottawa Evening Journal,* 18 January 1941, "Sunday Training Banned for Troops in General Order"; LDA 23, 21 February 1941, Webber to the Hon. J.L. Ralston, Minister of Defence; 8 March 1941, Ralston to Webber; 10 March 1941, (H.Q. 420-18-12) (Org.), (H.Q.C. 5208), "Department of National Defence, Army to G.O.C. in Central, Atlantic, Pacific Commands, and All District Officers Commanding," about Military Activities on Sunday.
20. Provincial Archives of British Columbia, RG1323, file L220-3, 9 June 1940, and telegram 20 June 1940, Famous Players Corporation to the Attorney General of British Columbia; Public Archives of Nova Scotia, RG10, series 'F', vol.1, 19 June 1940, telegram from the secretary-treasurer of Famous Players to the Attorney General of Nova Scotia; churches' response: LDA 22, 17 June 1940, "Re Proposed Trans-Canada Sunday Theatre Shows, July 1940" memo by Webber.
21. LDA 24, 16 November 1942, National Film Convener, IODE. To Naval, District, and Air Officers Commanding; 11 November 1942, National Film Convener, IODE, to Webber; copies to Provincial Film Conveners.
22. LDA 24, 10 August 1942, the Reverend W.N. Byers, Alberta and British Columbia field secretary, to Webber; 27 November 1942, Byers to Webber. "Sunday Entertainment of Uniformed Services" 10p., December memoranda of protests from Ministerial Associations. 1 December 1942, "The Council for Social Service of the Church of England in Canada to Dear Colleagues in the Ministry"; 27 November 1942, Alberta Provincial WCTU to Byers; Provincial Archives of British Columbia, RG1323, file L220-3, 31 August 1942, Local 168 of the International Alliance of Theatrical Stage Employees to the Attorney General; LDA 169, 1 December 1942, "On Guard."

23. Public Archives of Ontario, RG56, series A-2, file 4.13, "File Concerning the Lord's Day Alliance of Canada 1939-1945 from the Theatres Branch."
24. LDA 25, 24 March 1943, Ralph P. Bell, director general, Aircraft Production Branch, department of munitions and supply, to Webber.
25. LDA 25, 16 February 1943, 25 March 1943, Ralston to Webber; LDA 199, *Presbyterian Herald* (April 1943) "Sunday: Why? What?" by Webber, discussing *Hush*'s condemnation of the "Bible-toting pew warmers."
26. LDA 199, *Saskatoon Star-Phoenix,* 23 June 1943, "Sunday Movies in Canada? Majority Would Vote 'No'"; *Vancouver Province* "Majority of Canadian People Vote 'No' On Sunday Movies"; *Montreal Star* "Sunday Films?—'Yes' and 'No'"; LDA 25, 23 June 1943, Ralston to Webber; LDA 25, 10 December 1943, "Memorandum Re Sunday Theatre Entertainment For Members of the Active Service Forces" by Webber; *Presbyterian Record* (June 1943) "Sunday Cinemas and the Day of Rest" by Webber.
27. Public Archives of Ontario, RG4-32, file 1942-1008, 1 June 1942, "Report re Case against Chas. Biggart, Lessee of Biggart's Milk Shake Stand, Sunnyside Amusement Area, Toronto, for operating a Wurlitzer Phonograph on Sundays contrary to Section 4 of the Lord's Day Act"; *Evening Telegram,* 31 May 1943, "Seize Juke Box of Jitterbugs at Sunnyside. Determined to End Sunday Battles With Sailors, Police Swoop Down on Group of Dancers"; LDA 25, 18 May 1943, "Re Biggart's Restaurant" by Webber.
28. Provincial Archives of British Columbia, RG1323, file L220-3, 5 December 1940, the Red Cross to the Attorney General; 15 December 1943, executive secretary to the Attorney General; LDA 25, 12 May 1943, "Annual Meeting of the B.C. Branch of the Lord's Day Alliance."
29. LDA 24, *Windsor Daily Star,* 11 April 1942, "Endorses Opposition to Sunday Shows."
30. LDA 22, 25 October 1940, "Press Release for Friday, October 25, 1940, RE: SKI TRAINS" by Conant; *Globe and Mail,* "Sunday Ski Trains Dec. 1 Proposed in Conant Bill."
31. LDA 22, 22 February 1941; Public Archives of Ontario, RG3 (Premiers' Papers), box 216, file "Resolutions 1941" and Archives of the Roman Catholic Archdiocese of Toronto, MGPO05.06 a & b, 25 February 1941.
32. LDA 24, "Democracy, Law And Order in Ontario, a memorandum by the Christian Social Council of Canada, the Lord's Day Alliance of Canada, and the Ontario Temperance Federation, to Members of the Legislative Assembly of Ontario."
33. LDA 25, 20 October 1943, "Working on Sunday, York Farmers Charged."
34. LDA 25, 21 October 1943, "memo."
35. Supposedly to help the war effort, western farmers demanded the right to farm on Sundays long before the order-in-council. LDA 22, Edmonton Journal, 20 January 1940, "U.F.A. Convention"; LDA 169, *Saskatoon Star-*

Phoenix, 15 August 1942, "Sunday Will Be Harvest Working Day Around Here"; LDA 116, "The Lord's Day Alliance 1943 Annual Report for Manitoba, by J.S. Watson," p.3.

36. Barker, 117.

CHAPTER NINE

1. LDA 26, 17 May 1945, Webber to Mr. H.A. Lee, general Passenger Agent, CPR; 28 June 1945, Webber to Mr. J.D. Crabtree; LDA 27, 4 March 1946, Webber to the Rev. W.N. Byers, Calgary, re Powell River.
2. LDA 16, 20 June 1945, Angus J. MacQueen, Saint John, N.B., to Webber; LDA 25, 1944, 1945, United Church resolutions found in files on Service Stations; LDA 26, 30 May 1945, W.W. Judd, secretary of the Council for Social Service of the Anglican Church in a telegram to the Alliance; LDA 26, 14 June 1945, H.B. Snell, secretary of the Toronto Diocesan Council for Social Service, to Webber; *United Baptists Year Book,* 1944, p.314, "Report of the Board of Social Service"; also LDA 27, 14 September 1946, "Brief Submitted on Behalf of the Manitoba Board of the Lord's Day Alliance of Canada" 3p. to R.M. Fisher, Chairman, Committee re retail sale of gasoline.
3. LDA 27, *Globe and Mail,* 15 May 1946, "The New Bureaucracy": "The small owner may find that if his station is to provide him with a livelihood he must work longer than from dawn to dusk"; 28 May 1946, "Unnecessary Regimentation"; *Financial Post,* 25 May 1946, "Spurning the Customer."
4. LDA 27, 27 September 1946, "Look Not Thou Upon A Candy Apple When It Is Red," "Fined $10 for Selling Candy Apples—The Law Is A Hass!", 11 October 1946, "An Unpopular Federal Act," 18 October 1946, "Biggest 'Beef' Inconsistency of Enforcement; It Can't Be Done—Why Keep Up The Farce," and others.
5. For W.A. Lamport's membership, see LDA 71, 27 December 1909; Eric Hutton, "He Changed the Toronto Sunday," *Maclean's Magazine* vol. 65 (July 15, 1952):12-3, 58-9 and *The Canadian Parliamentary Guide 1941,* 525-6.
6. LDA 27, *Toronto Daily Star,* 30 May 1946, "Sunday Ball? 'No,' Say Clergy and Amateurs"; *Globe and Mail* "Champion of Sunday Ball."
7. LDA 29, *Globe and Mail,* 12 June 1948, "Blue Sundays. Ancient Statute, About to Be Repealed, Still Puts Crimp in Sabbath Activity"; 18 June 1948, "Two Ancient Ontario Sabbath Laws Ordered Repealed by Commons Vote"; "Bill 344. An Act to Amend the Lord's Day Act" 14 June 1948; HC (1948), columns 5149, 5358-64: 11-12 George VI ch.58 on 30 June 1948; "Ontario Government Press Release. Issued By Honourable L.E. Blackwell. Subject: Lord's Day Observance." September 10, 1948.

8. *Lord's Day Bulletin,* no. 10 (c.1949) "Canada's Sunday Law."
9. LDA 29, 7 September 1948, Webber to the Very Rev. G.N. Luxton, Dean of Huron, re Port Stanley.
10. Public Archives of Ontario, RG4-02, box 60.3, "1948-49 Lord's Day Act" Dana Porter, Attorney General to all crown attorneys, June 1949; LDA 30, "Ontario Government News Release. Issued by Dana Porter" 7 June 1949.
11. Lister Sinclair, "We All Hate Toronto," 256-78 in *A Play On Words & Other Radio Plays* was "First produced on the series *Panorama* on Thursday, January 17th, 1946, 9:00-9:30 EST on the Trans-Canada Network of the CBC." 267-8.
12. LDA 18, 20 March 1947, Webber to Charles Jennings, CBC; Jennings reply, 25 March 1947.
13. "At City Hall. By Frank Tumpane," 20 November 1948; a variant of the lyrics can be found in LDA 29; original words by Ozzie Williams and Lige McKelvy, *Sunday in Toronto* (Guelph, Ontario, Favorite Music Co., November 1948), 4p, republished here by permission.
14. LDA 30, 26 May 1949, Webber "to the Christian Ministers of Toronto" quotes the *Globe and Mail* of 24 May.
15. Public Archives of Ontario, RG4-32, file 1950-76, "Sunday Sports General File," 4 January 1950, "Memorandum for C.R. Magone ... Re: Sunday Sports."
16. LDA 30, *Windsor Daily Star,* 6 January 1949, "Now. By R.M. Harrison"; LDA 30, 24 June 1949, Webber to chief constable, Township of Sandwich East, Windsor; *Windsor Daily Star,* 9 July 1949, "Now. By R.M. Harrison": "Time is coming when the people of Ontario—particularly in the larger centres—will demand that enforcement of Sunday blue laws be handled on a local option basis."
17. LDA 30, September 1949; *St. Thomas Times-Journal,* 31 October 1949, "Seeks Wording Change on Windsor Sunday Sport Vote."
18. LDA 193, *Protestant Action,* December 1949, "An Open Sunday in Toronto?"
19. Public Archives of Ontario, RG4-02, box 60.4, file "1950-51 Lord's Day Act," *Globe and Mail,* 4 January 1950, "By Jim Coleman"; LDA 126, "Minutes of the Council of the Corporation of the City of Toronto 1950" 9 January 1950, "Appendix 'C'" (Mayor's Address. 117th Inaugural Meeting of the City Council), p.6.
20. LDA 31, 12 January 1950, Webber to McGrath; misquoted in LDA 164, *Canadian Register,* 21 January 1950, "Majority Votes and the Third Commandment" by Henry Somerville.
21. Archives of the Roman Catholic Archdiocese of Toronto, MGPO05.09-16.

22. LDA 164, *Globe and Mail,* 8 May 1950, "Sunday Ball Inaugural Spoiled for 17,388 Fans As Teams Toy With Time."
23. Public Archives of Ontario, RG4-02, box 60.4, file "1950–51 Lord's Day Act," 5 February 1951, Alliance to the Attorney General.
24. *Lord's Day Bulletin,* No.6, "An Esteemed Veteran Worker" [Spring 1946] No.10. for the death of A.R. Skinner; LDA 30, 9 May 1949, Byers to Webber; Presbyterian Church in Canada Archives, Toronto, "Mingie, George W.", obituary file; LDA 31, 10 November 1950, Webber to McGrath; *Toronto Daily Star,* 14 August 1951, "Crusader for a New Order" (obituary for C.H. Huestis); also *United Church Observer,* 15 November 1951; LDA 135, 1951 Annual Report announces the retirement of Miss M.W. Davidson in 1951; *London Evening Free Press,* 9 April 1953, "Pioneer Missionary, Dr. J. Watson, Dies."
25. LDA 31, 3 October 1950, Mrs. K. Seabrook, Brantford, Ontario, to Webber.
26. LDA 31, 25 October 1950, S.H. Adams, K.C., Calgary, to the Alliance.

EPILOGUE

1. JPA, 34-2, "Memoire de la Ligue du Dimanche à l'Episcopat de la Province de Québec" 4p. n.d. for letter to the Roman Catholic bishops of Quebec; bishops' reply is discussed in the minutes of 20 October 1966; See Clément, 285, for description of Vatican crisis.
2. E.g., *Mandements. Lettres Pastorales et Circulaires des Evêques de Montréal* "Circulaire de Son Excellence Msgr Paul-Emile Léger," p.884, 11 February 1952.
3. Steve Ross, "Sunday: Canada's Day of Arrest," *Church and State* (February 1987) 9-11.

CONCLUSION

1. Pettibone, 20. Reformers everywhere argued instead "for a theocratic union of religion and the state in which the state existed to serve the interests of the church."
2. Sironneau, 576-7.

Select Bibliography

A Century of Sundays from sacred to secular. People for Sunday Association of Canada. 1888–1988. Islington, Ontario: The People for Sunday Association of Canada, 1987.

Abella, Irving and Harold Troper. *None is Too Many. Canada and the Jews of Europe 1933–1948.* Toronto: Lester & Orpen Dennys, 1983.

Acta et decreta concilii plenarii quebecensis primi anno domini MCMIX. Quebec: L'Action Sociale, 1912.

Akenson, Donald H. *The Irish in Ontario. A Study in Rural History.* Kingston and Montreal: Queen's University Press, 1984.

Allen, Patrick, *et al. La pensée de Henri Bourassa.* n.p.: L'Action Nationale, (c. 1954).

Allen, Richard. *The Social Passion. Religion and Social Reform in Canada 1914–28.* Toronto: University of Toronto Press, 1971.

———. "The Social Gospel as the Religion of the Agrarian Revolt." pp. 174–86 in *The West and the Nation. Essays In Honour of W.L.Morton.* Ed. Carl Berger and Ramsay Cook. Toronto: McClelland and Stewart, 1976.

———, ed. *The Social Gospel in Canada. Papers of the Inter-disciplinary Conference on the Social Gospel in Canada, March 21-24 1973, at the University of Regina.* History Division of the National Museum of Man, Mercury Series. Paper No. 9. Ottawa: National Museums of Canada, 1975.

Archambault, Joseph-Papin, SJ *Figures Catholiques. Préface du juge Thomas Tremblay.* Montreal: Institut Social Populaire, 1950.

———. *Les Objectifs de l'Action Catholique.* Montreal: Ecole Sociale Populaire, c.1940.

———. *La Villa St.Martin. Retraites Fermées Pour les Hommes.* Abord-à-Plouffe: n.p., 1922. 20p.

Arès, Richard. "L'évolution de l'Eglise au Canada français de 1940 à 1975. Survivance et déclin d'une chrétienté." pp. 267–97 in *Idéologies au Canada Français 1940–1976 (t.III) Les partis politiques, L'Eglise.* Ed. Fernand Dumont, Jean Hamelin, and Jean-Paul Montminy. Quebec: Laval University Press, 1981.

Armstrong, Christopher and H.V. Nelles. *The Revenge of the Methodist Bicycle Company. Sunday Streetcars and Municipal Reform in Toronto, 1888–1897.* Toronto: Peter Martin Associates, 1977.

Bacchiocchi, Samuele. *From Sabbath to Sunday: A Historical Investigation of the Rise of Sunday Observance in Early Christianity.* Rome: Pontifical Gregorian University, 1977.

Barker, Ralph Whitehead. "The United Church of Canada and the Social Question." Ph.D., Victoria University, 1961

Beck, Jeanne R.M. "Henry Somerville and the Development of Catholic Social Thought in Canada: Somerville's Role in the Archdiocese of Toronto 1913–1943." Ph.D., McMaster University, 1977.

Bellefleur, Michel. *L'Eglise et le loisir au Québec avant la Révolution tranquille.* Quebec: Quebec University Press, 1986.

Berger, Carl. *The Writing of Canadian History. Aspects of English-Canadian Historical Writing since 1900.* Second Edition. Toronto: University of Toronto Press, 1986.

———. and Ramsay Cook, ed. *The West and the Nation: Essays in Honour of W.L. Morton.* Toronto: McClelland and Stewart, 1976.

Betcherman, Lita-Rose. *The Swastika and the Maple Leaf. Fascist Movements in Canada in the Thirties.* Toronto: Fitzhenry & Whiteside, 1975.

Bibby, Reginald. *Fragmented Gods: The Poverty and Potential of Religion in Canada.* Toronto: Irwin Press, 1987.

Bland, Salem Goldworth. *The New Christianity. Or the Religion of the New Age.* Introduction by Richard Allen. Toronto: University of Toronto Press, 1973 (1920).

Bliss, Michael. *A Canadian Millionaire. The Life and Business Times of Sir Joseph Flavelle, Bart. 1858–1939.* Toronto: Macmillan, 1978.———. "The Methodist Church and World War I." *Canadian Historical Review* 49:3 (September 1968) 213-33.

———. *Northern Enterprise. Five Centuries of Canadian Business.* Toronto: McClelland and Stewart, 1987.

Bothwell, Robert, Ian Drummond and John English. *Canada Since 1945; Power, Politics, and Provincialism.* Toronto: University of Toronto Press, 1981.

Bray, R. Matthew. "The Canadian Patriotic Response to the Great War." Ph.D., York University, 1977.

Brown, Robert Craig. *Robert Laird Borden: A Biography.* Toronto: Macmillan Press, 1975.

———. and Ramsay Cook. *Canada 1896–1921. A Nation Transformed.* The Canadian Centenary Series 14, Toronto: McClelland and Stewart, 1974.

The Canadian Parliamentary Guide and Work of General Reference ... Ottawa: 1905, 1908, 1910, 1912, 1941.

Carson, D.A., ed. *From Sabbath to Lord's Day: A Biblical, Historical, and Theological Investigation.* Grand Rapids, Michigan: Zondervan, 1982.

Carter, Paul A. *The Decline and Revival of the Social Gospel. Social and Political Liberalism in American Protestant Churches, 1920–1940.* n.p.: Archon Books, 1971. (First Edition 1956.)

Chadwick, Owen. *The Secularization of the European Mind in the Nineteenth Century.* The Gifford Lectures in the University of Edinburgh for 1973–74. London: Cambridge University Press, 1975.

Chamlee, Jr., Roy Zebulon. "The Sabbath Crusade: 1810–1920." Ph.D., The George Washington University, 1968.

Charlton, John. *Sabbath Observance. Speech on the Bill to Provide for Better Observance of the Lord's Day.* Ottawa: Roger Maclean, 1885. 24p.

———. *Speech of Mr. John Charlton, M.P. House of Commons, May 2nd 1894. Lord's Day observance; the Sabbath for man, the toiler's right to Sunday rest.* Ottawa: 1894. 16p.

Christianizing the Social Order. A Statement Prepared by a Commission Appointed by the Board of Evangelism and Social Service. Toronto: The United Church of Canada, 1934.

Clark, C.S. *Of Toronto the Good.* Montreal: The Toronto Publishing Co., 1898. Reprint edition: Coles Canadiana Collection, 1970.

Clément, Gabriel. *Histoire de l'Action catholique au Canada français. Commission d'étude sur les laïcs et l'Eglise. Deuxième annexe au rapport.* Montreal: Fides, 1972.

Clifford, N. Keith. *The Resistance to Church Union in Canada 1904–1939.* Vancouver: University of British Columbia Press, 1985.

Cohn, Norman. *The Pursuit of The Millenium. Revolutionary messianism in medieval and Reformation Europe and its bearing on modern totalitarian movements.* Second edition. New York: Harper & Row, Harper Torchbooks, 1961.

Connor, Ralph. *The Man from Glengarry.* New Canadian Library 14, Toronto: McClelland and Stewart, 1960 (1901).

Cook, Ramsay. *The Regenerators: Social Criticism in Late Victorian English Canada.* Toronto: University of Toronto Press, 1985.

Cox, Harvey. *Religion in the Secular City. Toward a Postmodern Theology.* New York: Simon and Schuster, 1984.

———. *The Secular City—Urbanization and Secularization in Theological Perspective.* New York: Macmillan, 1965.

Crysdale, Stewart. *The Industrial Struggle and Protestant Ethics in Canada. A Survey of Changing Power Structures and Christian Social Ethics.* Toronto: Ryerson Press, 1961.

———. and Les Wheatcroft, ed. *Religion in Canadian Society.* Toronto: Macmillan of Canada, 1976.

Dennison, James T., Jr. *The Market Day of the Soul. The Puritan Doctrine of the Sabbath in England, 1532–1700.* Lanham, Maryland: University Press of America, 1983.

Desrosiers, Yvon, ed. *Religion et culture au Québec. Figures contemporaines du sacré.* Montreal: Fides, 1986.

Dupont, Antonin. *Les relations entre l'Eglise et l'Etat sous Louis-Alexandre Taschereau 1920–1936.* Montreal: Guérin, 1973.

Edwards, Jonathan. *Twenty Sermons on Various Subjects.* Edinburgh: 1804.

Eider, Shimon D. *Halachos of Shabbos.* 4 volumes. Lakewood, New Jersey: 1973.

Eliade, Mircea. *The Sacred and the Profane. The Nature of Religion.* New York: Harcourt, Brace, Jovanovich, 1959. Reprinted 1961.

Emery, G.N. "The Lord's Day Act of 1906 and the Sabbath Observance Question" pp. 23–51 in *Documentary Problems in Canadian History.* Volume II *Post-Confederation.* Georgetown, Ontario: Irwin-Dorsey, 1969.

Flanagan, Thomas. *Louis 'David' Riel. Prophet of the New World.* Toronto: University of Toronto Press, 1979.

Fraser, Brian J. *The Social Uplifters. Presbyterian Progressives and the Social Gospel in Canada, 1875–1915.* SR Supplements Volume 20. Waterloo, Ontario: For the Canadian Corporation for Studies in Religion by Wilfrid Laurier University Press, 1988.

French, Goldwin. "Egerton Ryerson and the Methodist Model for Upper Canada." pp. 45–58 in *Egerton Ryerson and His Times.* Ed. Neil McDonald and Alf Chaiton. Toronto: Macmillan, 1978.

Friesen, Gerald. *The Canadian Prairies. A History.* Toronto: University of Toronto Press, 1984.

Grant, Barry J. *When Rum was King. (The Story of The Prohibition Era In New Brunswick.)* Fredericton, N.B.: Fiddlehead Poetry Books, 1984.

Grant, John Webster. *The Church in the Canadian Era. The First Century of Confederation.* Vol. 3 of *A History of the Christian Church in Canada.* General Editor: John Webster Grant. Toronto: McGraw-Hill Ryerson, 1972.

———. *George Pidgeon. A Biography.* Toronto: Ryerson Press, 1972.

———. *Moon of Wintertime. Missionaries and the Indians of Canada in Encounter since 1534.* Toronto: University of Toronto Press, 1984.

Hamelin, Jean. *Le XXe siècle. Tome 2. De 1940 à nos jours.* Vol. 3 of *Histoire du catholicisme québécois.* General Editor: Nive Voisine. Montreal: Boréal Express, 1984.

———. and Nicole Gagnon. *Le XXe siècle. Tome 1. 1898–1940.* Vol. 3 of *Histoire du catholicisme québécois.* General Editor: Nive Voisine. Montreal: Boréal Express, 1984.

Hallowell, Gerald A. *Prohibition in Ontario, 1919–1923.* Ottawa: Ontario Historical Society Research Publication No. 2, 1972.

Handy, Robert T., ed. *The Social Gospel in America 1870–1920. Gladden. Ely. Rauschenbusch.* New York: Oxford University Press, 1966.

Hargrove, Katharine T., ed. *The Paradox of Religious Secularity.* Englewood Cliffs, New Jersey: Prentice-Hall, 1968.

Heschel, Abraham Joshua, *The Sabbath: Its Meaning for Modern Man. With Wood Engravings by Ilya Schor.* New York: Farrar, Straus and Giroux, 1951.

Hewett, Phillip. *Unitarians in Canada.* Toronto: Fitzhenry & Whiteside, 1978.

Hogan, Brian. "'Salted With Fire': Studies in Catholic Social Thought and Action in Ontario, 1931–1961." Ph.D., University of Toronto, 1986.

Holmested, George Smith. *The Sunday Law in Canada.* Toronto: Arthur Poole & Co., Law Publishers, 1912.

Homel, Gene Howard. "Sliders and Backsliders: Toronto's Sunday Tobogganing Controversy of 1912" *Urban History Review.* X:2 (October 1981): 25–34.

Hopkins, Charles Howard. *The Rise of the Social Gospel in American Protestantism 1865-1915.* New Haven: Yale University Press, 1940. Fifth Printing 1957.

Horn, Michiel. *The League for Social Reconstruction: Intellectual Origins of the Democratic Left in Canada 1930–1942.* Toronto: University of Toronto Press, 1980.

Howell, David Francis. "The Social Gospel in Canadian Protestantism, 1895–1925: Implications for Sport." Ph.D., University of Alberta, 1980.

Huestis, Charles H. *Saving a Great Institution: Commemorating Forty Years of Service. By the General Secretary.* Toronto: The Lord's Day Alliance of Canada, 1930.

———. *Sunday in the Home.* Ryerson Essay 36. Toronto: Ryerson Press, 1928.

Hulliger, Jean. *L'Enseignment social des évêques canadiens de 1891 à 1950.* Montreal: Fides, 1958.

Hunt, Claude W. *Booze, Boats and Billions: Smuggling Liquid Gold!* Toronto: McClelland and Stewart, 1988.

Hutton, Eric. "He Changed the Toronto Sunday." *Maclean's Magazine.* Vol. 65 (July 15, 1952): 12-3, 58-9.

Indig, Sheldon. "Canadian Jewry and their struggle for an exemption in the federal Lord's Day Act of 1906." M.A., University of Windsor, 1976.

International Labor Office. *Report of the governing body of the International Labor Office upon the working of the convention concerning the application of the weekly rest in industrial undertakings.* Geneva: League of Nations, 1923.

Jable, J.T. "Pennsylvania's Early Blue Laws: A Quaker Experiment in The Suppression of Sport and Amusements. 1682–1740." *Journal of Sport History.* 1:2 (Fall 1974): 107-21.

Jameson, Sheilagh S. with Nota B. Erickson. *Chautauqua in Canada.* Calgary: Glenbow-Alberta Institute, 1979.

Johnston, T.J. *The Lord's Day Observance Vindicated and Seventh-Day Sabbatarians Answered.* Toronto: W. Briggs, 1919.

Jones, Richard. *L'Idéologie de L'ACTION CATHOLIQUE. (1917–1939).* Quebec: Laval University Press, 1974.

Kealey, Gregory and Peter Warrian, ed. *Essays in Canadian Working Class History.* Toronto: McClelland and Stewart, 1976.

Lachance, Micheline. *Le Prince de l'Eglise. Le cardinal Léger.* Montreal: Les éditions de l'homme, 1982.

Lacroix, Benoit and Jean Simard, ed. *Religion populaire. Religion de clercs?* Quebec: Institut Québécois de Recherche sur la Culture, 1984.

Landon, Fred. *Western Ontario and the American Frontier.* Toronto: McClelland and Stewart, Carleton Library No. 34, 1967.

Laskin, Bora. "Freedom of Religion and the Lord's Day Act—The Canadian Bill of Rights and the Sunday Bowling Case" *The Canadian Bar Review/La Revue du Barreau Canadien.* XL (March 1964): 147-56.

Laverdure, Paul. "Canada's Sunday: The Presbyterian Contribution, 1875–1950." William Klempa, ed., *The Burning Bush and a Few Acres of Snow. The Presbyterian Contribution to Canadian Life and Culture.* Carleton University Press: Ottawa, 1994, 83-99.

———. "The Future of Protestant Historiography" in *Status Quaestionis. Proceedings of the Colloquium Commemorating the 25th Anniversary of the Research Centre in Religious History of Canada, December 4, 1992.* Pierre Hurtubise, O.M.I., and Jean-Marie LeBlanc, ed. Saint Paul University: Ottawa, 1994, 61-6.

Law Reform Commission of Canada. *Report on Sunday Observance.* Ottawa: Minister of Supply and Services Canada, 1976

Leith, John H., ed. *Creeds of the Churches. A Reader in Christian Doctrine From the Bible to the Present.* Third Ed. Atlanta: John Knox Press, 1982.

Lemon, James. *Toronto Since 1918. An Illustrated History.* Toronto: National Museum of Man, James Lorimer & Co, 1985.

Levitt, Joseph. *Henri Bourassa and the Golden Calf. The Social Program of the Nationalists of Quebec (1900–1914).* Ottawa: University of Ottawa, 1972.

Marsden, George. *Fundamentalism and American Culture: The Shaping of Twentieth-Century Evangelicalism, 1870–1925.* New York: Oxford University Press, 1980.

Marshall, David B. "The Clerical Response to Secularization: Canadian Methodists and Presbyterians, 1860–1940." Ph.D., University of Toronto, 1986.

———. *Secularizing the Faith. Canadian Protestant Clergy and the Crisis of Belief, 1850–1940.* Toronto: University of Toronto Press, 1992.

Martin, David. *The Religious and the Secular. Studies in Secularization.* London: Routledge & Kegan Paul, 1969.

Masters, Donald Campbell. *The Rise of Toronto 1850–1890.* Toronto: University of Toronto Press, 1947.

McGowan, Mark G. *The Waning of the Green. Catholics, the Irish, and Identity in Toronto, 1887–1922.* Montreal & Kingston: McGill-Queen's University Press, 1999.

McLean, Robert I. "A 'Most Effectual Remedy.' Temperance and Prohibition in Alberta, 1875–1915." M.A., University of Calgary, 1969.

Meen, Sharon Patricia. "The Battle for the Sabbath; The Sabbatarian Lobby in Canada, 1890–1912." Ph.D., University of British Columbia, 1979.

———. "Holy Day or Holiday? The Giddy Trolley and the Canadian Sunday, 1890–1914" *Urban History Review.* IX:1 (June 1980): 49-63.

Metcalfe, Alan. *Canada Learns To Play: The Emergence of Organized Sport, 1807–1914.* Toronto: McClelland and Stewart, 1987.

Mol, Hans. *Faith and Fragility. Religion and Identity in Canada.* Burlington, Ontario: Trinity Press, 1985.

Moir, John S. *Christianity in Canada: Historical Essays,* edited by Paul Laverdure. Yorkton: Redeemer's Voice Press, 2002.

———. *The Church in the British Era. From the British Conquest to Confederation.* Vol. 2 of *A History of the Christian Church in Canada.* General Editor: John Webster Grant. Toronto: McGraw-Hill Ryerson, 1972.

———. *Early Presbyterianism in Canada: Essays,* edited by Paul Laverdure. Gravelbourg: Gravelbooks, 2003.

———. *Enduring Witness. A History of the Presbyterian Church in Canada.* New edition. Toronto: Presbyterian Church in Canada, 1987.

———. *Church and State in Canada West. Three Studies in the Relation of Denominationalism and Nationalism, 1841–1867.* Toronto: University of Toronto Press, 1959.

Morgan, Henry James, ed. *The Canadian Men and Women of the Time: A Hand-book of Canadian Biography.* Toronto: W. Briggs, 1898. Second Edition 1912.

Morrow, Don, Mary Keyes *et al. A Concise History of Sport in Canada.* Toronto: Oxford University Press, 1989.

Moyles, Robert G. *The Blood and Fire in Canada. A History of the Salvation Army in the Dominion 1882–1976.* Toronto: Peter Martin Associates, 1977.

Norman, Edward R. *The Conscience of the State in North America.* London: Cambridge University Press, 1968.

O'Dea, Thomas F. *The Sociology of Religion.* Englewood Cliffs, New Jersey: Prentice-Hall, 1966.

Olitzky, Kerry M. "Sundays at Chicago Sinai Congregation: Paradigm for a Movement." *American Jewish History* 74 (June 1985): 356-68.

O'Neill, R. Dennis. "The Temperance Movement, Prohibition and Scarcity in Ontario, 1900–1916." D.Ed., University of Toronto, 1984.

Ontario Reform Commission. *Report on Sunday Observance Legislation.* Toronto: Department of Justice, 1970.

Owram, Doug. *Promise of Eden: The Canadian Expansionist Movement and the Idea of the West, 1856–1900.* Toronto: University of Toronto Press, 1980.

Parker, Kenneth L. "Thomas Rogers and the English Sabbath: the Case for a Reappraisal." *Church History* 53 (September 1984): 332-47.

Peddie, Gordon A. *'The King of Kings.' The Basis of Union of the Presbyterian Church in Canada and its Relationship to the Present Need of the Church for a Confession of Faith in Jesus Christ as Lord of Church and State. Together with The Petition of a Memorial of the Presbytery of Paris to the General Assembly, 1942.* Toronto: 1942.

Penton, M. James. *Apocalypse Delayed. The Story of Jehovah's Witnesses.* Toronto: University of Toronto Press, 1985.

Pettibone, Dennis Lynn. "Caesar's Sabbath: The Sunday-Law Controversy in the United States, 1879–1892." Ph.D., University of California, Riverside, 1979.

Pinno, Erhard. "Temperance and Prohibition in Saskatchewan." M.A., University of Saskatchewan, 1971.

Pitman, Walter G. *The Baptists and Public Affairs in the Province of Canada, 1840–1867.* New York: Arno Press, 1980.

Pulker, Edward. *We Stand on Their Shoulders. The Growth of Social Concern in Canadian Anglicanism.* Toronto: Anglican Book Centre, 1986.

Le Repos dominical. Montreal: Ligue du dimanche, 1927, 84p.

Rochester, Lloyd B., ed. *The John Rochester Family in Canada.* Ottawa: Private printing, Fourth Edition, 1976.

Rochester, William M. *Report of World Commission On The Christian Sabbath. Read at the Third World's Christian Citizenship Conference.* Pittsburgh, Pennsylvania: National Reform Association, [1920?], 11p.

Rohrbach, Peter Wagner. "Puritan Attitudes Towards Physical Recreation In 17th Century New England." *Journal of Sport History.* 3:2 (Summer 1976): 139-51.

Rome, David, ed. *Jewish Archival Record of 1935. With Preface by Victor Sefton.* New Series, No. 7. Montreal: National Archives, Canadian Jewish Congress, 1976.

———. ed. *The Jewish Congress Archival Record of 1936. With a Report on Sabbath Rest (in lieu of a Preface).* New Series, No. 8. Montreal: National Archives, Canadian Jewish Congress, 1978.

———. ed. *On Sunday Observance, 1906.* New Series, No. 14. Montreal: National Archives, Canadian Jewish Congress, 1979.

Rordorf, Willy. *Sunday. The History of the Day of Rest and Worship in the Earliest Centuries of the Christian Church.* Translated by A.A.K. Graham. London: S.C.M. Press, 1968.

Rouillard, Jacques. *Histoire de la CSN (1921–1981).* [Montreal]: Confédération des syndicats nationaux et Boréal Express, 1981.

Rumilly, Robert. *Henri Bourassa. La vie publique d'un grand canadien.* Montreal: Chantecler, 1953.

Saunders, Leslie H. *An Orangeman in Public Life. The Memoirs of Leslie Howard Saunders.* Toronto: Britannia Printers, n.d.

Schrodt, Barbara. "Sabbatarianism and Sport in Canadian Society." *Journal of Sport History.* 4:1 (Spring 1977): 22-33.

Shore, Marlene. *The Science of Social Redemption. McGill, the Chicago School, and the Origins of Social Research in Canada.* Toronto: University of Toronto Press, 1987.

Silver, Arthur I. *The French-Canadian Idea of Confederation, 1864–1900.* Toronto: University of Toronto Press, 1982.

Sinclair, Lister. *A Play On Words & Other Radio Plays.* Toronto: J.M. Dent and Sons, 1948.

Sinclair-Faulkner, Charles Thompson. ""For Christian Civilization": The Churches and Canada's War Effort, 1939–1942." Ph.D., University of Chicago, 1975.

Sironneau, Jean-Pierre. *Sécularisation et religions politiques.* The Hague: Mouton Publishers, 1982.

The Six Lambeth Conferences. 1867–1920. Compiled Under the Direction of the Most Reverend Lord Davidson of Lambeth. Archbishop of Canterbury, 1903–1928. London: Society for Promoting Christian Knowledge, 1920, reissued 1929.

Smith, Ronald Gregor. *Secular Christianity.* New York: Harper & Row, 1966.

Socknat, Thomas P. *Witness Against War. Pacifism in Canada 1900–1945.* Toronto: University of Toronto Press, 1987.

Solberg, Winton. *Redeem the Time. The Puritan Sabbath in Early America.* Cambridge, Massachusetts: Harvard University Press, 1977.

Spence, Ruth E. *Prohibition in Canada. A Memorial to Francis Stephens Spence.* Toronto: Ontario Branch of the Dominion Alliance, 1919.

Swainson, Donald. *Oliver Mowat's Ontario. Papers Presented to the Oliver Mowat Colloquium.* Toronto: Macmillan, 1972.

Swartley, Willard M. *Slavery, Sabbath, War, and Women: Case Issues in Biblical Interpretation.* Foreword by Albert J. Meyer. Scottdale, Pennsylvania: Herald Press, 1983.

Thompson, John Herd. *The Harvests of War. The Prairie West, 1914–1918.* Toronto: McClelland and Stewart, 1978, reprinted 1981.

Thompson, John H. "The Prohibition Question in Manitoba 1892–1928." M.A., University of Manitoba, 1969.

———. with Allen Seager. *Canada 1922–1939. Decades of Discord.* Canadian Centenary Series Volume 15. Toronto: McClelland and Stewart, 1985.

Tucker, Robert C. "The Theory of Charismatic Leadership" *Daedalus.* 97:2 (1968): 731-56.

Vahanian, Gabriel. *The Death of God. The Culture of Our Post-Christian Era.* New York: George Braziller, 1957. Paperback edition 1966.

Voisine, Nive. *Histoire de l'Eglise catholique au Québec (1608–1970).* Commission d'étude sur les laïcs et l'Eglise. Première annexe au rapport. Montreal: Fides, 1971.

Waite, Peter B. *The Man from Halifax. Sir John Thompson. Prime Minister.* Toronto: University of Toronto Press, 1985.

Walker, James W. St.G. "Race and Recruitment in World War I: Enlistment of Visible Minorities in the Canadian Expeditionary Force" *Canadian Historical Review* LXX:1 (March 1989) 1-26.

Waterman, A.M.C. "The Lord's Day in a Secular Society: A Historical Comment on the Canadian Lord's Day Act of 1906" *Canadian Journal of Theology.* XI (1965): 102-23.

Way, Frank. "Stability and Change in Constitutional Litigation: the Public Piety Cases." *Journal of Politics.* 47 (August 1985): 910-25.

Westfall, William, Louis Rousseau, Fernand Harvey, and John Simpson, ed. *Religion/Culture. Comparative Canadian Studies/Etudes canadiennes comparées. Proceedings of a Conference Sponsored by the Association for Canadian Studies and the Graduate Centre for Religious Studies, University of Toronto, Held at the Ontario Institute for Studies in Education, Toronto, on May 23–26, 1984.* Volume VII of Canadian Issues/Thèmes canadiens. Ottawa: Association for Canadian Studies, 1985.

White, F.I. "The Sunday Observance Laws" *Faculty of Law Review.* (University of Toronto) 15 (April 1957): 58-64.

Wigley, John. *The Rise and Fall of the Victorian Sunday.* Manchester, England: Manchester University Press, c. 1980.

Whitaker, Reginald. "Mackenzie King in the Dominion of the Dead." *Canadian Forum.* (February 1976) 6-11.

Williams, Ozzie and Lige McKelvy. *Sunday in Toronto.* Guelph, Ontario: Favorite Music Co., November, 1948.

Zeman, Jarold K., ed. *Baptists in Canada. Search for Identity Amidst Diversity.* Burlington, Ontario: G.R. Welch, 1980.

Zolf, Dorothy and Paul W. Taylor. "Redressing the balance in Canadian broadcasting: A history of religious broadcasting policy in Canada." *Studies in Religion/Sciences Religieuses* 18:2 (Spring 1989): 153-70.

INDEX

BROTHER REGINALD:
A Poet in Moose Jaw

by Paul Laverdure

The biography and religious poetry of a Depression-era writer.

(Gravelbourg 2002) softcover, 6x9, 64pp, illus. $8.00.

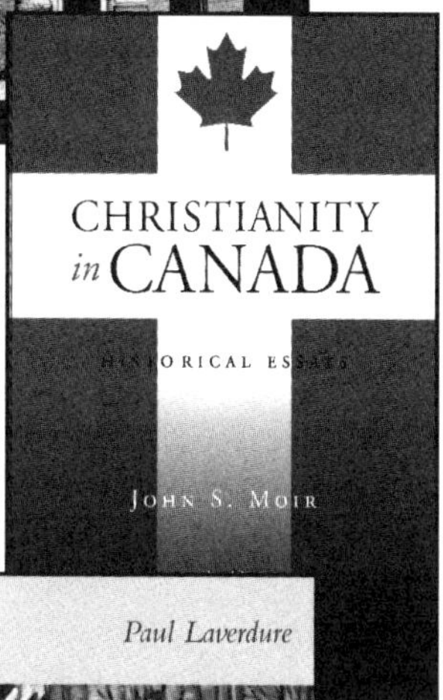

CHRISTIANITY IN CANADA

Historical Essays by John S. Moir
with a foreword by Mark G. McGowan

Seminal essays and speeches exploring the role of Christianity in Canadian society.

(Yorkton 2001) softcover, 6x9, xix+187pp, bibliographic notes. $20.00.

SUNDAY IN CANADA:
The rise and fall of the Lord's day

by Paul Laverdure

Holy day or holiday? Is Sunday different? Should it be? This book explores how Canadians faced and still struggle with these questions.

(Yorkton 2005) softcover, 6x9, 280pp., illus. $30.00.

Send cheque payable to:

LAVERDURE & ASSOCIATES
194 Second Avenue North, Yorkton, Saskatchewan, S3N 1G7

prices subject to change without notice.